Economic change in the Balkan States

To Birgitta, my wife
ÖS

With love, to my parents, Henry and Marjorie, for their inspiration and encouragement in all my personal and professional undertakings
MLW

Economic Change in the Balkan States:

Albania, Bulgaria, Romania and Yugoslavia

Edited by
Örjan Sjöberg and Michael L. Wyzan

Pinter Publishers
London

First published in Great Britain in 1991 by
Pinter Publishers Limited
25 Floral Street, London WC2E 9DS

British Library Cataloguing in Publication Data

A CIP catalogue record for this book is available from the British Library
ISBN 0 86187 0557

Typeset by DP Photosetting, Aylesbury, Bucks
Printed and bound in Great Britain by Biddles Ltd of Guildford and Kings Lynn

Contents

List of contributors

Anders Åslund Stockholm Institute of Soviet and East European Economics, Sweden

Ivo Bicanic Faculty of Economics, University of Zagreb, Yugoslavia

Will Bartlett School for Advanced Urban Studies, University of Bristol, United Kingdom

Gramoz Pashko Faculty of Economics, University of Tirana, Albania

Ognian Pishev Ambassador to the United States, Republic of Bulgaria

Per Ronnås Department of International Economics and Geography, Stockholm School of Economics, Sweden

Örjan Sjöberg Stockholm Institute of Soviet and East European Economics, and Department of International Economics and Geography, Stockholm School of Economics, Sweden

Alin Teodorescu Centre for Sociological Research, University of Bucharest, Romania

Alan H. Smith School of Slavonic and East European Studies, University of London, United Kingdom

Michael L. Wyzan Stockholm Institute of Soviet and East European Economics, Sweden, and Department of Economics, Illinois State University, United States

Preface

This book represents the first major project of the Institute of Soviet and East European Economics at the Stockholm School of Economics. It is a result of a conference on Economic Change in the Socialist Balkan Countries that we organised here on 12–13 June 1990.

We saw many reasons for this undertaking. First, we had three resident scholars who specialise in the economies of Balkan countries, Michael L. Wyzan on Bulgaria, Per Ronnås on Romania and Örjan Sjöberg on Albania. Second, political changes in the Balkans had been slower to come about than in East Central Europe, and at least initially there seemed to be few places in the world where such a conference could be organised. We were particularly happy to receive qualified and freely speaking economists from all four countries concerned. Third, the Balkan countries receive far too little scholarly attention, and the time seemed right for a common perspective on the economies of the four still socialist Balkan countries. All the major questions were raised, and new statistics had started to emerge, allowing for a new more appropriate assessment. Finally, we were happy to receive a substantial grant for this purpose from Prince Bertil's Foundation.

Our hope is therefore that this volume will be a substantial contribution to the study of the Balkan economies. Because of the extraordinary dearth of information that has long prevailed, little academic research has been possible on Albania, Romania and Bulgaria, while the Yugoslav economy has mostly been discussed outside the Balkan context. Our intention has been to provide the reader with up-to-date assessments based on statistics and information that have recently become available.

Furthermore, our ambition is not only to provide the reader with previously unknown facts. We also want to offer a forceful analysis. Far too many publications in this field have been, not least because of the necessary political caution, excessively timid and descriptive. The common view of the authors of this volume has been that at long last, the truth must be stated. Alas, there is rarely a common view of the truth. Our authors do present their perceptions, but also try to offer the facts upon which they base their judgements in order to allow the reader to scrutinise and question their opinions. Indeed, this is in line with the concept of objectivity as the late historian E.H. Carr saw it.

All our contributors belong to the younger generation of scholars in the field, though mature. Typically, none of them seems to be much impressed by market socialism, signifying a generational divide that is characteristic of both the Eastern and Western halves of Europe. Increasingly, the question that is posed is no longer what is the ideal society, but rather how do we move to a 'normal' society, that is a market economy of a West European type with predominantly private ownership. Inevitably, this becomes the starting point both for assessments of the current situation and for probing into the eternal question of what is to be done.

Anders Åslund
Stockholm
August 1990

Acknowledgements

This volume is an outgrowth of a conference on the four Balkan socialist economies, held in Stockholm on 12 and 13 June 1990. The conference was sponsored by the Stockholm Institute of Soviet and East European Economics, with funding from the Prince Bertil Fund. We are grateful to the Institute for the use of its facilities and funds in preparing for and holding the conference and in putting together this volume. Anders Åslund, the Institute's Director, provided both the original inspiration for this endeavour and continuing encouragement in our efforts to see it through to its completion. We are also indebted to the staff of the Institute, especially Marion Cutting, Sten Luthman and Kristian Uppenberg, for various forms of assistance.

Organising a conference on relatively short notice that entails the participation of individuals from Albania, Bulgaria, Romania and Yugoslavia is a daunting logistical undertaking. We are particularly appreciative of Jan af Sillén's assistance in facilitating the appearance in Stockholm of Gramoz Pashko, our Albanian participant, and for his insightful comments at the conference. We are also grateful for the active participation of several distinguished Swedish scholars, including Gun Eriksson, Anu-Mai Köll, Örjan Sturesjö and Stefan de Vylder.

Considerable effort was required in turning the various conference papers, which were diverse in style and content, into chapters of a single book. We are grateful to Per Ronnås for translating Alin Teodorescu's contribution into English, and to Marion Cutting and David Kendall for their excellent editorial assistance on the other chapters.

Needless to say, none of the aforementioned bears responsibility for any deficiencies that may remain. We both shared equally the burden of the editorial work on this book and will gladly share on the same basis whatever credit or blame greets its publication.

1 The Balkan states: struggling along the road to the market from Europe's periphery

Örjan Sjöberg and Michael L. Wyzan

Introduction

During the post-war period the Balkan countries have displayed a greater variety of political and economic systems than any area of comparable size on earth. If we consider only the four socialist states that are the subject of this volume and recall the situation on 9 November 1989, we find the following:

1. the last true European Stalinist state, for decades angrily denouncing the revisionism of virtually all other socialist countries while eschewing most foreign economic relations, despite a certain opening-up in the four years since the death of its original leader (Albania);
2. the Soviet Union's closest European ally, still operating a fairly traditional planned economy, despite a decade of abortive attempts at reform and unending institutional upheaval under a leader who had held power for thirty-five years (Bulgaria);
3. a wayward member of the Warsaw Pact that had managed to attain a certain independence of the USSR in foreign policy while simultaneously running its economy into the ground in a mad attempt by its long-term leader — who had built a personality cult around himself rarely equalled anywhere — to pay off its foreign debt at the expense of the standard of living, with horrifying consequences for the welfare of the population (Romania); and
4. the world's only economy run on the basis of workers' self-management, an experiment carried out in a loose federation of republics with no central government role in managing the economy and with constant nationalistic tensions seemingly threatening the very existence of the country (Yugoslavia).[1]

If all of these were not enough, the Balkan peninsula also encompasses Greece and (part of) Turkey, two medium-developed NATO members characterised by varying degrees of political instability.

Even more interesting, perhaps, than the great diversity of experiences with socialism of the four socialist Balkan states are the dramatic events in these countries since 9 November. Bulgaria's Zhivkov and Romania's Ceausescu have been dispatched from the scene. The former was put on trial as his country, evenly divided between the remnants of the Communist party and those totally rejecting its legacy, struggles to deal with the debt crisis he left behind. The latter was executed in the throes of the revolution that unseated him. Yugoslavia has instituted the Marković plan, its first serious economic reform since the mid 1970s, which at least initially had considerable success in meeting its stabilisation goals, but which is taking place against the backdrop of unprecedented ethnic tension. Even Albania shows signs of instability and popular discontent.

Despite the great diversity of these experiences, however, one should not lose sight of the fact that the 'Balkans' are once again an integral unit whose component states have sufficient in common to make the concept meaningful. During the late and unlamented Cold War, of course, it was typical to view all issues, especially in the European context, as part of a contest between mythical 'East' and 'West' blocs. Indeed, the Truman Doctrine initiated in 1947 was aimed primarily at the two capitalist Balkan states. As early as 1948, however, Yugoslavia had bolted from Stalin's Cominform, by 1960 Albania had expressed its preference for China, and Soviet troops were removed from Romania as early as 1958, long before Ceausescu's defiant stance on the 1968 invasion of Czechoslovakia. Only Bulgaria remained a classic Soviet ally, and even there the absence of Soviet troops and of a common border with the USSR meant that the country's obsequiousness was really a matter of conscious strategy on the part of Zhivkov. Needless to say, the formal end of the Cold War has only reinforced the notion that regional ties based on shared cultural and historical experiences — including those taking place long before there was a Soviet Union — are truly meaningful and worthy of study. Readers should perhaps be forewarned that they will find few references to the USSR in the pages that follow.

It might be argued that the four states covered here are pursuing different paths — or are at different points along the path — towards a market economy. Yugoslavia's Marković plan is at least as radical, and successful in its stabilisation goals, a move in that direction as the Jeffrey Sachs-inspired programme in Poland. Moreover, the 'former' communists who have ruled Bulgaria (until 29 November 1990) and Romania both profess their commitment to creating a market economy. Despite well-justified scepticism on the part of the West concerning the sincerity of that commitment and the ability of the present leaders to see it through, there is a sense of inevitability in the air. Albania's attempts at economic reform in 1990 create a feeling of *déjà vu* — where can such unintentional attempts to imitate Brezhnev or Zhivkov lead but to the same impasse at which all other European socialist nations now find themselves?

This volume includes two chapters on each country, one by a Western scholar and another by an indigenous one, in addition to a comparison of the situation in East Central Europe with that in the Balkans (Smith), and a concluding chapter bringing together the various strands presented in the country studies and suggesting reform directions (Åslund). The eight country study chapters are designed not only to cover the salient aspects of the recent past but also to provide clues to future developments.

The contributions are organised as follows. Each country is covered by two authors, the division of labour between whom was decided upon by the contributors themselves. Between them, the pair of chapters on a given nation treat the nature and genesis of the ongoing economic crisis in that country, the reform efforts that have been attempted to date, and the prognosis for the future. The individual chapters are as diverse as the situations in the respective countries. Some chapters focus on economic policy and performance in the 1980s (Bartlett, Ronnås, Sjöberg, Teodorescu), while others concentrate on the economic reform proposals of either the new regimes and their rivals (Bićanić, Pishev, Wyzan) or, in the case of Albania, an increasingly apprehensive old guard (Pashko).

The fact that one of the two chapters on a given country is written by a scholar from that country might in the past have meant merely that the official view of the situation would be presented to a Western audience.[2] However, in the aftermath of the events of 1989 this is no longer the case in any of the four nations. Although still presenting insiders' views, all of the Balkan contributors belong to a generation of young, critical scholars motivated largely by the pursuit of an improved understanding of the situation in their countries. This is not to suggest that they are disinterested observers of the local scenes. Indeed, three have been actively engaged in the opposition to the immediate post-totalitarian regimes (if we can describe the Alia government in Albania as such) in their respective countries. None the less, they clearly indicate in their chapters where they can no longer take a detached stand on the events or policies they analyse, and the Western observer benefits greatly from learning of their individual experiences.

The remainder of this Introduction is organised as follows. The next section looks at the increasingly harsh external environment in which the Balkan economies find themselves. The third section contains a brief discussion of the recent Greek and Turkish economic experiences, which provide important lessons for the other Balkan states. The final section describes the reform experiences of each of the four countries and summarises the arguments of each chapter.

The external environment

Among the many well-known unsatisfactory features of Balkan socialist economic performance, balance of payments and foreign debt problems stand out with particular clarity. Yugoslavia has generally been viewed as having debt problems second in severity only to Poland's (see e.g. Kunkle, 1989), and Bulgaria is currently in the throes of a debt crisis unprecedented in its history. As a result of the two oil shocks of the 1970s, Romania, the only member of the Council for Mutual Economic Assistance (CMEA) that is a major purchaser of OPEC oil, had built up a large foreign debt by 1981, before strangling its domestic economy to pay it off completely by the end of the 1980s. Only Albania has remained immune to foreign debt problems — foreign credit was proscribed by Hoxha — but even there the tentative opening up of its economy in the last few years, coupled with the inherent weakness of that economy, suggest that balance of payments difficulties cannot be avoided forever.[3]

The problems that the Balkan socialist states have experienced in the sphere of foreign economic relations are the result of both fundamental systemic weaknesses shared by all such economies and the unfavourable developments in the international economic environment in the past two decades. The price shocks of the 1970s, the continued sluggish overall economic performance throughout much of the 1980s, and the consequent external debt pressures have contributed to a trade pattern in which the CMEA predominates. In the 1980s the USSR alone accounted for 35 to 40 per cent of East European exports and imports, and intra-East European trade, excluding Yugoslavia, represented another 20 to 23 per cent (Woods, 1989: 396). Moreover, the share of the overall foreign trade of the developed West accounted for by the East European countries as a whole fell from about 2 per cent in the 1970s to about 1 per cent in the 1980s (Woods, 1989: 391. See also Kanet, 1986; and Smith, 1986: 217). Even in the case of Yugoslavia, the USSR became the main trading partner in the early 1970s and has so remained (Reuter–Hendricks, 1987: 111).

The rise to prominence in the 1980s of the newly industrialised countries (NICs) of East Asia (especially Hong Kong, South Korea, Singapore, and Taiwan) was particularly detrimental to the interests of the East European states. The East Asian NICs almost tripled the value of their exports to the West between 1980 and 1987, while East European exports in that direction rose by only 10 per cent (Woods, 1989: 393). Particularly striking is the stagnating and unfavourable commodity composition of East European exports to the West, which display 'a markedly "less advanced" and more resource-intensive composition . . . than [those of] most other country groups' (Woods, 1989: 415). For the East Asian NICs, machinery rose from 13 per cent of their exports to the indusrialised West in 1970 to 32 per cent in 1987; comparable figures for Eastern Europe are 9 and 11 per cent, respectively (Woods, 1989: 408).

To a large extent, of course, this state of affairs is the result of consciously inward-looking import-substituting development strategies (see, e.g. Winiecki, 1989a and 1989b). Domestically, such strategies helped to create and perpetuate the current inefficient economic structures — based on metallurgy, heavy engineering, and petrochemicals — that are so ill-suited to modern economic life. Moreover, agriculture and services (e.g. tourism), two major potential earners of hard currency, have suffered from serious neglect in several of the Balkan countries.

Having committed themselves to opening their hitherto autarchic economies to the rest of the world, the new leaderships of Bulgaria, Romania, and Yugoslavia are coming under increasing pressure from the international financial community to abandon these priorities. Given the degree of isolation of these nations, such a change will be nothing short of revolutionary.

Attempting to adapt the economy to the demands of the world market will require massive and painful structural change, in which inefficient plants and perhaps entire branches of industry will have to be shut down. This will put regions — and more importantly to the new more democratic political conditions, constituencies — in peril, quite likely contributing further to the political disorder that has already appeared in all four countries. This is, of course, especially true if a substantial increase in unemployment occurs.

The task is made no easier by the fact that the external environment is rapidly changing. Whatever understanding of and experience with dealing with foreign markets the East European countries may possess is rapidly becoming obsolete; recourse to trade on soft terms is vanishing at a staggering rate.[4] Under such circumstances, the changing conditions in inter-CMEA trade and the arrival of the European Community's unified market in 1992 are both significant events, either of which alone could prove disastrous to the Balkan states.

During 1990, the USSR reached agreements with its CMEA trading partners (e.g. on 23 April with Bulgaria), stipulating that beginning on 1 January 1991 all bilateral trade would be on a hard currency basis. Roughly simultaneously, the disappearance of the German Democratic Republic as an independent entity will further constrict the ability of the remaining CMEA nations to sell their low quality 'soft' goods. The latter will increasingly face the same dificulties within the CMEA as they do today in their trade with the developed market economies, not merely in terms of their inability to produce acceptable goods, but also reflecting their lack of experience with marketing techniques and their slow adaptation to changing market conditions. By the summer of 1990, the small, energy import-dependent CMEA states, such as Bulgaria and Hungary, were already suffering the effects of cut-backs of 10–15 per cent and 22 per cent, respectively, in Soviet oil deliveries (Jackson, 1990: 44). This move has caused six-hour petrol lines in Bulgaria, and forced it to double the prices of petrol, diesel fuel and heating oil on 23 July and to start shutting down power plants in August to save fuel for the winter (Gavrilov, 1990).[5]

On top of all this comes the establishment of the internal EC market, and the further relative reinforcement of the concomitant entry barriers against non-member countries (see e.g. Winiecki, 1989a, for a pessimistic assessment of the prospects in the absence of fundamental systemic reform). Competition within the EC will become stiffer than ever now that firms can no longer hide behind national barriers; this in turn will put a premium on competitiveness, which many Western (both within and outside the EC), let alone Balkan, exporters will find difficult to establish. Albania, Bulgaria and Romania continue to suffer from the legacy of the Stalinist autarchic and heavy industry-centred development strategy, so that the differences among them in the structure of productive capacity are less than they otherwise would have been.[6] Thus, there is little complementarity among their economies, which in turn implies that until restructuring is accomplished, they will by and large compete with each other for the same markets with similar products.[7]

The Balkan socialist economies will find it extraordinarily difficult to deal with all of these fundamental changes in the international economic order, given their shortages of investment resources, out-dated technology, lack of know-how (technical and economic), pressures for maintaining present employment levels and, not least, lingering ideological preferences. The continuing existence of soft budget constraints and the unwillingness to let enterprises go under and workers become unemployed in substantial numbers — practices that only in 1990 are finally starting to give way in the more reform-minded nations — have of course done nothing to improve matters. And the irony is that the new, more democratically constituted regimes may be less able to institute painful structural change than were their totalitarian predecessors.[8]

The Greek and Turkish experience

Space limitations preclude a detailed examination of the recent economic experience of Greece and Turkey. None the less, we cannot resist the temptation to take note of the fact that the socialist Balkan states, unlike the countries of East Central Europe, the USSR or China, have two capitalist countries with which they can be justifiably compared.[9] We are particularly struck by the fact that political instability and foreign debt problems have afflicted both Greece and Turkey, with varying degrees of severity, from time to time during the post-war period. Greece, of course, has been a member of the EC since January 1981, while Turkey's April 1987 application to join it is still under consideration pending the resolution of a number of economic and human rights questions.

The post-war Greek economy, while certainly avoiding the worst problems of the centrally planned economies to its north, has had its share of difficulties. Freris (1986: Chapter 5), for instance, sees the economy of the 1960s and 1970s as characterised by a 'take off that never was'. After US economic assistance dried up in 1949, with the victory of the Right in the civil war, the Greek government could not afford to sponsor an industrialisation drive, which the United States and international financial community seem in any case to have discouraged. A major devaluation in 1953 was unable to solve the country's balance of payments problems, although it is credited with a

> shifting of gear towards greater freedom for private enterprise, an opening of the . . . economy to internatinal [*sic*] trade by dismantling most of the complex import controls and export subsidies, and by eliminating some of the price and income distribution distortions caused by extensive use of multiple exchange rates. (Freris, 1986: 143).

A noteworthy characteristic of the Greek economy is the continuing, if diminishing, marginality of its industrial sector. As late as 1987 industry and construction accounted for only 28 per cent of total employment, and in 1988 mining and manufacturing contributed only 19.4 per cent to GDP (*OECD: Greece*, 1990: 7). Unlike the socialist Balkan countries, the machinery and transport equipment sectors in Greece remain relatively small and dominated by multinational corporations (Freris, 1986: 179); interestingly, the private sector has tended to shun investment in machinery in favour of construction (Freris, 1986: 166–81). The service sector remains extremely important to the economy, accounting for 58.6 per cent of GDP in 1988 (*OECD: Greece*, 1990: 7). The balance of trade has run persistently in the red, but severe balance of payments problems have been avoided due to substantial receipts from tourism and guest-worker remittances (for recent data, see *OECD: Greece*, 1990: 122). Overall, Freris (1986: 195–6) observes that the state has played a very minor role relative to such issues as unemployment, the balance of payments and industrial policy.

In the last two or three years, the Greek macro-economy has not performed well, and the EC is reportedly unhappy with the way the socialist governments of the 1980s managed the country's affairs. The termination of the 1986–7 Stabilisation Programme and relaxation of fiscal and incomes policies have resulted in 15 per cent inflation, public sector borrowing running at over 20 per cent of GDP and a huge current account deficit (*OECD: Greece*, 1990; 'Try Again', 1990). As it turns out, the election of a Conservative prime minister in April 1990 may result in macroeconomic policies more to the EC's liking.

Turkey has also had a turbulent post-war economic history. In view of the foreign debt problems that have afflicted the socialist Balkan countries, it is interesting to find that

> Turkey was the first major developing country . . . debtor to face a payments crisis after 1973. Turkey's debt debacle began in mid 1977, before the oil shock of the late 1970s. Indeed, Turkey's debt reschedulings prior to 1982 were the largest ever undertaken. (Celâsun and Rodrık, 1989: 193)

Yet, by the end of the 1980s it was possible to write that a 'model of stabilisation and adjustment for long, Turkey [has] been perceived as one of the few examples of a successful transition from inward- to outward-oriented policies during the turbulent economic conditions of the 1980s. (Aricanlı and Rodrık, 1990: 1).

Celâsun and Rodrık (1989) identify three periods of foreign exchange stringency (1957–8, 1969–70 and 1978–80), associated in each instance with both military takeovers and IMF-sponsored programmes of stabilisation and devaluation. Focusing on the 1970s, one is able to observe governments attempting to stimulate economic growth via overvalued exchange rates and other price distortions, large public sector budget deficits and easy money. The resulting current account deficits were financed by external borrowing until foreign lenders became nervous and the flow of new lending virtually dried up. The remedy tried in the late 1970s was administrative import controls, which led to sharp declines in investment and growth and rising inflation.

If none of this is particularly distinctive for a developing country, the radical policy turnaround in January 1980 is much more so. As described by Baysan and Blitzer (1990: 10–11), these measures included the following, among others:

1. flexible and realistic exchange rate policy;
2. more effective export promotion;
3. gradual import liberalisation (beginning in earnest at the end of 1983);
4. enhanced foreign debt management;
5. tighter monetary policy;
6. decontrol of interest rates; and
7. privatisation in sectors heretofore dominated by state enterprises.

These policy manoeuvres are credited with the chief responsibility — along with the highly favourable attitude of the United States in the wake of the fall of Iran (see Arıcanlı, 1990) — for the success of the Turkish economy in the succeeding years. Some results are as follows: the dollar value of exports grew by 25.4 per cent p.a. between 1980 and 1985, while imports grew by 16 per cent p.a.; by 1985 the current account deficit (in US dollars) was less than a third of its 1980 level; although the foreign debt grew, the debt/export ratio fell so that by 1985 it was about two-thirds of its 1980 level; real GNP grew at about 5 per cent p.a. between 1980 and 1986; and wholesale price inflation fell from 107.2 per cent p.a. in 1980 to 25.3 per cent by 1982, although it was as high as 52 per cent in individual years (Baysan and Blitzer, 1990:

23–30; Senses, 1988: 14). None the less, a number of serious economic problems, including insufficient private sector investment in manufacturing, the political and social ramifications of declining real wages, and persistently high inflation, were never overcome and seemed to be worsening by the end of the decade (see, e.g. Baysan and Blitzer, 1990).[10]

This brief discussion of Greece and Turkey should be sufficient to suggest that an understanding of the recent economic experience of these two nations is invaluable for those concerned with how the socialist Balkan states can extricate themselves from their present predicaments. The exploration of the implications of that experience for the four countries that are the main concern of this book seems a most promising research direction.

Reform experience of Albania, Bulgaria, Romania and Yugoslavia

The chapters contained in this volume provide ample discussion of the recent reform experiences of the countries in question; from their bibliographies the reader can trace the prior reform experiences thereof.[11] They demonstrate that the attemps of the socialist Balkan states to keep up with the times have so far not been particularly successful, and since the near future can reasonably be expected to produce increasing strains on their economies, pressure for more comprehensive reform will continue to build up.

Most of the countries under discussion, except Albania where such propositions in the past were normally inhibited on ideological or political grounds,[12] have at one time or another produced proposals for economic reform of varying degrees of ambition. As with the parallel attempts at reform in the Soviet Union and East Central Europe, the restructuring of the Balkan economies in the 1960s amounted to virtually nothing. To the extent that a genuine decentralisation took place, it soon gave way to the process of recentralisation that characterised much of the subsequent decade (Schlüter, 1988b: 25–6). The centre lost little time in reasserting its power, and whenever the enterprise incentive structure was perceived to produce unsatisfactory results, shorter planning horizons and an ever increasing number of plan indicators were reintroduced.

Yugoslavia, of course, is a special case, inasmuch as Soviet-style central planning was abolished at an early stage. None the less, some of the difficulties and biases normally associated with such planning seem to have remained as valid there as elsewhere in the socialist Balkans. The arguably most important characteristic of self-management in its Yugoslav guise is the fact that it is not a competitive economy, but a socialist one (Lydall 1989: Chapter 3). Political interference, sometimes down to the minutest detail, is a fact of life. Precisely because of this unwillingness to recognise the importance of sound commercial criteria, local authorities and banks — the latter often politically controlled or manipulated — continually assist loss-making firms to stay in business. Coalitions between enterprises and the authorities, with management, labour and local politicians often sharing in a communion of interests, cannot be expected to welcome and still less to encourage the entry of new competitors. The necessary structural change, which requires not only the closing down of uncompetitive enterprises, but also freedom of entry, has therefore never been implemented.

Moreover, self-management has, among other things, helped create or at least to uphold a 'fractured' economy (Bićanić, 1988), that is, an economy with less regional and sectoral integration than one would have expected on the basis of its level of development. This is not to suggest that the economy is totally fragmented — empirical studies (e.g. Bookman, 1990) indicate otherwise — but pressure for autarchy remains strong and duplication is frequent. As both the foreign trade barriers (including, before 1990, the non-convertibility of the dinar) and internal barriers largely remain in place, true competition from without seldom makes itself felt, thereby eliminating the only alternative test of competitiveness.

It is our contention, then, that Yugoslavia is not necessarily so distinct from the other economies under discussion as to invalidate its inclusion in a common 'Balkan socialist' category. On the contrary, the Yugoslav experience may well present the others with a warning that half-hearted reform produces its own dilemmas, with, for instance, open inflation taking the place of shortages.

The two chapters on Yugoslavia contained in this volume, besides providing general discussions on the ongoing reforms, focus on specific issues of great contemporary significance. Ivo Bićanić is concerned with the role of labour in the transition to a market economy led by Prime Minister Ante Marković. Bićanić focuses on five aspects of the labour market that impinge on this transition: (1) the absence of labour markets under the ideology of self-management; (2) labour discipline; (3) populist egalitarianism regarding income distribution; (4) the role of knowledge-intensive producer services; and (5) entrepreneurship. He then provides a critical survey of the economic reform attempts of the 1980s and of both phases of the Marković plan. On the whole, he is sceptical regarding the ability of Yugoslav society to withstand the enormous structural and behavioural changes required of it.

Will Bartlett describes the extraordinarily severe Yugoslav economic crisis of the 1980s, focusing on its foreign trade and payments problems and macro-economic imbalances. In order to deal with these difficulties, the dinar was devalued, exports were subsidised and exporters were allowed to keep varying amounts of their foreign earnings. The heart of his chapter is an original empirical analysis of the responsiveness of Yugoslav export supply to these changes in relative prices. Interestingly, he finds very low — although positive — price elasticities of export supply, a result consistent with both the Yugoslav experience and the standard theory of the self-managed firm.

Although similar in size and population, Romania is in many respects the opposite of Yugoslavia. Planning and the role of and attitude towards foreign economic relations are only two areas where they part. Nevertheless, structural problems abound in both countries, as economic criteria have not had much influence on investment decisions and living standards have suffered as a consequence of political decisions inimical to sound economic development. Few would object, however, to the contention that the Romanians have suffered the most in Eastern Europe under communism. Those aspects of reform that enhanced the forcefully executed austerity policies were implemented, while others were not; self-management in the Romanian context thus meant local responsibility without corresponding powers.

Ceausescu's tragic legacy is described and analysed at some length in Per Ronnås's chapter. Pointing out that the 1960s and early 1970s were a favourable period for the Romanian economy, he goes on to describe the causes of the stagnation and decay that set in during the 1980s. He draws our attention to the structural deformities wrought by years of economic policy strongly at variance with the economic logic; as the crisis deepened, responses became more and more absurd. Two particularly deleterious policies stand out: the draconian response to a self-induced energy crisis, and the inflexible and ideologically charged response to the problems of agriculture. Ronnås concludes by warning that some of the worst effects of Ceausescu's reign will be with us for years to come. This is not least true of the rapidly expanding labour force and the concomitant need to increase employment opportunities without putting the viability of the economy as a whole in jeopardy.

Alin Teodorescu provides a vivid picture of life under the old regime and discusses, from the vantage point of someone who lived through the Ceausescu era, the effects of the external debt repayment strategy. He also analyses the economic policies of the two major contesting parties in the May 1990 elections, as outlined in their respective election platforms. Against the background of previous mismanagement and the difficulties ahead, his disheartening prediction is that the economy would not fare very well in the hands of any party that heeded its own advice from the election campaign. Far more radical steps are needed to remedy the defects of the Romanian economy, Teodorescu asserts, with 'shock therapy' the only viable option.

During the 1980s Bulgaria went through the most attempts at economic reform and experienced the highest degree of institutional upheaval of all the countries covered here. Todor Zhivkov, its paramount leader for thirty-five years, one of communism's most puzzling characters, at once espoused the need for substantive change in the country's economic and political systems and guided one of the world's most repressive totalitarian states. Michael L. Wyzan begins by describing Decree no. 56, issued in January 1989, which lays down the rules according to which a new type of economic organisation known as a 'firm' is to run itself. This confusing and ambiguous document was left in force since the post-Zhivkov leadership saw fit to amend it rather than replace it. Wyzan goes on to describe the economic programme of the Socialist (formerly, Communist) party government that won the elections in June 1990. He finds that the stabilisation aspects of that programme do not go nearly far enough to rectify the country's enormous macro-economic imbalances and balance of payments problems, while its restructuring aspects are too timid in their support for the country's nascent private sector.

Ognian Pishev, currently the Bulgarian ambassador to the United States and at the time of writing one of the Bulgarian opposition's top economic advisers, compares the economic platforms of the main contenders in the June 1990 elections — the socialists, the agrarians and the opposition Union of Democratic Forces (UDF). He views the 'three principal axes of market reform' to be the transformation of property relations, the creation of a labour market, and the creation of financial intermediaries. He also presents five fundamental features of economic reform agreed upon by economic experts from all political parties. His analysis of the current transitional period is highly critical of the Socialist government's attempts to deal with inflation, unemployment, the creation and stimulation of private enterprise, autonomy for state enterprises, and foreign debt. He concludes on an optimistic note with the presentation of the UDF's anti-crisis agenda.

The final pair of country studies, of Albania, draw attention to developments of a different order. Here, Örjan Sjöbert leads off, arguing that in contradistinction to the view of some Western authors that Albanian economic policy has increasingly diverged from the pure Stalinist model, orthodoxy remained the centrepiece of economic policy throughout the 1980s. While Sjöberg sees Ramiz Alia as a pragmatic leader, he finds little to suggest that by the time Alia assumed power from Enver Hoxha, the new leader had come up with a coherent design for reforming the economy. Sjöberg describes the vagaries of economic policy during the 1980s, devoting particular attention to the dominant agricultural sector. He sees the policy manoeuvres towards the end of the decade as designed largely to rectify the worst effects of previous, almost invariably ill-conceived policies, rather than forming part of a reform programme as such. His examination of such data as exist for the late 1980s confirms this interpretation.

Indeed, in spite of all this activity, the Albanian economy remains the most centralised of the four. Given this and the fact that the tumultuous events of 1989 have not yet reached the 'final domino' with full force, it is perhaps logical that the experience of neighbouring countries will be repeated in Albania. The recently launched reform proposals, and this time they form a package, immediately call to mind the Romanian designs of the 1980s. Certainly, the 'new economic mechanism' as described by Gramoz Pashko, who since his chapter was written has emerged as a leader of the opposition Democratic party, resembles in no small part — and decidedly so in such important aspects as organisational set-up, pricing and the role of self-financing — the officially endorsed reports provided on Romania by, for example, Iancu (1989). Pashko's view is a more detached one, however, and he conscientiously points out the inherent weaknesses of the reform as outlined in official documents as well as the gross neglect of the need for the structural change that must accompany any such reorganisation of economic management.

In the penultimate chapter, Alan H. Smith takes a broader view and draws on the richer reform experience of the East Central European states, identifying points of similarity and divergence between the two major East European regions. Smith finds that as far as common problems are concerned, the South-East European socialist states are in many respects in a worse position than their more northern and more highly developed counterparts. Moreover, some of the Balkan countries face obstacles to economic recovery not experienced by the former Soviet-type economies in East Central Europe. These include a lower level of development and a weaker infrastructure (except in the Habsburg parts of Yugoslavia), as well as a higher degree of population pressure (especially in Albania, Romania and parts of southern Yugoslavia) and the possibility of national disintegration (Yugoslavia). It is thus no surprise that they also lag behind in the volume of foreign investment and in attractiveness to prospective foreign investors. However, foremost among the differences that work to the detriment of the formerly Ottoman portions of the region is the lack of the civil society that can support the process of peaceful social change and create alternative political structures as necessary. The economics of change may be the central theme of this book, but it would be a mistake not to give politics its due.

Anders Åslund, the organiser of the workshop from which this volume originates, provides a concluding chapter drawing together some of the major threads emerging from the discussion. Here the road ahead is in the spotlight, as strategies, or the lack thereof, with respect to marketisation and privatisation are heralded as the critical issues for the future.

On the whole, the papers suggest that reform as traditionally conceived has had no fundamental impact on the systemic features responsible for poor economic performance. The same can also be said for such 'fashionable non-solutions' (Winiecki, 1989b: 377–80) as membership in the IMF, unified exchange rates, equity joint ventures with Western firms and free trade zones. All of these measures have been manipulated virtually at will by, in Winiecki's (1989b: 377) words, 'the central planners and their political masters'. In any event, from the perspective of the events of late 1989, these reforms were the product of a doomed economic system, a failed experiment in social engineering whose days on earth must surely be numbered.

Notes

1. We are aware, of course, that not all regions of the four countries that we are calling 'Balkan' are physically on the Balkan peninsula, and, more importantly, that not all share an Ottoman past. Indeed, the multi-party elections in Slovenia and Croatia in the spring of 1990 reinforce the suspicion that the formerly Habsburg portions of Yugoslavia may have more in common with, say, Czechoslovakia than with the rest of the country; Transylvania has also demonstrated a certain distinctiveness from the rest of Romania in recent times. None the less, throughout this work we shall apply the 'Balkan' label to all four nations in their entirety, with apologies to any offended parties.
2. Of course, this statement is not equally true of all four countries, given the considerable scope for frank discussion and foreign travel long afforded Yugoslav, and more recently and to a lesser extent Bulgarian, economists.
3. Indeed, recent reports in the Albanian press (e.g. Korbeci, 1990) indicate a rapidly mounting trade deficit, the size of which is a source of concern.
4. The benefits to Bulgaria, the only 'orthodox' Soviet ally among our four nations, of obtaining 95 per cent of its coal, 90 per cent of its crude oil, 85 per cent of its electricity, and all of its natural gas from the USSR on soft terms, as it did in 1989 (Gavrilov, 1990: 3), need no elaboration. Bulgaria was even allowed to re-export Soviet oil against hard currency; indeed, according to PlanEcon ('Bulgarian Foreign Trade', 1988: 3), such re-exports made up 40 per cent of total Bulgarian exports to the developed West in 1987. Adding further to the complexity of this picture is Bulgaria's practice of purchasing oil of Middle Eastern origin via the Soviets at least partly for soft currency, even though such imports show up in Bulgaria's accounts as coming from the (capitalist) Third World ('Bulgarian Foreign Trade', 1989: 2). Such options were of course unavailable to Romania, which became quite dependent on OPEC oil to feed its petrochemical complex (Smith, 1986). Albania, an exporter of crude oil and some basic derivatives — although an importer of the finer grades of refined petroleum products — has been seen by some as realising net gains thanks to the elevated petroleum prices prior to the 1985–6 slump (Artisien, 1987: 238); see, however, the dissenting view in Sandström and Sjöberg (Forthcoming).

5. Bulgaria, as part of a move to reduce its energy dependence on the USSR, signed an agreement with Iraq in July providing for Iraqi oil deliveries to Bulgaria to pay off the US$1,200 million that Iraq owes it (Sudetic, 1990). Hence, Bulgaria's agreeing on 8 August to support the United Nations (UN) sanctions against Iraq over the latter's invasion of Kuwait carried a very high price for a nation so deeply in debt; Bulgaria immediately appealed to the UN for emergency financial assistance. Much the same is true of Romania, which is also one of Iraq's main creditors. In addition, Yugoslavia has long maintained a large presence and has over the years built up a substantial business in the area (Kusin, 1990).
6. Indeed, Khruschchev's attempts in the 1950s and the early 1960s to create a 'socialist division of labour' within the CMEA were fiercely rebuffed by Romania; Albania's leaving the fold is also partly the result of its desire for autarchic ('self-reliant') economic development. Even the Yugoslav economy, although considerably more open to trade with the developed West than the others in Eastern Europe, suffers from autarchic tendencies.
7. Albania, with its highly underdeveloped and resource-rich economy, is something of a special case here, but it too must overcome the inertia of its current industrial structure and badly performing extractive sector.
8. On the other hand, the continuing popularity of Yugoslav Prime Minister Ante Marković in the face of the very severe stabilisation programme introduced there — an opinion poll in late July 1990 found that 79 per cent of Yugoslavs would vote for him (Silber, 1990) — suggests that matters are not hopeless.
9. Comparative studies of the Balkan economies that include both socialist and capitalist countries have been rare. Gianaris (1982) takes a broad overview of all six countries, while Hoffman's (1972) examination of the spatial aspects of development strategy and Lampe's and Jackson's (1982) economic history includes Greece and the four socialist countries. Also worthy of mention is Gianaris (1984), which compares the economies of Greece and Yugoslavia.
10. On the other hand, 1990 has seen very rapid economic growth, predicted in September to be over 10 per cent. Trouble may be on the horizon, however, given that Turkey's commitment to support the UN embargo against Iraq had already cost it US$4,000 million by mid September (Silk, 1990).
11. There is an enormous volume of literature on economic reform in Eastern Europe in the 1970s and 1980s. In addition to the regular US Congress Joint Economic Committee and NATO compendia, Schönfeld (1985), Althammar (1987), Altmann (1988), Schlüter (1988a), and *Economic Reforms* (1989) are recommended as recently published descriptions and analyses of these reform efforts in South-Eastern Europe.
12. For instance, the suggestion during the first half of the 1970s that Albania might do well to pursue a less isolationist economic policy (including a foreign trade policy more receptive to relations with the industrialised West) was killed in its infancy. Indeed, its major proponents, a number of ministers with economic portfolios, were literally among the victims of the reaction to these proposals (see Kaser, 1986: 3). Later on, the break with China in the late 1970s brought home to the leadership the necessity of maintaining good terms with neighbouring countries, as attested to by the changing pattern of trade (Masotti Christofoli, 1985).

References

Althammar, Walter, ed. 1987. *Südosteuropa in der Ära Gorbatschow. Auswirkungen der sowjetischen*

Reformpolitik auf die südosteuropäischen Länder (Südosteuropa Aktuell, 2. Munich: Südosteuropa-Gesellschaft).

Altmann, Franz-Lothar. 1988. 'Wirtschaftsreformen in Südosteuropa und der CSSR — Versuch einer vergleichenden Gegenüberstellung', *Südosteuropa*, Jg. 37: 6, pp. 280–94.

Arıcanlı, Tosun. 1990. 'The political economy of Turkey's external debt: the bearing of exogenous factors', in Tosun Arıcanlı and Dani Rodrık, eds, *The Political Economy of Turkey: Debt, adjustment and sustainability* (New York, NY: St Martin's), pp. 230–53.

Arıcanlı, Tosun and Dani Rodrık. 1990. 'Introduction and overview', in Tosun Arıcanlı and Dani Rodrık, eds, *The Political Economy of Turkey: Debt, adjustment and sustainability* (New York, NY: St Martin's), pp. 1–7.

Artisien, Patrick. 1987. 'Albania at the Crossroads', *Journal of Communist Studies*, vol. 3:3, pp. 231–49.

Baysan, Tercan and Charles Blitzer. 1990. 'Turkey's trade liberalization in the 1980s and the prospects for its sustainability', in Tosun Arıcanlı and Dani Rodrık, eds, *The Political Economy of Turkey: Debt, adjustment and sustainability* (New York, NY: St Martin's, 1990), pp. 9–36.

Bićanić, Ivo,. 1988 'Fractured economy'. In Dennison Rusinow, ed., *Yugoslavia: A fractured federalism* (Washington, DC: Wilson Center Press), pp. 120–41.

Bookman, Milica Zarkovic. 1990. 'The economic basis of regional autarchy in Yugoslavia', *Soviet Studies*, vol. 42:1, pp. 93–109.

'Bulgarian foreign trade performance in 1987: quadrupling of trade surplus with the Third World fails to improve country's hard-currency payments picture', *PlanEcon Report*, vol. 4:22–3 (3 June 1988).

'Bulgarian foreign trade performance in 1988 and during January–March 1989: non-socialist exports continue to fall and the rise in trade deficit heightens concern about a potential upcoming payments crisis', *PlanEcon Report*, vol. 5:27–8 (14 July 1989).

Celâsun, Merih and Dani Rodrık. 1989. 'Turkish experience with debt: macroeconomic policy and performance', in Jeffrey D. Sachs, ed., *Developing Country Debt and the World Economy* (Chicago, Ill.: University of Chicago Press), pp. 193–211.

Economic Reforms in the European Centrally Planned Economies, (United Nations Economic Commission for Europe, Economic Studies, 1. New York, NY: United Nations, 1989).

Freris, Andrew F. 1986. *The Greek Economy in the Twentieth Century* (New York, NY: St Martin's).

Gavrilov, Vera. 1990. 'Energy crisis looming', *Report on Eastern Europe*, vol. 1:34 (24 August), pp. 3–5.

Gianaris, Nicholas V. 1982. *The Economies of the Balkan Countries: Albania, Bulgaria, Greece, Romania, Turkey, and Yugoslavia* (New York, NY: Praeger).

Gianaris, Nicholas V. 1984. *Greece and Yugoslavia: An economic comparison* (New York, NY: Praeger).

Hoffman, George W. 1972. *Regional Development Strategy in Southeast Europe: A comparative analysis of Albania, Bulgaria, Greece, Romania and Yugoslavia* (New York, NY: Praeger).

Iancu, Aurel. 1989. 'Role and functioning of the enterprise in Romania', *Economic Reforms in the European Centrally Planned Economies* (United Nations Economic Commission for Europe, Economic Studies, 1 (New York, NY: United Nations), pp. 123–35.

Jackson, Marvin. 1990. 'The impact of the Gulf crisis on the economies of Eastern Europe', *Report on Eastern Europe*, vol. 1:35 (31 August), pp. 40–5.

Kanet, Roger E. 1986. 'East European trade in the 1980s: reorientation in international economic relations', in Phillip Joseph, ed., *The Economies of Eastern Europe and their Foreign Economic Relations/L'Économie des pays d'Europe de l'Est et leurs relations économiques extérieures* (Brussels: NATO), pp. 291–310.

Kaser, Michael. 1986. 'Albania under and after Enver Hoxha', in *East European Economies: Slow growth in the 1980s*, vol. 2: *Country Studies on Eastern Europe and Yugoslavia. Selected papers submitted to the Joint Economic Committee of the United States, March 28, 1986* (Washington, DC: US Government Printing Office), pp. 1–21.

Korbeci, Shane. 1990. 'Milionat për import kemi në duart tona', *Zëri i popullit*, 8 August.

Kunkle, William. 1989. 'East European balance of payments prospects', in *Pressures for Reform in the East European Economies*, vol. 2: *Study Papers Submitted to the Joint Economic Committee of the Congress of the United States, October 27, 1989* (Washington, DC: US Government Printing Office), pp. 352–76.

Kusin, Vladimir, V. 1990. 'Iraq, Kuwait, and Eastern Europe', *Report on Eastern Europe*, vol. 1:34 (24 August), pp. 41–4.

Lampe, John R. and Marvin R. Jackson. 1982. *Balkan Economic History, 1550–1950: From imperial borderlands to developing nations* (Bloomington, Ind.: Indiana University Press).

Lydall, Harold. 1989. *Yugoslavia in Crisis* (Oxford: Clarendon Press).

Masotti Christofoli, Angelo,. 1985. 'Albania's economy between the blocs', in Roland Schönfeld, ed., *Reform und Wandel in Südosteuropa*, Untersuchungen zur Gegenwartskunde Südosteuropas, 26. (Munich: R. Oldenbourg), pp. 285–305.

OECD Economic Surveys: Greece (Paris: OECD, 1990).

Reuter-Hendricks, Irena, 'Jugoslawiens Beziehungen zur Sowjetunion, in Walter Althammar, ed., *Südosteuropa in der Ära Gorbatschow, Auswirkungen der sowjetischen Reformpolitik auf die südosteuropäischen Länder*, Südosteuropa Aktuell, 2 (Munich: Südosteuropa-Gesellschaft), pp. 111–17.

Sandström, Per and Örjan Sjöberg, Forthcoming. 'Albanian economic performance: stagnation in the 1980s', *Soviet Studies*.

Schönfeld, Roland, ed. 1985. *Reform und Wandel in Südosteuropa*, Untersuchungen zur Gegenwartskunde Südosteuropas, 26. (Munich: R. Oldenbourg).

Schlüter, Rolf, ed. 1988a. *Wirtschaftsreformen im Ostblock in den 80er Jahren. Länderstudien: Sowjetunion, DDR, Polen, Rumänien, Tschechoslowakei, Bulgarien, Ungarn* (Paderborn: Schöningh).

Schlüter, Rolf. 1988b. 'Einleitung', in Rolf Schlüter, ed., *Wirtschaftsreformen im Ostblock in den 80er Jahren. Länderstudien: Sowjetunion, DDR, Polen, Rumänien, Tschechoslowakei, Bulgarien, Ungarn* (Paderborn: Schöningh), pp. 13–30.

Senses, Fikret. 1988. 'An overview of recent Turkish experience with economic stabilization and Liberalization', in Tevfik F. Nas and Mehmet Odekon, eds, *Liberalization and the Turkish Economy* (New York, NY: Greenwood Press), pp. 9–28.

Silber, Laura. 1990. 'Markovic prepares for a legendary struggle', *Financial Times*, 31 July.

Silk, Leonard. 1990. 'Turkey's stake in the Mideast crisis', *The New York Times*, 14 September.

Smith, Alan, H. 1986. 'Romania: internal economic development and foreign economic relations', in Phillip Joseph, ed., *The Economies of Eastern Europe and their Foreign Economic Relations /L'Économie des pays d'Europe de l'Est et leurs relations économiques extérieures* (Brussels: NATO), pp. 255–74.

Sudetic, Chuck. 1990. 'East block to sell masks to Saudis', *The New York Times*, 6 September.

'Try Again', *The Economist*, 31 March 1990, p. 49.

Winiecki, Jan. 1989a. 'Eastern Europe: challenge of 1992 dwarfed by pressures of system's decline', *Aussenwirtschaft*, vol. 44:3/4, pp. 345–65.

Winiecki, Jan. 1989b. 'CPEs' structural change and world market performance: a permanently developing country (PDC) status?', *Soviet Studies*, vol. 41:3, pp. 365–81.

Woods, Leyla. 1989. 'East European trade with the industrial West', in *Pressures for Reform in the East European Economies*, vol. 2: *Study Papers Submitted to the Joint Economic Committee of the Congress of the United States, October 27, 1989* (Washington, DC: US Government Printing Office), pp. 388–419.

2 The role of labour in the great transition to a market economy in Yugoslavia

Ivo Bićanić

Introduction

This chapter will deal with whether labour market issues can further, hinder or even prevent the 'Great Transition' to a market economy in Yugoslavia. It is composed of three sections. The first will try to justify the notion that labour has a special place that warrants special attention. The second will point out the five main characteristics of labour that can influence the transition, while the last will describe policy attempts to turn the tide of the Yugoslav crises of the 1980s.

Each of the formerly socialist East European economies, the Balkan ones included, has embarked down a new growth path that will attempt to provide its inhabitants with a 'decent level of welfare' by relying on radically different means. The cornerstone of this new economic system is the introduction of a modern market economy capable of participating in the world economy. For these societies the development of the institutions of a market economy and market exchange represents a great transition. This great transition entails many demanding and complicated tasks requiring these societies to shed their previous political and economic systems.

Due to the complexity of the process it is impossible to deal with more than one of its aspects in a chapter such as this. Hence, this chapter will attempt to address one aspect in only one country. Namely, it will deal with the present role of labour in the Yugoslav economy and, more specifically, whether labour by its behaviour can facilitate or hinder, perhaps even prevent, Yugoslavia's great transition to a market economy.

This topic was chosen for a number of reasons, the first two of which are applicable primarily to Yugoslavia while the third and fourth are relevant to all the formerly socialist countries. First, the need for a transition to a market economy is the only issue on which there is consensus. For at the time of writing (June 1990), all aspects of the country's future are being heatedly debated, and the President of the Federal

Executive Council has only just announced the second phase of the current reform. Thus at present the wider issues concerning the redistribution of policymaking power, the form and very existence of the country are on the agenda, as are narrower ones regarding the nature, asymmetric impact, cost and time horizon of the chosen economic policy measures. The former have been put on the agenda by the victory of non-Communist parties in the two north-western republics, the latter by all as the distribution of costs of the reform is being bargained over before they start to take effect.

However, while the differences on these issues are very big, all the parties concerned agree on one issue: that the great transition is unavoidable and must proceed without delay (although admittedly the way to proceed differs). The second reason for choosing this topic is that all economic policy attempts described in the third section to turn the tide of the Yugoslav crises of the 1980s assumed the population had an infinite capacity to absorb welfare loss and adapt. Whether through price increases, wage control or wage restraint, unemployment or consumer loans, the policymakers first turned to the population, expecting it to pay the cost of change. Third, and in line with this policy choice, most of the literature has concentrated on the institutional changes required for a successful transition in individual formerly socialist economies. This is true both of official documents and of professional papers. Such an approach has meant that concern for the non-institutional requirements of the transition has been out of the limelight. Since the non-institutional requirements define the constraint space within which institutional change must optimise, this disregard does not seem justified. The fourth reason for concentrating on labour is that among the non-institutional requirements for the transition it has a special position. For apart from being the prime target, ultimately it is the population which has to provide the efficient labour input without which no transition is possible, and, conversely, if incentives and motives are lacking, it can hinder the whole endeavour, perhaps even prevent it.

The role of labour during the great transition

Among the generally disregarded non-institutional underpinnings required for the transition, labour has received the least attention. All the other non-institutional requirements, such as foreign reserves, foreign trade capabilities, the structure and nature of capital goods, infrastructure and natural resources, and so on, have received more attention. This is surprising, given that these countries had previously declared their adherence to socialist principles, and had professed to 'build' socialism.

Five aspects seem especially important when discussing labour's role in the transition. These are the following: (1) labour allocation without official labour markets; (2) working habits and labour discipline; (3) populist egalitarianism in distribution; (4) the position of knowledge-intensive producer services; and (5) the channelling of entrepreneurial talent. Their common characteristic is that during past development the economy has adapted to them; they have become built in, and hence changing them is a slow process requiring time and wise economic policy.

Furthermore, to a large extent they determine the welfare of the population and the incentive to work, thus influencing labour inputs.

Labour allocation without official labour markets

In the official economy organised by the ruling élite with the purpose of developing self-managed socialism, labour markets had no place. The existence of labour markets was *a priori* unacceptable, for in Marxian political economy they imply exploitation and alienation, and admitting their existence under socialism would lead to many theoretical paradoxes. Furthermore, the 'Associated Labour Paradigm' applied since the early 1970s, and the concept of social ownership it included, justified the exclusion of labour markets from the system, a feature further underpinned by the concept of the leading role of the League of Communists of Yugoslavia (LCY), especially for 'positional jobs'. Apart from these ideologically based objections to labour markets, this state of affairs served other useful purposes. First, in an economy with surplus labour it provided the ruling élite with an important economic power; and second, it enabled the complete control of all positional jobs in the economy.

Thus for forty-five years labour was not allocated through officially sanctioned labour markets. Unofficial channels and ties involving personal favours dominated most employment decisions. For positional jobs considerations of political loyalty predominated, but for other jobs family and regional ties sufficed. This is not surprising, for it was already suggested in the theoretical literature, that explained the behaviour of the labour-managed enterprise in terms of negotiation and game theory. Recent empirical studies find that increasing employment is one of the major goals of the Yugoslav enterprise (see Prasnikar *et al.*, 1989). This created strong pressures, internal and external, to increase employment, which were further increased by the chosen industrialisation policy based on cheap part-time workers and shifting population from rural into urban areas (Crkvenac, 1985). Under such circumstances it is not surprising that employment was the one policy target that was regularly overshot in five-year plans (see Table 2.1) and yearly policy resolutions was employment (see Crkvenac, 1985, and Mencinger, 1986). Furthermore, three-quarters of GNP growth from 1948 to 1986 can be attributed to the quantity of labour

Table 2.1 Comparison of planned and achieved employment targets in post-war Yugoslav plans

Rate of growth	Planned	Achieved	Error
1957–61	4.4	7.7	+3.3
1960–65	6.2	4.2	−2
1966–70	2.5 to 3	0.7	−1.8 to −2.3
1971–75	3	4.3	+1.3
1976–80	3.5	4.1	+0.6
1981–85	2.5	2.7	0.2

Source: Respective five-year plans and *Statistički godišnjak SFRJ*.

input (Jovanović–Gavrilović, 1989: 139). This had a detrimental effect on labour productivity and on the efficiency of capital (Stipetić, 1985) and led to fictitious employment and serious overmanning.

On the other hand, for a variety of reasons employment could not fall and the economy had a built-in 'ratchet effect' regarding employment growth in the socialised sector. In enterprises it was a result of the workers' solidarity consideration built into the behaviour of the labour-managed enterprise. On the macro-economic level it resulted from labour laws that made it almost impossible to lay off workers and at times compulsory to employ school-leavers, and a very soft budget constraint preventing enterprises from going bankrupt and treating the shedding of labour as a predominantly social and political problem.

Both these phenomena, namely the pressure to overemploy and the ratchet effect, have led to job security for the employed and a high probability of finding employment for all but the unskilled.

In spite of the dominant non-market allocation of labour over time, some segments of the labour market were influenced by external labour markets. The opening of West European labour markets in the mid-1960s influenced primarily unskilled workers (traditionally the most mobile) and some 'convertible professions' (e.g. engineers, physicians). Seasonal labour in agriculture, tourism, and housing and construction is frequently employed on short-term contracts in unofficial markets even by the socialised sector. Those employed by the private sector are also in competitive employment. The self-employed professions (lawyers, actors, physicians) have always been in competitive official markets.

One of the most important tasks of the current reform is to introduce labour markets. First, it will attempt to introduce job insecurity into the Yugoslav economy, thus allowing firms to vary labour. Institutionally this will be achieved through collective employment contracts between labour (represented by trade unions of a different kind from the present ones), owners of capital (presently non-existent with the chambers of commerce unwilling to become representatives of surrogate owners), and the state; changing employment laws so that managers will be able to vary employment (by making the employment decision a discretionary power on the part of managers); and providing for the reduction in overmanning (through defining 'technological surplus employment' and offering retraining, golden handshakes and early retirement). Second, the existing employment office will evolve into a labour exchange, an idea not yet worked out. Furthermore, bankruptcy laws are to be implemented and profit-maximising banking is supposed to harden the budget constraint. However, one aspect of labour markets has not yet been dealt with: provision for the unemployed. This is a flaw in the effort to introduce labour markets, for it is expected that the reform will lead to a major increase in unemployment. The present unemployment benefit covers less than one-third of the unemployed and is far below the subsistence level, so that the costs of unemployment are still private family costs (faced by increasingly impoverished families).

Work habits and labour discipline

Due to the aforementioned employment policies, present Yugoslav enterprises are overmanned. This is a stylised fact about the Yugoslav economy, although there are nothing but guesstimates about the extent of this phenomenon, and these are in the range of 20 per cent (estimated as a lower boundary for 1988; see Mencinger, 1989: 23) to 50 per cent of the employed in the socialised sector. Officially, this would mean an increase in unemployment of between 600,000 and 1.6 million (in addition to the presently registered 1.2 million; see *Ekonomska politika*, 1987:88, p. 11). The same source reports that the registered 'technological surplus' is unreliable because of varied response, the uncertainty reporting has for the firm and the tailoring of the figures to meet other political needs. However, regardless of the inspiration, motive, or method of estimation, all cases give a large figure for overmanning, and perhaps even more importantly, regard it as a long-standing feature. Perhaps the only partly reliable data can be derived from employment policies of firms inheriting the capital stock of bankrupt enterprises. They tend to employ only about half of the previous labour force (and increase production, wages, and so on). These bankruptcies ('strategic bankruptcies' as they are being referred to) have increasingly become a favoured way by managers of enterprises of shedding surplus labour.

This stylised fact has had many effects both on Yugoslav enterprises and on household behaviour. Overmanning and the resulting low wages have necessitated second jobs for both men and women. Over a third of the employed are part-time workers/part-time peasants with neither income being sufficient for subsistence. Many of the skilled work in the unofficial economy, especially providing services. The professional classes, when possible, offer their services for a contracted honorarium or through the unofficial economy. All the aforementioned groups barter labour services. The political and business élite enjoy imputed earnings and privileges. In spite of this, 61 per cent of polled households in 1985 did not find their regular household income sufficient and over half found their total incomes to be below their expenditures (Sirotić, 1986).

This kind of behaviour has had a feedback effect causing a negative spiral. The practice of having second jobs has further decreased work incentives. Thus, a survey of enterprise managers reported major disruption of production during the high agricultural season (Maroević, 1984). Unofficial economic activities are practised by many but perhaps equally importantly, these activities are contracted or even performed during regular working hours, frequently with equipment and parts 'borrowed' from the enterprise (Vejnović, 1984). The first of these problems has been a major influence on the aforementioned falling productivity of labour and capital and has had a major role in maintaining low wages and poor labour discipline and work habits. Low wages resulting from overmanning have led to the need to have two wage-earners per family (and high female employment at discriminatory wages). Moreover, low wages have led to the importance of second jobs, either through mixed households or in unofficial economic activities.

Apart from overmanning, a disincentive effect on labour is provided by two other aspects of the position of labour in the enterprise: promotion and job security. Expertise and hard work are as insufficient for internal promotion as they are for finding employment. The higher one's position in the internal enterprise hierarchy, the less importance is given to one's work. Job security on the other hand discourages any extra effort. The importance of these aspects can be seen from Table 2.2.

Table 2.2 Negative features of the immediate working environment as perceived by the adult population

Negative feature	per cent
Privileges of individuals and groups	55
Privatisation of social ownership	43
Bribery and corruption	36
Loitering and avoiding work	34
Illegal activities	28
Moonlighting during office hours	26
Disorder, disorganisation and chaos	23
Apathy and political indifference	8
Other	2
Does not know	9
No negative features	8

Note: The totals add up to more than 100 since some of those polled listed more than one choice.

Source: Kroflin-Fišer (1985: 54).

The trade-off between high wages and job insecurity on one hand and low wages complemented with a second job and job security on the other clearly suggests what risk-adverse economic agents might prefer. The extent to which the latter is built into the social system is shown by Zupanov (1984), who explains social and economic stability during the crises by a tacit agreement between workers and the ruling élite. The former do not question the legitimacy of the latter and tolerate it as long as job security is maintained.

Obviously the current reform proposes to break this relationship. What results this may have are still unpredictable, for the first phase of the reform, price stabilisation and currency convertibility, was achieved in early 1990 without leading to significant increases in unemployment or changes in household behaviour. Restructuring, the second, longer-lasting and less glamorous phase of the reform, however, cannot succeed without eliminating overmanning and dealing with the consequent changes in labour discipline and household behaviour. With a 45-year history of influencing household behaviour it is difficult to expect there to be no opposition to such restructuring.

Populist Egalitarianism in Distribution

During the whole post-war period there has been a strong pressure towards egalitarianism. Thus, any effort to increase inequality was soon declared ideologically suspect; there were regular economic policy campaigns against the above-average income brackets; there was continual pressure to attach the stigma of illegal dealings and dishonest means to those who had a greater wealth; very narrow intra-enterprise differentials were recommended by policymakers; and last, but far from least, the ruling élite did not achieve its privileges through larger money incomes.

Furthermore, when incomes policies were being defined so as not to interfere with self-management, they concentrated exclusively on limiting total enterprise labour costs. The result was that the size of the resulting wage fund was such that any degree of inegalitarianism would leave too many workers with below-subsistence wages.

This 'populist egalitarian syndrome' influenced inequality levels in general as well as the distribution of income within enterprises. The former is clearly shown by Gini coefficients for the distribution of net personal income of the fully employed in the socialised sector. The more reliable calculations (the period of high inflation rates has been omitted since the data are unreliable due to overrepresentation of the high income brackets) are given in Table 2.3. Intra-enterprise inequality was not high either. A long-standing official recommendation of an intra-enterprise range of 1 to 3 (Mates, 1980) led most enterprises to accept narrowing wage differentials over time. Other results confirm this (Flakierski, 1989). The low inequality levels in general, the lower levels in the more developed parts of the economy, and the low intra-enterprise differentials conceal an important aspect of income inequality. The wage distribution system was such as to permit a high level of intra-occupational inequality. The wage of an occupation varied with the individual enterprise or sector of employment. This major deficiency has been attributed, among other things, to the lack of a price of capital, which permitted capital-intensive enterprises to distribute capital income to workers.

Table 2.3 Gini coefficients for those employed in the socialised sector of the Yugoslav economy

	IX 1970	III 1971	III 1974	IX 1974	III 1983
Yugoslavia	0.1918	0.1967	0.1873	0.1757	0.1683
Bosnia & Herzegovina	0.1829	0.1818	0.1774	0.1704	0.1643
Montenegro	0.1850	0.1839	0.1750	0.1804	0.1607
Croatia	0.1912	0.2078	0.1887	0.1766	0.1682
Macedonia	0.1857	0.1925	0.1727	0.1700	0.1656
Slovenia	0.1712	0.1771	0.1618	0.1471	0.1352
Serbia	0.1921	0.1936	0.1926	0.1757	0.1711
– Serbia proper	0.1958	0.1986	0.1901	0.1823	0.1763
– Kosovo	0.1760	0.1822	0.1993	0.1713	–
– Vojvodina	0.1822	0.1836	0.1925	0.1794	–

Source: The distributions were taken from the respective monthly Statistical Index of the Federal Statistical Office; the coefficients were calculated using the INEQ program written at the London School of Economics.

Regarding inequality measures derived from household surveys, there are some established relations in the structure of inequality (Bićanić), 1988). First, the more-developed regions have smaller inequality measures for households and the employed. Second, in all regions except the most developed, Slovenia, the structure of relative household inequality is the same and is characteristic of dualistic societies (rural incomes are lower with less variation while urban incomes are higher and more variable; over time, agricultural incomes vary inversely with non-agricultural incomes). The exception to this is Slovenia, where all household incomes show the same level of inequality and change simultaneously. The overall level of inequality is not high either.

The crisis itself, with falling living standards and real incomes, has increased the egalitarian 'equality in poverty' syndrome. On a national level inequality measures fell until the mid 1980s, since which time there has been a slight increase as intra-regional inequality has fallen and interregional differences have increased.

The development of labour markets and the consequent increase in income differentials with falling intra-occupational ones, the restructuring of the economy, the changes in the size distribution of enterprises as the 'black hole' is filling and a vigorous private entrepreneurial sector all necessarily lead to an increase in inequality that will be further increased by unemployment. Finally, inequality will rise as interregional differences increase even further.

Such large changes in inequality are visible and conspicuous. Historical experience (see Kaelble, 1986, or Phelps-Brown, 1977) shows that inequality is a very stubborn and deeply-rooted feature of an economy. Such sudden increases in inequality connected with increasing poverty as the welfare effects of the reform impinge can easily be a further breeding-ground for populist egalitarianism. This in turn can lead to opposition to the restructuring.

The position of knowledge-intensive producer services

Among producer services, business services have a special role, especially the knowledge-intensive producer services (KIPS) defined as 'finance, insurance, law, advertising, consulting, data processing and communications' (Spero, 1985: 179) and, according to some authors, real estate. Frequently they are considered to be the most dynamic part of the economy, both due to service externalisation resulting from restructuring and technical progress and because of their role in economic development and growth. In market economies they provide the services that operate the capital market, contractual relations, the know-how for managerial decisions, financial services, and so on. Obviously their role in the great transition is vital for setting up capital and money markets and paving the way to privatisation of, in the case of Yugoslavia, socially-owned capital. Equally, without adequate financial services the whole effort of putting banking on a profit-oriented basis is doomed. These are, arguably, the greatest tasks of the transition and both are still open. Indeed, the transformation of socially-owned capital into other forms of ownership (private, co-operative and state) is said to be the central task of the second phase of the current programme.

In order to estimate the contribution KIPS may give, it is important to evaluate the present level of their development. During the forty-five years of Communist rule, and especially since the mid 1970s, four main influences have dominated the position and development of KIPS. The first is the bias of the Marxian development path (Crkvenac, 1985) in favour of industry and heavy industry in particular. It has led to the well-known lag in the development of services (*Trade and Development*, 1988) while the bias in favour of 'productive work' has led to a lag in knowledge-based activities.

A second major influence was the bias against the private sector (Grbić, 1984). For KIPS this meant that their most common organisational form — partnerships and small or one-person firms — faced an unfavourable and uncertain economic environment, frequently forcing them into unofficial economic activities. The third is the bias in favour of large organisations (Petrin, 1986), which represents a rational reaction of Yugoslav enterprises to their business environment. In relation to KIPS this meant that there was a barrier to their externalisation and the setting-up of small specialised firms as well as an incentive to organise existing KIPS in big establishments (especially in finance). The fourth and perhaps most important influence was the bias towards politicising issues (Maksimović, 1985). The reduction of all economic issues to those of politics and ideology had an especially devastating effect on KIPS. Furthermore, politicians in a one-party state, as well as the enterprise managers whose appointments they controlled, could not respect independent expertise. Thus instead of being knowledge-based, these services are to a great extent based on ignorance. To what extent these services are underdeveloped can be seen from Table 2.4 which gives the employment in these services. These are the only available data since the national accounts still treat them in line with the Marxian approach which considers them unproductive.

Table 2.4 Employment in financial and other services in Yugoslavia in the socialised sector (yearly average in thousands)

	1965	1975	1980	1981	1982	1983	1984	1985	1986	1987	1988
Banking	27.7	38.9	68.4	71.0	71.1	73.2	75.4	79.7	84.3	88.4	89.7
Insurance	14.0	11.1	15.0	15.6	15.9	16.3	16.9	17.5	18.2	18.7	18.7
Commercial	14.0	22.2	28.9	29.7	31.6	31.4	34.0	41.3	42.4	47.9	49.8
Designing	18.0	27.3	45.2	46.6	48.1	49.6	50.2	52.1	55.5	55.8	54.4
Geological	5.9	6.9	8.4	8.8	8.3	9.3	9.2	9.7	9.6	7.0	6.7
R & D	6.3	8.3	15.8	16.7	17.6	18.5	20.0	22.5	22.6	22.7	22.5
Business	6.9	9.3	14.9	15.8	16.4	17.2	17.8	19.2	20.3	20.6	20.5
Total	87	124	197	204	209	216	224	242	253	261	262
Total empl.	3583	4667	5681	5846	5980	6097	6224	6378	6566	6703	6715

Source: Statistički godišnjak SFRJ, various years.

Given the importance of KIPS and the policymakers intent on swift change, this means that the reform has to tap existing human resources and existing services or import human capital. This, in turn, depends on how quickly they can 'catch up' both in quantity and quality on lost development and meet the rising demand for their services. The catching-up will involve three kinds of changes. The first kind of change involves their transformation from ignorance-based to KIPS. The second kind of catching-up is related to the number of enterprises. These will significantly increase as new ones are formed, existing ones are externalised and some leave the unofficial economy. The third kind of change involves the setting-up of institutions and services required in a market economy but which were previously non-existent.

The success with which this will be done and the quality of the services performed may significantly influence the outcome. A misevaluation of capital during privatisation, bad support for investment decisions when investments are low, and inadequate banking exposing banks to risks, are some of the results inadequate KIPS can cause in the short term and thereby bring about a slowing-down of the pace of reform.

The channelling of entrepreneurial talent

Assuming that entrepreneurial talent is an inborn talent that can be channelled by the economic environment and enriched by investing in human capital, Yugoslavia is still not tapping this scarce resource. The economic environment is not conducive to risk-taking, there are institutional barriers to the growth and expansion of enterprises and expertise has not been necessary for promotion to senior managerial posts.

The economic environment incited risk-adverse behaviour in many ways. The already-mentioned preference for large capacity created huge inert enterprises in which entrepreneurs lost out to administrators. Enterprise performance was determined by negotiating business terms (prices, import quotas, export subsidies, soft loans, and so on) with the ruling élite and not based on the market-channelled entrepreneurial talent in negotiating and bargaining, nor organising production and marketing. Indeed, some sectors by these means had achieved such extensive administrative monopolies as to cause the aforementioned large intra-occupational wage variations (Korosić, 1983). The importance of negotiating and the ageing of the ruling élite made seniority important. Entrepreneurship was further stifled by barriers to firm growth. There are two such barriers. The first was the placing of a maximum on the number employed in a private sector enterprise; there was a barrier when passing from the private sector into the socialised one by employing more than five workers. The second barrier resulted from the large social overheads required, which made the average social overhead per worker employed in small enterprises too high for them to compete. The result was that the size distribution of enterprises has a 'black hole' (Vahcic, 1989), for there are a large number of very small private firms (the average private firm employs fewer than two workers) and a large number of big firms (by Yugoslav standards). This prevented firms from starting small and growing; there was a large minimum size required that further incited 'administrating' and soft budget constraints. Many entrepreneurs from the private sector were thus forced into unofficial activities and devious methods in order to expand. In the socialised sector the entrepreneurs had to start either with the support of the ruling élite of big enterprises, or slowly in a time-consuming way by working their way up the hierarchy (Kos, 1986).

Lastly, no human capital was invested in entrepreneurs. The curricula of economic courses was old-fashioned both in economics and in the other related fields (electro-engineering, mechanical engineering, law) from which entrepreneurs are recruited. There was no business school until 1990 and investment in research was falling during the 1980s (Maricic, 1986).

In spite of these adverse circumstances one can marvel at the entrepreneurial drive and imagination of some socialist managers. They have managed to maintain production during a crisis that abounded with unintelligible regulations and excessive administration. However, to do this they frequently had to revert to unofficial activities: smuggling spare parts (to avoid import regulations), creating unofficial markets (to avoid shortages and carry out distribution), circumventing laws (to pay wages), issuing 'grey' money (to maintain liquidity), and so on.

The current reform attempts to change this. It has lifted the constraints on the size of private enterprises but the social overhead costs largely remain. A government-sponsored centre for small firms has been set up and many business schools are springing up. This, however, still does not change the existing human capital in enterprises, for the ruling business élite achieved its position through the old system and, most importantly, it knows how to operate in that kind of system.

Clearly all five features described can represent major obstacles to a successful transition of the economy. During the first phase of the transition, i.e. economic stabilisation, none of these issues was addressed, but the second phase, that is, restructuring, cannot avoid doing so. Since the latter implies much larger social costs and welfare losses for the population, it is understandable to expect opposition. It can be increased not only by bad policy measures and an inequitable distribution of the costs but also with the time between the two phases as the acute imperatives for change recede and the social consensus for stabilisation does not extend to a social consensus for restructuring. This last point is especially true with respect to prices. Given the initial success of the stabilisation phase in Yugoslavia, where inflation was reduced to zero, new regional non-Communist governments that will be unwilling to impose welfare losses on voters while interregional power redistribution is being negotiated, new administrations without adequate experience or knowledge in running the affairs of state and a population that has survived a decade of falling living standards and expectations may mean that the second phase will not be pursued with adequate vigour and speed. Without restructuring, however, the transition is impossible, and as previous Yugoslav experience has shown, none of the lasting benefits of markets can be achieved without completing the transition. The barriers imposed by the non-institutional economic features described in this section need not prevent the transition, provided they are harnessed into a new consensus for restructuring.

A survey of economic policy attempts

A surprisingly small amount of intellectual effort has been devoted both by Yugoslav and foreign economists as well as by politicians and government officials to the discussion of questions such as that which is addressed in this chapter. The question, 'Is the economy capable of the great transition to a market economy?' was not asked. It was implicitly assumed that the economy can and the population is willing to absorb any shock and change. Discussions were reduced to juggling institutional frameworks, for as Horvat (1970: 7) aptly stated, 'Problems which emerged were usually dealt with by changing the institutional framework . . . Lands economic policy was made up of an endless series of reorganisations.' This is even more interesting, given that all the previous attempts to reform radically the society and economy have failed. The introduction of centrally planned socialism in 1946, the introduction of self-management in 1950, the reform of 1965, and the associated labour paradigm of 1974, all represent efforts of transformation no smaller than that of 1989.

In the profession the most attention was devoted to questions related to the underlying causes of the economic and social crises of Yugoslavia in the 1980s and to the events that triggered them. It is understandable that the underlying causes of the crises were the dominant theme, for the crisis of the 1980s was the longest, deepest, and with regard to the welfare loss the biggest in the country's history (see Bićanić, 1986). These topics attracted the most authors and all the most famous economists tried their hand at it (see, for example, Bajt, 1985; Horvat 1985; Jerovsek *et al.*, 1986; Korosić, 1988; Pjanić, 1987; Vojnić, 1989). The contributions to the discussion took all forms (alas, the dominant ones were impressionistic, frequently anecdotal, contributions in round-table discussions for journals). A prominent role in this formidable library was played by blueprints for survival, policy proposals and scenarios.

The latter were, understandably, at the centre of the attention of politicians and the government. With the deepening of the crisis their number increased. Indeed, since the crisis was perceived by policymakers in 1981, there were two major social blueprints for survival offered, four types of policy approaches and an innumerable number of programmes (attempting to find the means by which the approaches were to be implemented).

The first of the two blueprints was the report of the so called Kraigher Commission (set up in July 1981), which reported its findings in four volumes in 1983 under the title of *Long-Term Programme of Economic Stabilisation* (1983). In spite of being accepted by everybody (the 12th Congress of the LCY, Parliament, Federal Executive Council), its more radical reforms were never implemented. The second blueprint was written by a different group of politicians (and social scientists they chose to support). Known as the Vrhovec Commission, it published its findings in 1986 under the title *Critical Analysis of the Functioning of the Political System*. Each of the reports represents a different and mutually exclusive vision. The differences, for example, concern markets, the former stressing their all-encompassing nature and the latter their historical temporality; the calculation of factor costs, the former using prices, but not the latter; the role of money and finance, the former seeing banks as independent instiutions, and the latter as suppliers of financial services; the enterprise, the former stressing the enterprise and the latter its constituent parts, that is, the basic organisation of associated labour; and so forth. Thus to a great extent the *Critical Analysis* implied a return from markets to the Associated Labour Paradigm. All other major policy statements, and there were many of these, were of a much more limited scope.

The first of the four economic policy approaches could be called 'administering an external equilibrium' and was implemented in the first three years of the government of Ms M. Planinc, that is, from 1982 to mid-1985. Influential in masterminding the approach (but not all the measures) was, arguably, the best-known Yugoslav economist, A. Bajt from Ljubljana. The primary task of this approach was to achieve an external balance and not deal with other macro-economic variables: inflation (which was rising), living standards (which were falling), production (which was stagnant), investment (which was negative in real terms). Such a set of priorities was imposed by the foreign debt difficulties. The dinar was devalued and a policy of 'realistic exchange rates' implemented, regions had to achieve net foreign earning targets, stringent import quotas even for raw materials and spare parts were imposed and administratively maintained, while the population faced harsh foreign currency and travel restrictions. In just over two years an external balance (with a surplus on the current account) was achieved, an agreement with the IMF was reached and the country continued to pay its rescheduled debt. But this approach also led to falling investments (by 10 per cent in the 1981–5 period) and a welfare loss (for the 1981–5 period per capita production fell yearly by 0.3 per cent, real incomes by 4.3 per cent).

In April 1985 the 17th Session of the Central Committee of the LCY (and subsequent meetings) initiated a major change in economic policy. This was done as part of the preparations for the 13th Congress of the LCY. After the government had reached an agreement with the IMF, politicians started fearing labour unrest and unpopularity caused by the welfare loss. The economic policy of the Planinc government was judged as over-restrictive, insufficiently selective, and inadequately anti-inflationary, while the introduction of real interest rates was too hasty. Following that, the government waited out the last year of its term in office without taking any major policy decisions. By the time the new government of Mr B. Mikulić came to power in May 1986 the new policy approach had a name: 'programmed inflation'. A more appropriate name for the second policy approach would have been 'programming inflation by complex indexation'. Masterminded by Belgrade economist M. Cirović and the staff of the National Bank of Yugoslavia, the purpose was to target macro-variables (wages, interest rates, exchange rates) to a programmed inflation rate and imagine that reality would conform to the envisaged course. For example, the desire to reduce inflation led to a major reduction of interest rates while prices were still rising. To keep the economy in this straight-jacket a large number of laws, regulations and rules were passed in three 'waves' during 1986. At the same time there was no control of the money supply, official or 'grey'. The result was inflation rates that were rising monthly, falling exports, stagnant production, and a severe wage freeze which was eventually abandoned by fearful politicians in the face of labour unrest. The far worse track record of this approach was achieved in spite of a more favourable economic environment than during the previous period (see Stiblar, 1988: 24).

Even before these results, immediately upon publication, the programmed inflation approach was criticised by the profession. However, the government stubbornly implemented it until May 1988 when a new policy approach was unveiled. This approach had two cornerstones, one dictated by the new IMF agreement and based on liberalising exchange rates and prices, and the other by the government which continued to place its faith in administration. The former was reflected in three liberalisations (of many prices, of imports, and the introduction of a foreign exchange market), and the latter by relating the rate of change of three macro-economic aggregates (personal incomes, public expenditure, and supply of money) to expected inflation. The system came to be called 'three liberalisations and three anchors'. Thus this approach could be called 'administering with partial liberalisation'. While the former was implemented, the latter macro-economic aggregates were not controlled; wages were controlled the longest. The approach survived the first post-war Yugoslav vote of non-confidence in the government of Mr Mikulić. It was implemented by the caretaker government run by him and for most of the first year of the new government Mr A. Marković, which started in 1989. During this period major new laws were passed (especially in 1989 concerning enterprises, foreign capital, banking, and so on); a policy of positive real interest rates and realistic exchange rates was maintained, although the inflation rate increased; real incomes and per capital GNP fell; and the economy increasingly used the Deutschmark as a measure of value and the dinar was endangered, even as a medium of exchange.

A new policy approach started in December 1989 under the name of an anti-inflationary programme, largely masterminded by the American economist J. Sachs. So far two stages of the programme have been unveiled, the first on 18 December 1989 and the second on 30 June 1990. The first stage concentrated on inflation and inflationary expectations, while the second one put privatisation in the limelight.

Inflation, whose monthly rate in December 1990 was 64 per cent, was to be reduced by decreasing the money supply (by monthly targets), fixing the exchange rate (at 7 denominated dinars to DM 1), freezing wages (at their indexed November levels) and liberalising foreign trade (achieved by high foreign reserves). The price stabilisation target was achieved in April when prices rose 0.2 per cent. This was later than planned, thus leading to an overvalued currency. The lag is largely blamed on loopholes in wage control which permitted their unplanned increase, and bad planning of the money supply which overlooked yearly interest rate payments and the amount of foreign currency in circulation. Apart from stabilising prices, the first phase brought about the expected liquidity problems for firms with a few firms going bankrupt, falling production, rising unemployment, increases in reserves as well as social tensions.

The second phase of the reform concentrated on privatisation, fiscal policy and the banking system. It was decided against transforming 'socialised ownership' into 'state ownership' and selling the capital stock below value. The mode proposed by the government is to revalue the existing capital stock and sell part of it to the employed (present and past) through 'internal shares' which have limited opportunities for resale and are payable in instalments. The internal shares can also be used instead of wage increases, thus providing a softening of the wage freeze and reducing social tension. The second phase leaves many questions unanswered; for example, privatisation is only partly defined, capital markets are not introduced in a full-fledged manner, monetary control may have been relaxed, and so on.

However, it is not only the deficiencies of the two stages of the reform programme which may bring its implementation into question. Equally important for its success is the fact that all republics have held multi-party elections and a renegotiation of the relationship between them is taking place. Both of these decrease the will to bear the social cost of restructuring by requiring politicians to retract from economic reform, and placing political issues in the limelight.

References

Bajt, Aleksander. 1985. *Alternativna ekonomska politika* (Zagreb: Globus).
Bajt, Aleksander. 1988. *Samoupravni oblik drustvene svojine* (Zagreb: Globus).

Bićanić, Ivo. 1986. 'Some general comparisons of the impact of the two world crises of the twentieth century on the Yugoslav economy and their effects', in Ivan T. Berend and Knut Borchardt, eds, *The Impact of the Depression of the 1930s and Its Relevance for the Contemporary World* (Budapest: Academy Research Centre), pp. 248–75.

Bićanić, Ivo. 1988. 'Mjerenje nejednakosti u jugoslavenskom selu u razdoblji od 1963 do 1983 godine', *Sociologija sela*, vol. 26, no. 100, pp. 101–15.

Bićanić, Ivo. 1990. 'Systemic aspects of the social crisis in Yugoslavia', in Stanislaw Gomulka, Yong-Chool Ha and Cae-One Kim, eds, *Economic Reforms in the Socialist World* (London: Macmillan), pp. 139–55.

Bićanić. 1990. 'Unofficial economic activities in Yugoslavia', in Maria Łos, ed., *The Second Economy in Marxist States* (London: Macmillan), pp. 85–100.

Crkvenac, Mato. 1985. *Politika razvoja i proizvodna orijentacija* (Zagreb: Liber).

Flakierski, Henryk. 1989. *The Economic System and Income Distribution in Yugoslavia* (Armonk, NY: Sharpe).

Grbić Cedo. 1984. *Socijalizam i rad privatnim sredstvima* (Zagreb: Zagreb).

Hirsch, Fred. 1977. *Social Limits to Growth* (London: Routledge & Kegan Paul).

Horvat, Branko. 1970. *Privredni sistem i ekonomska politika Jugoslavije* (Belgrade: Institut Ekonomskih Nauka).

Horvat, Branko. 1985. *Jugoslavensko drustvo u krizi: kriticki ogledi i prijedlozi reformi* (Zagreb: Globus).

Jerovsek, Janez, Rus, Veljko and Zupanov, Josip, eds. 1986. *Kriza, blokade i perspektive* (Zagreb: Globus).

Jovanović-Gavrilović, Predrag. 1989. *Kvalitet privrednog razvoja* (Belgrade: Savremena administracija).

Kaelble, Hartmuth. 1986. *Industrialization and Social Inequality in 19th Century Europe* (Leamington Spa: Berg).

Korosić, Marijan. 1983. *Ekonomske nejednakosti jugoslavenske privrede* (Zagreb: Liber).

Korosić, Marijan. 1988. *Jugoslavenska kriza* (Zagreb: Naprijed).

Kos, Marko. 1986. 'Kriza inovacija — kriza tehnicke inteligencije', in Janez Jerovsek, Veljko Rus and Josip Zupanov, eds, *Kriza, blokade i perspektive* (Zagreb: Globus), pp. 34–67.

Kraigher, Sergej. 1985. *Kako iz krize* (Zagreb: Globus).

Kroflin-Fiser, Nada. 1985. 'Jugoslavensko privredno i drustveno danas i sutra', *TRIN*, 3, pp. 52–8.

Maksimović, Ivan, ed. 1985. *Ekonomija i politika*, Naucni skupovi, 28 (Belgrade: Srpska Akademija Nauka i Umetnosti).

Maricić, Siuisa. 1986. 'Pamet pod opsadom', in Janez Jerovsek, Veljko Rus and Josip Zupanov, eds, *Kriza, blokade i perspektive* (Zagreb: Globus), pp. 320–35.

Maroević, Tonko. 1984. 'Nedostatnost prihoda — koliko nam i kako opada zivotni standard', *TRIN*, 3, pp. 19–30.

Mates, Neven. 1980. 'Ekonomski sadrzaj dogovora o raspodjeli dohotka', *Ekonomski pregled*, vol. 31: 7–8, pp. 333–48.

Mencinger, Joze. 1986. 'Drustveno planiranje — utvara i realnost ovladanja budućnosću', in Janez Jerovsek, Veljko Rus and Josip Zupanov, eds, *Kriza, blokade i perspektive* (Zagreb: Globus), pp. 97–124.

Mencinger, Joze. 1989. 'Privredna reforma i nezaposlenost', *Privredna kretanja Jugoslavije*, no. 193 (March).

Petrin, Tea. 1986. 'Kriza male privrede', in Janez Jerovsek, Veljko Rus and Josip Zupanov, eds, *Kriza, blokade i perspektive* (Zagreb: Globus), pp. 186–206.

Phelps-Brown, Henry. 1977. *The Inequality of Pay* (Oxford: Oxford University Press).

Pjanić, Zoran. 1987. *Anatomija krize* (Belgrade: Ekonomika).

Prasnikar, Janez, Svejnar, Jan, Mihaljek, Dubravlo and Prasnikar, Vesme. 1989. *A Test of*

Enterprise Behavior under Labor-Management, (Working Paper, 247. Pittsburgh: Department of Economics).

Sirotić, Sonja. 1986. 'Sto ove godine kazuju ocjene uvjeta zivota', *TRIN*, 3, pp. 3–10.

Spero, Joan. 1985. 'Comment: U.S. trade policy and International Service Transactions', in Robert P. Inman, ed., *Managing the Service Economy: Prospects and problems* (Cambridge: Cambridge University Press), pp. 179–81.

Statisticki godisnjak SFRJ (Belgrade: Savezni Zavod za Statistiku, various years).

Stiblar, Franjo. 1989. 'Iskustva stare i iskusenje nove ekonomske politike', *Privredna kretanja Jugoslavije*, no. 191 (January).

Stipetić, Vladimir. 19885. 'Ekonomska znanost i opadajuća efikasnost investicija o Jugoslaviji od sezdesetih godina naovamo', *Ekonomski pregled*, vol. 36:5–6, pp. 167–96.

Trade and Development Report (Geneva: United Nations, 1988).

Vejnović, M. 1984. 'Kradja kao oblik protesta', *Privreda*, 6.

Vahcic, Ales. 1989. 'Prestrukturiranje jugoslavenske privrede pomoću preduzetnistva', *Nase teme*, vol. 33:11, pp. 2906–15.

Vojnić, Dragomir. 1989. *Ekonomska kriza i reforma socijalizma* (Zagreb: Globus).

Zupanov, Josip. 1984. 'Opadanje standarda i drustvena stabilnost', *TRIN*, 3, pp. 7–18.

3 Economic change in Yugoslavia: from crisis to reform

Will Bartlett

Introduction

Yugoslavia was the first centrally planned economy, unique not only in the Balkans, but throughout the whole socialist bloc, to experiment with economic reforms involving extensive decentralisation of decisionmaking authority to enterprises on the basis of regulated market relations. In the early 1950s the post-war system of central planning was gradually wound down. Responsibility for enterprise management was passed to workers' councils under the system of self-management, based upon extensive employee involvement in decisionmaking, as well as an element of control and supervision by regional and local authorities. This Yugoslav system of socialist self-management and its effects, particularly upon income distribution, have been the subject of much critical analysis, including important studies of the institutional system and its effects upon income distribution and economic development by R. Bićanić (1973), Horvat (1976), Estrin (1983), Sacks (1983), Prout (1985), Lydall (1984), Lydall (1989), and Flakierski (1989). The system has undergone a variety of changes in the extent of enterprise autonomy, which broadly was greatest in the period between 1965 and the early 1970s. Following the introduction of the 1974 Constitution and the Associated Labour Law of 1976, the system stabilised into one of attenuated self-management. Under this framework, enterprise self-management was conducted within the restrictive confines of a form of devolved planning through 'self-management agreements' and 'social compacts', in which localised political and planning authorities exercised a major role. Alongside the decentralisation of economic power has gone a devolution of political power to the republics and provinces. This devolution has been so extensive that it is hardly an exaggeration to say that Yugoslavia could now be regarded as a loose federation of separate states that happen to share a common currency.

This sometimes chaotic experiment with the reform and marketisation of a planned economy appeared, for a while, to be immensely successful, at least up until the end of the 1970s. Then something went badly wrong. From about 1980 the Yugoslav economy has been in a state of what can only be called a profound crisis.

The crisis, eloquently catalogued by Lydall (1989), has included dramatic reductions in living standards, and soaring inflation that achieved Latin American levels of hyperinflation by 1989. In addition an acute political crisis has unfolded, involving a breakdown of the authority and influence of the Communist party in most republics and the emergence of a stridently nationalistic version of socialist politics in Serbia. The nationalities problem, apparently previously solved by the simultaneous devolution of large areas of economic and political responsibility to the republics and provinces, and the uniformity of political party processes and organisational forms at the federal level, began to re-emerge as the crisis deepened into bloody conflict between Serbs and Albanians in the southern province of Kosovo, and has begun to spread further afield.

The economic crisis of the 1980s

Yugoslavia has been unique among socialist countries in the extent of the development of its trade relations with the West. By 1980 Yugoslavia's exports to the West (i.e. the convertible currency area), amounted to US$5,655 million, compared with US$3,322 million with the Eastern bloc countries. However, whilst trade with the East showed a small surplus, with the West, Yugoslavia had a trade deficit of US$5,665 million (importing twice as much as it exported to the West). This structural imbalance has been a persistent feature of Yugoslavia's foreign trade, so that by 1980 Yugoslavia had built up a gross total foreign debt of US$21,096 million (Bartlett, 1987b). In the early 1980s increased interest rates on international financial markets, combined with an increasing reluctance on the part of the international banking system to increase exposure to foreign debt, caused difficulties in refinancing the debt in many countries. Yugoslavia was caught in this debt trap, a situation that was not helped by the fact that many of the investment projects that had been undertaken in the 1970s were economically unsound and did not provide a rate of return high enough to contribute effectively to debt repayment. This meant that Yugoslavia had to bring economic growth, which depended upon imports of Western machinery and materials, to an abrupt halt. Under the mantle of an IMF-style stabilisation policy, a contraction of demand and an expansion of production for the export market was required to correct the deficit and to ensure the continuation of short-term refinancing of the payments deficit. Stand-by loans from the IMF were a precondition of debt-service rescheduling by the international financial markets, and these loans were tied to the implementation of other elements of the policy package, which the IMF subjected to close 'monitoring'; these measures included a free float of the exchange rate, liberalisation of prices on the domestic market, cuts in government expenditure, and a contractionary monetary policy to deflate domestic demand so as to release resources for use in production for the export market. The effects of this policy orientation can be seen in Table 3.1.

Real gross domestic product stagnated between 1980 and 1985, real output per employee in the manufacturing sector fell by 5 per cent p.a., and real earnings per employee in the manufacturing sector by 8 per cent p.a. In addition, the inflation that had been a persistent, if as yet manageable, feature of the Yugoslav market economy

Table 3.1 Trends in growth, productivity and earnings, 1970–85 (per cent per annum growth)

	a	b	c	d	e
1970/75	4.5	10.09	0.5	4.79	17.28
1975/80	5.08	0.63	1.49	4.99	18.25
1980/85	–0.05	–5.18	–7.95	3.14	38.63

Notes:
a: Real GDP per capita.
b: Real output per employee in the manufacturing sector.
c: Real earnings per employee in manufacturing.
d: Employment in manufacturing.
e: Prices (GDP deflator).

Source: World Bank World Tables Database, University of Bath, United Kingdom.

began to accelerate. During the 1970s retail prices had been rising at a steady average rate of around 17 per cent. During the first half of the 1980s, however, the average rate more than doubled to 38 per cent, despite the imposition of a restrictive macroeconomic policy and a fall in the real money supply (Bartlett, 1987a). Further increases in inflation followed in the latter half of the 1980s. This occurred in the context of a policy orientation which — despite changes of emphasis and elements of a stop–go approach, as emphasised by Lydall (1989), and Ivo Bićanić in this volume — retained a basis in the stabilisation philosophy introduced in the early 1980s, particularly in its emphasis on price liberalisation, and devaluation as a means to overcome the balance of payments constraint. Indeed, by 1989 the rate of price increase was being openly referred to as hyperinflationary (*The Economic Scene*, 1990). The rate of inflation of retail prices for 1989 was 1,256 per cent, and by December the annual rate of inflation had risen to 2,665 per cent (*The Economic Scene*, 1990).

By the end of 1989 the crisis had reached intense proportions. Outlays for fixed investment declined by 26.2 per cent in real terms for the year as a whole, and by 38.4 per cent in December on an annual basis, while the volume of retail sales declined by 4.8 per cent during the year. Throughout this process, employment in the socialised sector of the economy continued to increase, exacerbating the decline in productivity, with all the unfavourable effects on the efficient utilisation of labour discussed by Ivo Bićanić in Chapter 2 of this volume.

Foreign trade performance

The onset of the crisis at the beginning of the 1980s was brought about by deteriorating foreign trade performance in the previous decade, the build-up of foreign debt, and the policy response to that situation following the changing international monetary situation after the 1979 oil price shock. The stabilisation policy was, in essence, designed to provide a way out of this debt trap, and to overcome the balance of payments constraint that faced the Yugoslav economy. By engaging in an aggressive depreciation of the value of the dinar it was hoped to reverse the terms of trade losses of the previous decade; to boost the relative dinar price of Yugoslav exports and imports, and simultaneously to stimulate the self-managed enterprises to increase production for the export market; and to reduce imports by increasing their relative cost to domestic consumers of imported goods. The extent of the changes in the exchange rate are shown in Table 3.2.

Table 3.2 Dollar/dinar exchange rate, cents per dinar, 1970–88

1970	1975	1980	1985	1986	1987	1988
8.00	5.56	3.41	0.32	0.22	0.08	0.02

Source: Main Economic Indicators (1990).

At the same time rapid domestic inflation meant that the relative price of exports to domestic goods, expressed in dinars, changed much less sharply, although the terms of trade did improve, and a real effective depreciation did take place. The change in the relative price of exports is shown in Figure 3.1. It is clear that a fundamental improvement in the relative price facing exporters took place during the 1980s, compared with the long-term trend during the previous two decades.

Clearly, a policy of this type is based upon the expectation that producers will actually respond to relative price signals in the desired fashion. Yugoslav economists were in disagreement over the likely effectiveness of such a policy, with some arguing that devaluation would be effective in reducing the balance of payments deficit, whilst others contended that the only effect would be an increase in inflation. Evaluating this debate, Prasnikar and Svejnar (1988) argue that devaluation would have only temporary effects and would not on its own bring about the fundamental increase in productivity required to place the economy on a long-term path of sustainable growth. As I indicate below, this would require a set of structural changes to the incentive structures facing economic agents in the economy.

It should also be pointed out that additional incentives were provided to exporters in the form of export subsidies, although in practice the impact of these subsidies was doubtful due to the frequent delays involved in their administration (Lydall, 1989). A further influence on the incentive to export operated through the varying regulations concerning the amounts of foreign exchange that individual enterprises were allowed to retain. These regulations were subject to a succession of laws on foreign trade and foreign exchange. However, under the 1985 Law on Foreign Trade and Exchange, put into effect in 1986, the previously established retention quota of two-fifths of foreign exchange earnings was abolished and firms were required to surrender all foreign exchange receipts to authorised banks at the official rate of exchange (Prasnikar and Svejnar, 1988). Policy changes in this area reflected the divergent interest of the northern and southern republics to a large extent, for the northern

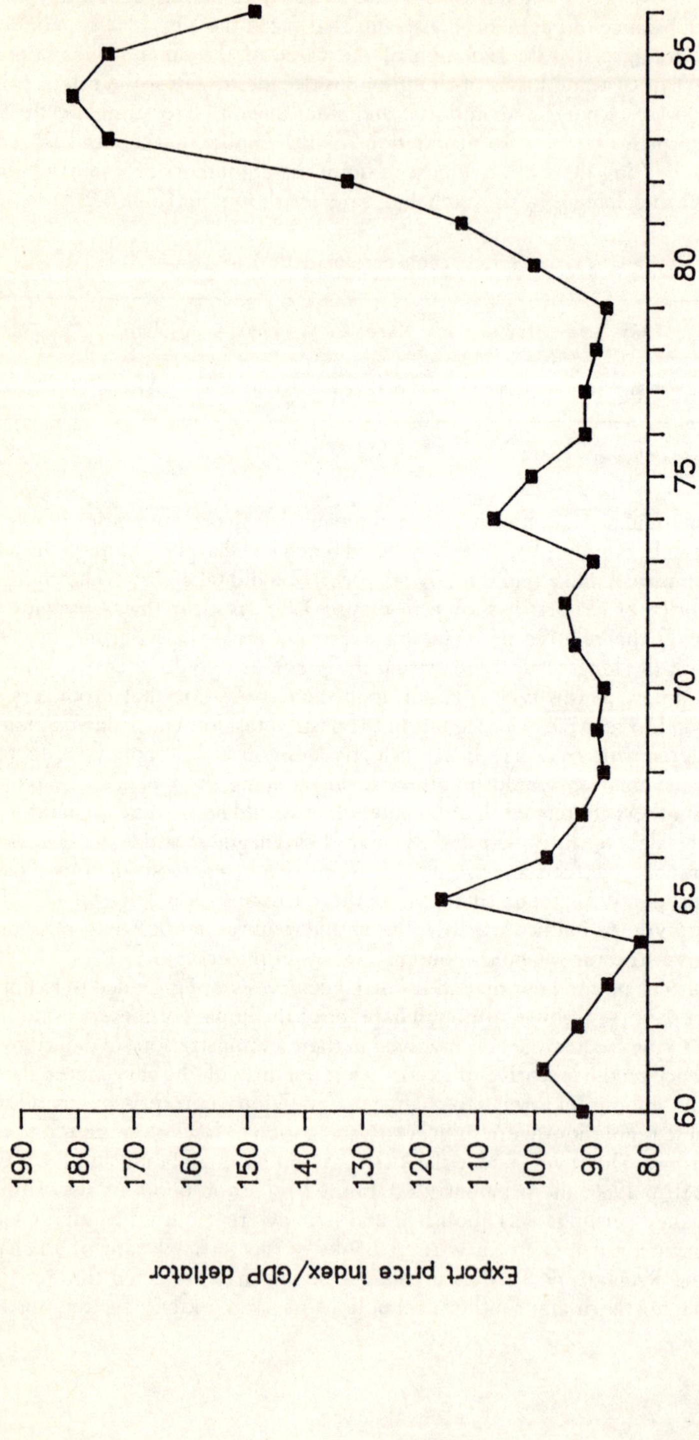

Figure 3.1 Relative export price index. *Source:* World Bank data

republics favoured high retention ratios, whereas the southern republics favoured an administrative reallocation of scarce foreign exchange. Probably the abolition of retention quotas in 1986 reduced incentives for some northern enterprises to export, but in the context of generalised scarcity of foreign exchange it is not clear that the policy changes in this area could have had much influence on the overall export propensity of the economy, as opposed to distributional effects among the individual republics and their enterprises.

The impact of the restrictive policy, and of the depreciation of the dinar on imports, was dramatic. Imports fell sharply, especially imports of investment goods from the West (Bartlett and Uvalić, 1985). Although exports increased only sluggishly, the trade balance improved and by the end of the decade there was a healthy surplus on current account. The extent of the impact of the policy measures is indicated in Table 3.3. Various methods of computing a series for real export and import volumes give somewhat different measures of rates of change of the aggregates. Two sets of estimates are presented in Table 3.3, from both World Bank and OECD sources.

Table 3.3 Rate of change of export and import volumes, 1965–85

	Exports		Imports	
	a	b	a	b
1965/70	8.39	n.a	13.44	n.a.
1970/75	4.74	5.12	5.54	5.56
1975/80	4.37	4.99	2.09	3.91
1980/85	–1.04	0.07	–7.84	–7.5

Notes:
a: Dinar basis, *World Bank World Tables*.
b: Dinar basis, *OECD Economic Surveys: Yugoslavia* (1988), Table A.

Whilst there is some disparity, the two sources indicate that, evaluated at dinar prices, real export growth rates fell continually, and in the early 1980s responded little to depreciation. Import volumes fell sharply on either a dinar or a dollar basis, but particularly so, at a rate of 7 per cent p.a. on a dinar basis.[1] The balance of payments outcomes in value terms as shown in Table 3.4.

Table 3.4 Balance of payments, current prices (US$m), 1980 and 1989

	1980	1989
Exports (goods)	8,978	13,560
Imports (goods)	–15,064	–15,002
Trade balance	–6,086	–1,442
Net services	3,795	3,895
Current balance	–2,291	2,427

Sources: OECD Economic Surveys: Yugoslavia (1988), Table 8; *The Economic Scene* (1990).

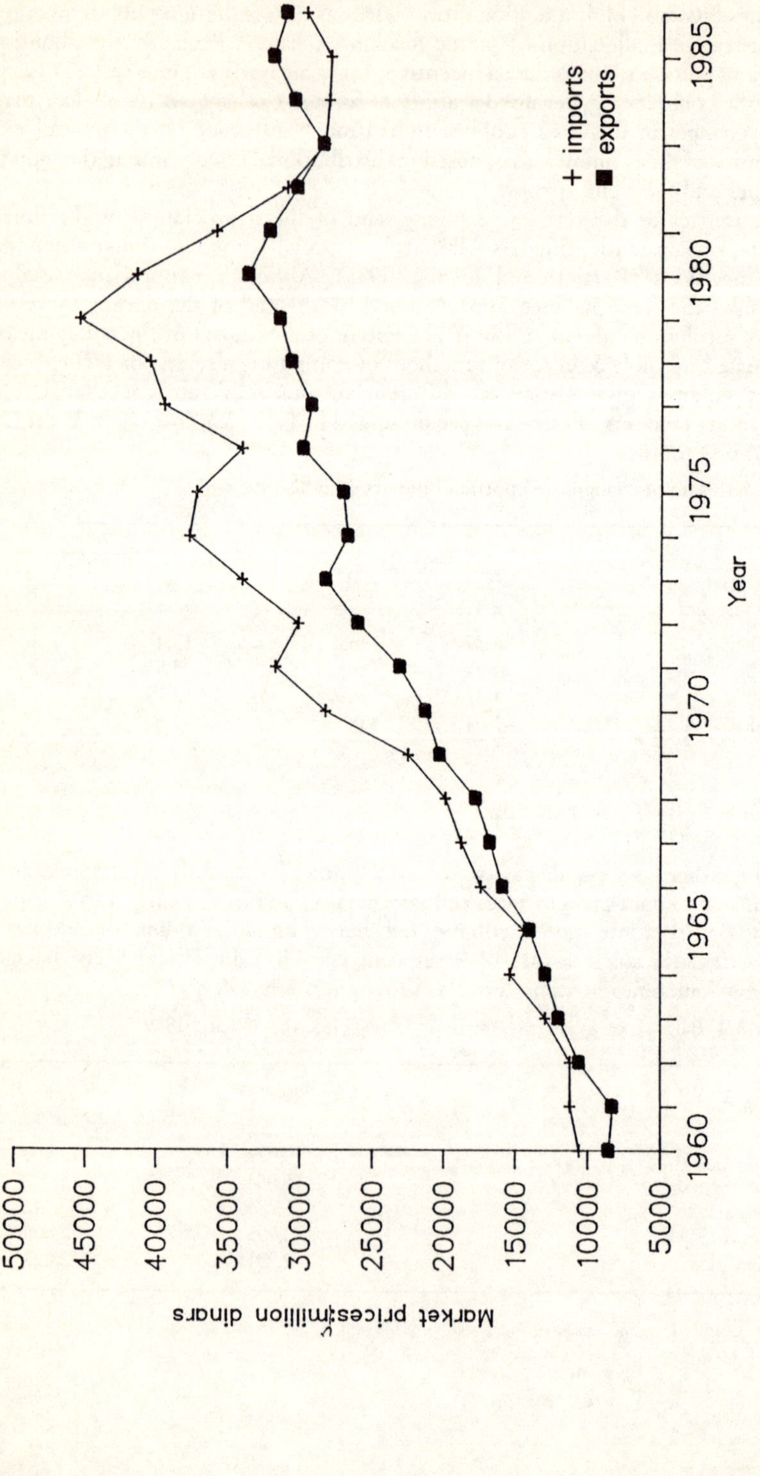

Figure 3.2 Exports and imports of goods and non-financial services in current prices. *Source:* World Bank Data

Remarkably, the value of imports in 1989 was less than it had been in 1980, while export values had increased by about 50 per cent. At least during the 1980s, then, while the stabilisation policy was in force, imports appear to have been more price-responsive than exports. The effect of the abrupt halt in import growth has been to turn a balance of payments deficit of US$2,291 million in 1980 into a surplus of US$2,427 million by 1989. The extent of the turnaround to long-established trends can be seen in Figure 3.2, which shows the pattern of export and imports of goods and non-financial services, in current dinar prices, over the period 1960 to 1985. For the first time during this whole period, from 1983 import expenditures were brought down below export proceeds, yielding a sustained improvement in the balance of payments position. This is a remarkable achievement, though it has not been without considerable costs to the health of the Yugoslav domestic economy, and has plunged not only the economy, but the political and social systems as well into a deep crisis from which they are now struggling to emerge.

In the absence of large-scale private portfolio capital flows, the net effects of a devaluation on the balance of payments is given by the combined effect of import demand responsiveness and export supply responsiveness to a change in the price of imports and exports brought about by a change in the exchange rate. It can easily be shown that for a country which is a price-taker on international markets, the necessary condition for a devaluation to improve the balance of payments is

$$e_m + s_x > 0 \qquad (1)$$

where e_m is the elasticity of import demand and s_x is the elasticity of export supply. This is a modified version of the traditional Marshall–Lerner condition, which requires that the elasticities of demand for exports and imports should add up to a figure in excess of unity in order to ensure a stable response to a devaluation. The traditional Marshall–Lerner condition is usually presented on the assumption that the elasticity of export supply is infinite, and that of import demand is less than infinite (Thirlwall, 1980). For a small country whose exports do not influence the world price, the last assumption is unreasonable. For a self-managed economy, the Ward theorem (Ward, 1958) on the low (and possibly negative) elasticity of the supply function of a labour-managed firm suggests that the first assumption is unreasonable as well. The above condition has been developed, therefore, on the assumption that the elasticity of export demand is infinite and that of export supply less than infinite.[2] Clearly, if the elasticity of export supply were actually negative as the simple Ward theorem suggests, then the possibility of a perverse reaction to a devaluation can exist in a self-managed economy even though the traditional Marshall–Lerner conditions may be satisfied. The stark features of the Ward theorem are somewhat modified in the case of joint production for two distinct markets such as an export market and a domestic market (Bartlett, 1987a), and yet the possibility of a low level of responsiveness is still present and could render ineffectual policies that depend upon eliciting increased output through changes to relative prices.

Direct estimates of these price elasticities can be made by econometric estimation of import demand and export supply functions for the Yugoslav economy, on the basis of World Bank data for the period 1965–86. The specification of the functions adopted here takes account of the fact that adjustment will not normally be instantaneous but will proceed with a lag as actual quantities traded adjust to desired quantities. The simplest way to model this effect is through a stock adjustment hypothesis of the form:

$$\ln X_t - \ln X_{t-1} = k(\ln X(^*)_t - \ln X_{t-1}) \qquad (2)$$

so that the increment in any one period is a proportion, k, of the gap between optimal levels in period (t) and actual levels in period (t–1).

The export supply function is:

$$\ln XE(^*)_t = a_0 + a_1 \ln PE_t + u_t \qquad (3)$$

where PE_t is a measure of (relative) export prices and u_t is a disturbance term. The estimate of the supply elasticity is given by a_1. The import demand elasticity is:

$$\ln XM(^*)_t = b_0 + b_1 \ln PM_t + b_2 \ln Y_t + v_t \qquad (4)$$

where PM_t is a measure of (relative) import prices, Y is real income per capita and v_t is a disturbance term. Using the stock adjustment hypotheses these become:

Export supply

$$\ln XE_t = a_0 k + a_1 k \ln PE_t + (1-k) \ln XE_{t-1} + u'_t \qquad (5)$$

Import demand

$$\ln XM_t = b_0 k + b_1 k \ln PM_t + b_2 k \ln Y_t + (1-k) \ln XM_{t-1} + V'_t \qquad (6)$$

The short-term demand and supply elasticities are given by the estimated coefficients on the price terms (defined negatively for the import demand elasticity) and the long-run elasticities can be recovered by dividing the short-run elasticities by [1–(1–k)], i.e. by one minus the coefficient on the lagged dependent variable. Parameter estimates are presented in Table 3.5. Two versions of each function are presented. One involves using a relative price term defined from the implicit price deflators for exports, imports and GDP, on a dinar basis. The other uses dollar-based export and import price indices. In a situation of foreign exchange rationing the absolute price indices may be a better measure of the price term relevant to enterprise decisionmaking. Exporting firms are keen to earn foreign exchange, and so a high absolute foreign exchange price will elicit a supply response, irrespective of the level of prices on the domestic market.

The implied long-run elasticities are between 0.58 and 0.00 for export supply and between 3.39 and 1.1 for import demand, elasticities depending on the specification of the price term. Although one cannot rule out the possibility of a Ward-type negative supply elasticity in the export sector, the relatively strong response of import demand to prices (and to per capita income) implies that there appears to be no danger of an unstable response to the depreciation. This does not mean that there may be no overall perverse supply response. Output supplied to the domestic market might be contracting faster than the export market is expanding. Figures for the volume of retail sales in the socialised sector bear this out. The index of real retail sales fell from a peak of 116 in 1980 to a level of 97 by 1988.[3]

Table 3.5 Export supply and import demand function estimates, 1966–86

Dependent variable:	Ln XE_t		ln XM_t	
Model:	a	b	a	b
Regressor				
Const	9.708 (2.717)	1.928 (0.2.21)	–3.039 (0.982)	3.259 (2.452)
Ln PE_t	0.276 (2.365)	–0.065 (1.138)		
Ln PM_t			–0.3346 (2.372)	–0.355 (3.017)
Ln Y_t			0.6331 (1.841)	0.417 (1.964)
Ln XE_{t-1}	0.523 (2.936)	0.922 (29.652)		
Ln XM_{t-1}			0.901 (8.237)	0.673 (5.044)
R-bar sq	0.958	0.976	0.910	0.964
Durbin's h	0.479	0.418	0.007	1.7566
Long-run elasticity	0.577	0.000	3.387	1.100

Notes:
a: Absolute price model; Price indices are dollar based, 1980 = 100; quantities in 1980 US$. t-ratios are in brackets.
b: Relative price model; Price indices based on GDP deflators; quantities in constant dinars. t-ratios are in brackets.

Taken together with the decline, or at least stagnation, in GDP this suggests that there may well be an overall inelasticity in the supply response. In any case the elasticities of export supply are disturbingly low. A 1 per cent change in the dollar-based export price index induces only ½ per cent change in exports in the long run at best; changes in relative prices induce no response in exports at all. On the other hand the estimated income elasticities of demand for imports are between 0.63 and 0.42, and the long-run import price elasticities of demand lie between –3.3 and –1.1, so that much of the work of adjustment needs to be done on the import side. This is exactly the approach taken by policy makers in the 1980s, with all the consequences that severe reductions in imports have for economic growth and stability that are discussed above.

Previous work by Tyson and Neuberger (1979), who estimate import demand functions over the period 1968–76, provides similar estimates of short-run income and relative price elasticities of import demand of 0.79 and –0.33, respectively. Their estimated long-run price elasticity is –0.94. These estimates, particularly those for the price elasticities, are remarkably close to those presented in this chapter, which have been estimated over a much longer period. This suggests that the relationships reflect some stable structural features of the Yugoslav economy. Tyson and Neuberger attempt without success to estimate export demand functions rather than export supply functions (since they were concerned, mistakenly in my view for reasons explained above, with providing the information required by the traditional Marshall–Lerner condition on demand elasticities of both exports and imports). The only comparable estimate is provided by Burkett (1983), and again, the findings from that research include a relatively inelastic supply response which has been identified here.

Thus, in Yugoslavia, although the extreme currency depreciation has been effective in correcting the balance of payments deficit, turning an overall deficit of US$2,000 million in 1980 into a surplus of US$2,500 million in 1989, the cost of the policy has been high, because exports have responded only sluggishly to the price incentives that have been presented to producers. In particular, the depreciation policy has been associated with a severe contraction of imports, in production for the domestic market, and in living standards, with the development of hyperinflation, and a rise in regional conflicts over the distribution of an ever-diminishing pie.

Restructuring incentives: the 1990 reform

The main cause of the crisis must eventually be traced to those factors that underlie the relatively low supply responsiveness of the Yugoslav economy. These factors include the spatial immobility of both capital and labour due to the trends towards regional autarchy, and the lack of effective financial discipline which is associated with the 'soft-budget constraint' that enterprises face when they become 'illiquid' (Uvalić, 1988). Ultimately, these problems with the Yugoslav self-management system have to do with the institutional structures that condition the incentives to producers, more than with policies designed to fine-tune the macro-economy. Whilst devaluation and currency depreciation will not solve this problem, alternative macro-economic policies will be unlikely to have much success either without a fundamental institutional reform.

The sources of inelastic supply response are not hard to find. They are located in the 'social ownership' of enterprise assets. Under this system no single economic agent has the incentive to use the assets of the enterprise in a productive manner. Alchian and Demsetz (1972) have pointed to the disincentive effects of loose property rights in enterprise assets. They argue that the internal monitoring of workers' effort is required to reduce free-riding by the individual members of a work collective. However, the monitor herself requires some form of material incentive to carry out this function efficiently. Whilst Alchian and Demsetz argue that the required incentive is provided by the right to appropriate the residual income from the use of the firm's assets, and so provide a theoretical foundation for the optimality of private enterprise, recent work on incentives and monitoring by Ireland and Law (1988) has shown how the monitor herself may be an 'agent' (in the sense of the principal agent literature) of the work collective. Monitoring in a labour-managed enterprise in this model will be carried out on behalf of the workforce (the principal), which owns the collective assets, by the firm's manager (the agent). Experience with co-operative forms of organisation in Western Europe is instructive. There, co-operative enterprises are formed under various ownership structures that vary from individual employee ownership of capital shares, as in Mondragón in Spain, through pure collective ownership of assets as in the UK ICOM co-operatives. Various mixed arrangements can be found in the well-developed co-operative sectors elsewhere in Western Europe, e.g. in France, Portugal, Italy and Catalonia in Spain (Bartlett and Pridham, 1990). Studies of the determinants of productivity in these co-operative enterprises tend to show that individual employee participation in profits or in firm's equity has positive productivity effects, whilst collective ownership of assets has negative productivity effects (Estrin, Jones and Svejnar, 1987).

Economic reform and the new economic policy

The new economic policy introduced in Yugoslavia in January 1990 has sought to engage many of these issues. The policy has involved pegging the dinar to the Deutschmark, a temporary wage freeze, free market price-setting and a tight monetary policy including an end to soft budget constraints, with the object of reducing inflation to a rate of 13 per cent for the year as a whole. At the same time a wide variety of new forms of ownership of enterprise assets has been legitimised through the substitution of a new Enterprise Law, introduced in July 1989, for the 1976 Law on Associated Labour. The new forms of ownership include social ownership where, as before, assets are managed by the workers in the enterprise; now, however, other forms of ownership may be adopted, including private ownership, co-operative ownership and mixed ownership. Correspondingly, a large number of enterprise legal forms are available, including joint-stock companies, limited liability companies, limited partnerships, companies with unlimited liability, and co-operative enterprises. Of particular interest are the arrangements whereby socially owned firms may form joint ventures with other socially owned firms through the acquisition of shares. This is designed to stimulate the mobility of capital across local and regional boundaries.

The reforms have achieved some rapid results. The rate of disinflation was rapid. From the rate of 64 per cent p.m. in December 1989, inflation fell to 17 per cent p.m. in January, and to 2.5 per cent p.m. in March. By April, inflation had been eliminated and prices had actually begun to fall at a rate of –0.2 per cent p.m. (*Privredni Pregled*, 2–4 June 1990). It appeared that a downward spiral in prices would ensue, owing to the peculiar instability of prices in a labour-managed economy as has been analysed by Bartlett and Weinrich (1985). However, by July inflation had returned (producer prices rose at an annual rate of 25 per cent during that month) and real wages, which had fallen by 42 per cent between November 1989 and April 1990, have been on the rise since then. As a result of the short-run success of the reform, Yugoslavia was able to arrange new credits from Western financial institutions and government organisations, including US$400 million from the World Bank, US$500 million from EFTA, and US$2,500 million from the EC. Success in making repayments of principal on the foreign debt in the previous year when some US$3,600 million had been repaid, led to the prospect of a favourable response to discussions on further rescheduling with the Club of Rome group of financial institutions (*Privredni Pregled*, 2–4 June 1990, p. 3). Yet some serious obstacles remain. Severe problems of enterprise illiquidity presented many firms with difficulties in paying their wage bills. The political crisis has intensified with the election of non-Communist governments in Slovenia and Croatia. And the crisis of the ethnic nationalities shows no sign of going away, with the virtual collapse of the economy in Kosovo.

On the positive side, successful experiments have been made in the promotion of new forms of enterprise organisation and the entry of several thousand new small and medium-sized enterprises (SMEs). In Slovenia an enterprise promotion project has been initiated to restructure the economy. In 1989 about 13,000 new enterprises were created and it is expected that there will be a considerable increase in their number in 1990. There is an explosion in the number of SMEs seeking investment funds, with about 500 contracts concluded in the first two months of 1990 (*Privredni Pregled*, 4 April 1990, p. 1). Under the project, promoted by the Slovenian government, it is hoped to set up advice centres and pilot projects in the other Yugoslav republics as well, and the World Bank has provided funds to assist this restructuring process. The concept of small-firm enterprise zones or 'incubators' has been utilised to encourage this development, drawing on experience from other countries such as Italy where the development of 'industrial districts' has been so successful as a means to create local economic development and a dynamic export base. Such districts group together thousands of small enterprises into a closely knit geographical and social nexus. Similarly the experience of restructuring declining industries in the 'rustbelt' areas of the United States (such as Pittsburgh) has influenced the thinking of the promoters of the new wave of small enterprises such as Istok Kremser of the firm ININ (*Privredni Pregled*, 2–4 June 1990, p. 6). The development of new forms of enterprise able to take advantage of the opportunities that are increasingly opening up with the development of the European Single Market is a vital prerequisite of the success of the reforms. As the EC begins to open itself to East European members, a successful export industry, with a high elasticity of response to price movements, will be essential if Yugoslavia is to meet the full force of international competition. Only then will it be able to make the transition from crisis to reform, and take her full place in the European and world markets of the 1990s.

Notes

1. Evaluated on a dollar basis, merchandise exports continued to increase at a rate of over 3 per cent p.a. between 1980 and 1985, although this was a noticeably slower rate of growth than attained previously, while merchandise imports fell by only 2 per cent p.a. between 1980 and 1985.
2. A full derivation is presented in Bartlett (1987a).
3. The index is based on 1985 = 100.

References

Alchian, Armen A. and Demsetz, Harold. 1972. 'Production, information costs, and economic organization', *American Economic Review*, vol. 62:5, pp. 777–95.

Bartlett, Will. 1987a. *Foreign Trade and Stabilization Policy in a Self-Managed Economy: Yugoslavia in the 1980s*, Bath Papers in Political Economy, No. 01/87 (Bath: University of Bath; forthcoming in John Allcock, ed., *Yugoslavia in Transition* (Leamington Spa: Berg).

Bartlett, Will. 1987b. 'The problem of indebtedness in Yugoslavia: causes and consequences', *Rivista Internazionale di Scienze Economiche e Commerciali*, 34:11–12, pp. 1179–95.

Bartlett, Will and Pridham, Geoffrey. 1990. *Co-operative enterprises in Italy, Portugal and Spain: history and development* (Bristol: Centre for Mediterranean Studies, University of Bristol, mimeo.).

Bartlett, Will and Uvalić, Milica. 1985. 'Yugoslavia and EEC trade relations: problems and prospects', *EUI Colloquium Papers* (Florence: European University Institute), DOC. IUE 133/85 (COL 47).

Bartlett, Will and Weinrich, Gerd. 1985. *Instability and indexation in a labour-managed economy: a general equilibrium quantity rationing approach*, EUI Working Paper, No. 85/186 (Florence: European University Institute, 1985), forthcoming in Derek Jones and Jan Svejnar, eds, *Advances in the Economic Analysis of Labor Managed and Participatory Firms*, vol. 4, 1991.

Bićanić, Rudolf. 1973. *Economic Policy in Socialist Yugoslavia* (Cambridge: Cambridge University Press).

Burkett, John P. 1983. *The Effects of Economic Reform in Yugoslavia: Investment and trade policies, 1959–1976*, Research Series, 55 (Berkeley, CA: University of California, Institute of International Studies, 1983).

The Economic Scene of Yugoslavia December 1990 (Belgrade: National Bank of Yugoslavia, March 1990).

Estrin, Saul. 1983. *Self-management: Economic theory and Yugoslav practice* (Cambridge: Cambridge University Press).

Estrin, Saul, Jones, Derek C., and Svejnar, Jan. 1987. 'The productivity effects of workers' participation: producer cooperatives in Western economies', *Journal of Comparative Economics*, vol. 11:1, pp. 40–61.

Flakierski, Henryk. 1989. *The Economic System and Income Distribution in Yugoslavia* (New York: Sharpe).

Horvat, Branko. 1976. *The Yugoslav Economic System* (White Plains, NY: International Arts and Sciences Press).

Ireland, Norman J. and Law, Peter J. 1988. 'Management design in labor-managed firms', *Journal of Comparative Economics*, vol. 12:1, pp. 1–23.

Lydall, Harold. 1984. *Yugoslav Socialism: Theory and practice* (Oxford: Clarendon Press).

Lydall, Harold. 1989. *Yugoslavia in Crisis* (Oxford: Clarendon Press).

Main Economic Indicators: Historical statistics, 1969–88 (Paris: Organisation for Economic Co-operation and Development, 1990).

OECD Economic Surveys: Yugoslavia (Paris: OECD, 1988).

Prasnikar, J. and Svejnar, Jan. 1988. 'Economic behaviour of Yugoslav enterprises', in Derek C. Jones and Jan Svejnar, eds, *Advances in the Economic Analysis of Participatory and Labor-Managed Firms*, vol. 3, pp. 237–311.

Prout, Christopher. 1985. *Market Socialism and Yugoslavia* (Oxford: Oxford University Press).

Sacks, Stephen R. 1983. *Self-Management and Efficiency: Large Corporations in Yugoslavia* (London: Allen & Unwin).

Thirlwall, Alan. 1980. *Balance of Payments Theory and the United Kingdom Experience* (London: Macmillan).

Tyson, Laura D'Andrea and Neuberger, Egon. 1977. 'The impact of external economic disturbances on Yugoslavia: theoretical and empirical explorations', *Journal of Comparative Economics*, vol. 3:4, pp. 346–74.

Uvalić, Milica. 1988. *Investment in Labour-Managed Firms: Theoretical problems and empirical evidence from Yugoslavia*, unpublished Ph.D. thesis (European University Institute, Florence: Cambridge: Cambridge University Press, forthcoming).

Ward, Benjamin. 1958. 'The firm in Illyria: market syndicalism', *American Economic Review*, vol. 48:3, pp. 566–89.

4 The economic legacy of Ceausescu

Per Ronnås

Introduction

Few regimes have been subjected to such drastic reassessment, in terms of both their overall and economic performance, over such a short time, as has Romania under Ceausescu. It has hardly been more than a decade since Ceausescu was praised in the West as 'the maverick of the Soviet bloc' and economic development under his rule was described in the most positive terms. Today, he stands out as one of the worst tyrants modern Europe has known and as the chief culprit for the present disastrous state of the Romanian economy.

Yet, an examination of the overall development strategy and economic policies pursued in Romania over the past decades clearly brings out a very high degree of continuity and consistency over time. Indeed, dogmatic inflexibility in the face of changing external conditions was one of the main reasons behind the economic decline and the gradual disintegration of the economic system in Romania in the 1980s. Ceausescu's ideological conviction and perception of the world were apparently firmly moulded in his early years and remained essentially unaltered throughout his life.

> Not an intellectual, not even educated through primary school, Ceausescu understands the outlines of Marxism, its simplifications of the complex development of human history, rather than its subtle philosophical ponderings on human capacities and alienation. In his youth he studied other communists' interpretations of the mature Marx and, most notably, the Stalinist doctrine of rapid and autarchic industrialisation as it was being applied in the Soviet Union. This was to dominate Ceausescu's understanding of revolutionary socialism. (Fischer, 1989: 32–3).

The creation of a homogeneous 'socialist' population modelled on the urban working class out of the traditionally peasant-based Romanian people remained a prime development objective throughout Ceausescu's reign, that is, long after such targets were de-emphasised in the rest of Eastern Europe. Linked to this was the probably equally important, albeit not officially acknowledged, objective of subjugating the population to the will and control of the regime by minimising its independence and scope for individual decisionmaking and manoeuvring. On the economic front the pivotal goal remained to create a strong industrial economy, based on heavy industry, within the framework of a centrally planned economy. Combined, these objectives go a long way towards explaining the policies and programmes pursued by the Ceausescu regime. In the 1980s it became increasingly clear that there was an inherent conflict between the economic goal on the one hand and, on the other hand, the strategy of economic development spearheaded by heavy industry as it dismally failed in creating the necessary preconditions for fully integrating the population into the socialised economy. Seen in this light, Romania provides an interesting case study of a traditional, unreformed Stalinist development strategy pursued for a long period of time.

The incompatible economic and societal development objectives provide the framework for analysis in the present study of the economic and social development of Romania during the second half of Ceausescu's reign. Special attention is given to agriculture and to employment in an attempt to highlight the nature and depth of the conflict between economic and societal objectives. An examination of the energy sector serves to illustrate in more general terms the effects on and costs to society of the priority development of heavy industry.

The study shows that the development strategy that was pursued proved to be singularly ill-suited as an instrument for achieving the regime's overall societal objectives. It failed to create sustainable economic growth, to provide the labour force with adequate employment and income opportunities, and to ensure an adequate supply of food products and other consumer goods and services through the socialised sector. Consequently, it failed to create the basis for social homogenisation and for integrating the entire population into the socialist economy and development process. Indeed, the flawed economic development strategy had rather the opposite effect. Yet, dogmatic intransigence precluded any modification of the economic system and development strategy. Instead, the regime resorted increasingly to coercion on all fronts and as the economic situation deteriorated, there was a consequential shift in emphasis from integration to subjugation.

This study includes with (1) an assessment of the Ceausescu legacy; (2) an examination of the initial changes and reforms in the short period between the fall of Ceausescu in December 1989 and the elections in May 1990; and (3) a brief discussion of the road ahead.

The successful years

The Romanian development strategy was initially very successful, since the preconditions for an 'extensive' development were ideal. At the time of the collectivisation campaigns in the late 1950s and early 1960s Romania was still a backward agrarian economy. On the eve of the final collectivisation drive some two-thirds of the labour force were still in the primary sector (Ronnås, 1984: 143), only a few percentage units below the level immediately after World War I. In absolute terms the agricultural population was considerably larger than it had been at the turn of the century, some sixty years earlier. As the yields of the main crops were only slightly above the level registered at the turn of the century[1] and because agricultural prices were low, it is safe to conclude that by 1960 labour productivity and incomes in agriculture were barely higher than they had been sixty years earlier.

The collectivisation of agriculture in the early 1960s was followed by a concerted effort to mechanise agriculture and to develop the manufacturing sector. As a consequence, the vast pool of underutilised labour in agriculture was mobilised and transferred to the non-agricultural sectors. The share of the non-agricultural population in the total labour force increased from 30.3 per cent in 1956 to 42.9 per cent in 1966, and to 63.5 per cent in 1977 (Ronnås, 1984: 143). In absolute terms the non-agricultural labour force increased from 4,442,000 in 1966 to 6,818,000 in 1977.

This shift of the labour force led to huge gains in productivity, even though productivity in the industrial sector was still low by international standards. The high overall economic growth rates in the 1960s and early 1970s[2] were largely a result of these transfer gains. As a prognosis for the future they were very deceptive indeed.

The industrial strategy after the collectivisation of agriculture remained essentially unaltered, in spite of a shift in the emphasis of the development strategy from creating a strong industrial base to creating a strong and numerous working class. The predominantly heavy industrial 'Group A' branches continued to receive 85–90 per cent of all industrial investments (Table 4.1). However, there was a pronounced shift in the location of new plants from the traditional raw material-based centres of heavy industry to the capitals of counties with large agricultural population. Typically, a few huge industrial plants would be constructed in a county to soak up the surplus agricultural labour.[3]

Table 4.1 Investment patterns in the socialist sector: percentages

Sector	1961–65	1966–70	1971–75	1976–80	1981–85
Industry	46.5	50.0	50.5	49.2	49.0
– Group A	41.5	42.4	42.1	42.1	42.9
– Group B	5.0	7.6	8.4	7.1	6.1
Construction	3.4	3.9	4.7	5.9	3.9
Agriculture	19.4	16.0	14.4	13.8	16.5
Transportation	8.8	10.3	10.2	10.6	11.3
Communal housing	11.5	9.5	9.3	10.2	10.3
Education & Culture	2.2	2.0	1.9	1.5	0.6
Health	1.2	1.2	0.9	0.7	0.5
Other sectors	6.9	7.1	8.1	8.1	8.0
All sectors	100.0	100.0	100.0	100.0	100.0

Notes: Agriculture includes silviculture; transportation includes communication; others include trade, communal services except housing, science, administration and other sectors. Figures for 1961–65 in 1959 constant prices; for 1966–75 in 1963 constant prices; 1976–80 in 1977 constant prices and for 1981–85 in current prices.

Source: Anuarul Statistic (1986: 222–3).

Towards the end of the 1970s economic growth slowed down considerably and the economy displayed signs of severe imbalances. The growth rate of national income fell from an average of over 10 per cent in the first half of the 1970s to only 3 per cent in 1980. Other indicators, such as employment, investments and gross industrial and agricultural output registered similar declines. Gross agricultural production actually dropped by 4 per cent in 1980 (*Anuarul Statistic*, 1981: 97) and total investment declined by 7 per cent the following year (*Anuarul Statistic*, 1982: 43). Shortages of food products became increasingly widespread in the domestic market after 1979–80.

Table 4.2 Economic development 1970–89: selected indicators

Indicator	Unit	1970	1980	1989	% yearly change 1970–80	% yearly change 1980–89
Population	1,000	20,252.5	22,201.4	23,151.6	0.92	0.47
Wage workers	1,000	5,108.7	7,340.0	7,996.6	3.69	0.96
Fixed assets	bil. lei	757.1	1,864.2	3,524.7	9.43	7.33
Social product	bil.lei	523.4	1,250.9	1,934.6	9.10	4.96
National income	bil.lei	212.1	508.7	613.7	9.14	2.11
Gross ind. prod.	bil. lei	307.2	936.1	1,270.4	11.79	3.45
Gross agr. prod.	bil. lei	68.6	129.1	193.4	6.53	4.59
Investments	bil. lei	80.0	210.5	236.4	10.16	1.30
Mean wage	lei/month	1,289	2,238	3,063	5.67	3.55
Peasant income	lei/month	589	1,388	1,920	8.95	3.67
Retail sales	bil. lei	93.7	213.1	297.3	8.53	3.77
Electric energy	mil. kwh	35,088	67,486	75,770	6.76	1.29
Coal	1,000 tons	20,531	35,164	61,343	5.53	6.38
Crude oil	1,000 tons	13,377	11,511	9,173	–1.49	–2.49
Steel	1,000 tons	6,517	13,175	14,415	7.29	1.00
Tractors	No.	29,287	70,873	24,500	9.24	–11.13
Cars	No.	23,604	88,232	122,800	14.09	3.74
TV sets	1,000	280	541	511	6.81	–0.64
Fertilisers	1,000 tons	895	2,451	2,805	10.6	1.51
Concrete	1,000 tons	7,966	15,611	13,265	6.96	–1.79
Timber	mil. cu m	5,305	4,593	3,784	–1.43	–2.13
Woven fabrics	mil. sq m	608	1,154	1,206	6.62	0.49
Knitwear	mil. units	134	296	261	8.25	–1.39
Shoes	1,000 pairs	65,804	113,401	111,400	5.59	–0.28
Meat	1,000 tons	425	993	686	8.86	–4.03
Milk	mil. litres	433.6	732.5	568	5.38	–2.77
Cooking oil	1,000 tons	274	369	247	3.02	–4.33
Refined sugar	1,000 tons	377	509	693	3.05	3.49
Butter	tons	30,700	34,600	45,600	1.21	3.10
Cheese products	tons	68,200	112,900	81,600	5.17	–3.54

Sources: Anuarul Statistic (1981: 97, 186–99); *Buletin de informare* (1990/3: 1–4).

Stagnation and decay in the 1980s

Official economic statistics were increasingly falsified after 1980[4] and indeed very few data were published after 1985. The absence of reliable data makes it impossible to offer a detailed year-by-year scrutiny of the economic development in the 1980s. Any comprehensive analysis of the anatomy of economic decay in the 1980s will have to wait for a recalculation of the economic data for the 1980s. However, a comparison of the development of economic indicators in the 1970s and 1980s (Table 4.2) casts light on the contrast between the dynamic development of the 1970s and the stagnation, not to say retrogression, of the 1980s.

Two factors which directly contributed to the break in the trend deserve special mention. First, the transfer gains arising from the shift of a large part of the labour force from agriculture to industry had been largely exhausted by the end of the 1970s. At the same time, a domestic energy crisis arose as the development of highly energy-intensive industries resulted in a rapid increase in energy consumption, an increase which could not be met by domestic supplies. As a consequence oil imports increased sharply — from 2.3 million tons in 1970 to 16.0 million tons in 1980 — at the same time that energy prices on the world market were at their peak. However, the simultaneous occurrence of these two phenomena should not distract our attention from the fact that at the heart of the problem were system-determined inefficiencies, increasing sectoral imbalances and erratic and often harmful policies.

Romania was bypassed by the waves of genuine attempts at economic reforms aimed at improving economic efficiency through decentralisation and deregulation which swept through Eastern Europe in the 1960s and 1970s.[5] By the end of the 1970s Romania and Albania remained the most centralised and rigidly planned economies in Eastern Europe. Although such an economy had proved its worth at mobilising resources in the preceding two decades, it was totally unsuited to meeting the challenge of continued economic growth through more efficient resource utilisation in the 1980s. Romania faced the classic and seemingly impossible task of changing from extensive to intensive growth within the framework of a centrally planned economy. The rapid decline in the availability of surplus agricultural labour and of cheap domestic sources of energy and the very rigid nature of the economic system made the task particularly troublesome.

The response to the crisis

Throughout the 1980s Ceausescu's response to the economic crisis was marked by an intransigence and rigidity of mind and a decreasing contact with reality. It also revealed a willingness to impose any amount of material hardship on the population in the futile pursuit of a vision. Thus the crisis was perpetuated and aggravated by several factors:

1. the determination of the regime to continue the rapid development of large-scale heavy industry at all costs;
2. a refusal to reform the extremely centralised economic system; and

3. a failure to revitalise the agricultural sector, which suffered from a depletion and degradation of its human resources and adverse economic conditions.

The 7th and 8th five-year plans, for 1981–5 and 1986–90, respectively, paid little heed to the difficult economic situation, but called for continued rapid growth along the same lines as previously.[6] As a consequence, imbalances and shortages were aggravated by structurally inappropriate and unrealistically taut plans. In addition, the sharp curtailment of imports following the decision to pay off the entire external debt led to acute shortages of many industrial inputs. Thus capacity utilisation fell in many industries and periodic closures of enterprises for lack of inputs became a common feature. Yet, investments in new plants of 'Group A' industries continued more or less unabated. The result was a sharp drop in the return to investment (Table 4.3). Overall returns to investment, measured as the growth of national income per 1,000 lei invested, fell from 273 in 1971–5, to 157 in 1976–80 to 50 in 1981–9.

Table 4.3 Investments, growth and employment, 1970–89

Period	Total investments	Incremental national income	Incremental employment	A	B	C
1971–75	549,000	149,800	1,192,100	0.27	2.17	0.33
1976–80	931,940	146,800	1,039,200	0.16	1.12	0.41
1980–89	2,110,575	105,000	656,600	0.05	0.31	0.43

A: Incremental national income in lei per invested lei.

B: Incremental employment per million lei investments.

C: Employment elasticity; per cent change in employment/per cent change in national income.

Note: Figures on investments and incremental national income are in million lei at 1963 fixed prices for the years 1971–5 and current prices for the subsequent years.

Sources: Anuarul Statistic (1988: 3); (1987: 3); (1986: 222–223); (1981: 97, 385); *Buletin de informare* (1990/3: 1); *Scînteia* (4 February 1988; 4 February 1989).

As the discrepancy between vision and reality became increasingly glaring, Ceausescu's attention turned more and more to grandiose projects, such as the Danube–Black Sea canal, the new civic centre of Bucharest, giant chemical and metallurgical complexes, and not least to the 'systematisation' of the countryside.

The crisis in the rigid centrally planned economic system was met with further centralisation of decisionmaking. Failure to meet plan targets at the sectoral and enterprise level resulted in increased interference from the top in the detailed management of enterprises. Detailed instructions and directives were issued to individual enterprises, often arbitrarily and *ad hoc* following a 'flying inspection' by Ceausescu. Plan targets, both on the macro and enterprise level, were increasingly based on Ceausescu's personal directives rather than on realistic calculations and assessments. Consequently, production results were increasingly falsified at all levels, in order to avoid the wrath of the leader. Such falsification is obviously a common phenomenon in all centrally planned economies. However, in Romania it reached an unprecedented extent in the late 1980s.[7] It created a make-believe economy, which fooled nobody, but clearly played havoc with planning. On the whole, it is safe to conclude that during the 1980s the economy because a highly personalised command economy.

The policy of developing heavy industry at all costs resulted in a further accentuation of the priority given to this sector in the 1980s, so that the already serious sectoral imbalances were further aggravated. The priority allocation of scarce resources — energy, capital, labour, and so on — to 'Group A' industry took place at the expense of other economic sectors and of consumers.

The policy-induced energy crisis

The energy crisis which hit the country in the early 1980s illustrates well how unrealistic rigid planning, policy-induced sectoral imbalances and erratic policy decisions in the face of crisis aggravated the economic situation and, not least, had severe repercussions on the standard of living.

In 1985 Romania produced 3,160 kwh of electricity per capita, about the same amount as Italy (3,413), Spain (3,263) or Yugoslavia (3,220) (*Anuarul Statistic*, 1986: 377). Yet, the streets were dark at night, houses were feebly lit with a single 40 watt bulb and small children and old people died from the cold in their homes in the winter. By 1989 electricity production had increased slightly to 3,279 kwh/per capita, while household consumption of electricity had fallen to a mere 167 kwh/per capita, that is, 5.1 per cent of total consumption and a decline in absolute terms of 53 kwh or 24 per cent since 1980 (*Buletin de informare*, 1990/93: 2; *Anuarul Statistic*, 1981: 55, 203). The sharp increase in the industrial demand for energy was matched by overoptimistic plans for the domestic supply of energy. A long-term perspective plan for the energy sector in 1980 (*Programul-Directiva*, 1979: 5) projected that self-sufficiency in energy would be reattained by the year 1990. This target was subsequently scaled down. At the 13th Congress of the Romanian Communist Party in late 1984 the self-sufficiency target was abandoned and the production targets were set at 95,000 million kwh and 100 million tons of coal by the year 1990 (Ceausescu, 1984: 17). By contrast, electricity production reached only 75,700 million kwh and coal production 61, 343 million tons in 1989. A 16.7 per cent increase in the capacity to generate electricity between 1985 and 1989 resulted in a mere 5.4 per cent increase in production because of faulty installations and a shortage of imported coal (*Buletin de informare*, 1990/3: 2). Rather than approaching self-sufficiency, the proportion of imports in total energy consumption increased from 28.2 per cent in 1980 to 39.2 per cent in 1989 (*Buletin de informare*, 1990/3: 2).

The policy response to the shortfall in energy supply was first and foremost the imposition of draconian curbs on the use of energy by households and by the 'non-productive' economic sectors. Consequently, the fall in sales of consumer durables such as refrigerators and washing machines between 1980 and 1989 (see Table 4.5 below) was not so much due to a shortage of supply as to a fall in the demand for energy-consuming appliances. The savings made through these measures bore no relationship to the hardship they caused, since the share of these sectors in the total energy consumption was in any case small.

Ultimately, other economic sectors were also affected. A quarter of the irrigaion capacity in agriculture remained unutilised in 1989 due to a lack of energy, and many industries were forced to run at less than full capacity. Yet, up until the very end of the high development priority given to heavy, energy-intensive industries remained unchallenged.

Table 4.4 Development of agriculture, 1970–89

	Unit	1970	1980	1989
Arable area	1,000 ha	9,373	9,834	9,500
– irrigated		686	2,125	2,900
Labour force	1,000	4,849	3,048	3,487
Global production	mil. lei	68,600	129,100	196,300
Tractors	no.	107,290	146,600	152,000
Chemical fertilisers	1,000 tons	594	1,114	1,200
Fixed assets	mil. lei	87,100	199,500	428,900
Production				
Cereals	1,000 tons	10,631	20,200	18,379
– wheat & rye	1,000 tons	3,399	6,467	7,935
– maize	1,000 tons	6,536	11,182	6,769
Sunflower	1,000 tons	770	817	656
Soya	1,000 tons	91	448	304
Sugarbeat	1,000 tons	2,921	5,562	6,771
Potatoes	1,000 tons	2,064	4,135	4,420
Vegetables	1,000 tons	2,004	3,585	3,727
Milk				
– state farms	litre/cow	2,855	2,341	2,801
– collective farms	litre/cow	1,297	1,367	1,516
Eggs				
– state farms	per hen	215	207	159
– collective farms	per hen	79	210	152
Animal stock				
Horned cattle	1,000	5,216	6,485	6,283
– dairy cows	1,000	2,625	3,188	2,453
Pigs	1,000	6,359	11,542	11,659
Sheep & goats	1,000	5,216	15,865	15,442

Notes: Global production for 1970 in 1963 prices, for 1980 in 1977 prices and for 1989 in current prices.

Sources: Anuaral Statistic (1986: 50, 134, 143, 174–6, 198, 210); *Buletin de informare* (1990/3: 1–5).

Ideological response to the stagnation in agriculture

Romania's agricultural performance in the 1980s was dismal (Table 4.4). Production of most products declined or, at best, stagnated. The number of horned cattle declined, in the case of dairy cows by as much as a quarter. Only the number of horses registered a marked increase — from 555,000 to 686,000 in 1987 — as a consequence of demechanisation in the trail of the energy crisis.

There were several reasons behind the poor performance of agriculture. The rapid industrial transition had eroded the human resource base in agriculture, quantitatively as well as qualitatively. By 1977 women made up 70 per cent of collective farm-workers and the mean age of the entire agricultural labour force had risen to 43.2 years. Only 30 per cent of the agricultural labour force had more than four years of formal education, as compared to 75 per cent of the non-agricultural labour force (Ronnås, 1984: 148–9).

The massive transfer of labour from agriculture to the other economic sectors had not significantly improved the living conditions of the agricultural population and the rural–urban divide remained as large as ever. In contrast to the other centrally planned economies in Eastern Europe the gap between collective farm incomes and non-agricultural incomes remained large. In 1989 the average remuneration per work norm (i.e. approximately a day's work) in collective farming was 41 lei, while the average remuneration for waged workers was reportedly 3,063 per month or about 125 lei per day (*Buletin de informare*, 1990/3: 8). However, as the private production by collective farm members exceeded the collective farm production for important products such as milk, meat, eggs, wool, potatoes and fruit, and equalled it for vegetables (*Anuarul Statistic*, 1986: 170–207),[8] there can be little doubt that for most collective farm members income from work on the collective farm was only a minor part of their total incomes.[9] There were large regional variations in collective farm incomes,[10] and it is clear that in many parts of the country collectivised agriculture had become relatively unimportant as a source of income for the rural population, although it maintained a two-thirds share of the most productive asset in rural areas, namely arable land (see e.g. Ronnås, 1987: 41–53). The difficulties in mobilising labour, which had plagued collective agriculture since the 1970s, reflected not so much an absolute shortage of labour as the simple fact that remuneration had fallen below the supply price of labour in many areas. As a consequence collective farms came to rely increasingly on compulsion and on temporary recruitment of non-agricultural labour (e.g. students, soldiers and rural non-agricultural workers) to meet the demand for labour during peak periods. Intransigent centralised decision-making on crop and product mixes and a shortage of inputs and of functioning machinery were other important reasons for the poor performance of agriculture.

As a result of the crisis in the agricultural sector, the supply of food through the socialist trade network fell sharply from an already very low level. Most staples virtually disappeared from the shops (Table 4.5). Food rationing was introduced in 1981 (Decretul 306/1981; Decretul 313/1981) and was combined with draconian measures to combat hoarding and 'speculation'. In reality the picture was even grimmer than Table 4.5 indicates. A more detailed analysis would probably reveal that the supply of food did not fall gradually between 1980 and 1989, but instead fell

Table 4.5 Per capita retail sales of selected goods through the socialist trade system, 1980 and 1989

	Unit	1980	1989
Bread	kg	101.3	111.1
Fresh meat	kg	20.8	9.7
Meat products	kg	10.7	11.1
Fish	kg	3.3	3.3
Milk	litre	32.3	24.1
Fresh milk products	litre	23.4	8.8
Cheese	kg	4.3	2.5
Butter	kg	1.3	1.0
Edible oil	kg	9.2	8.6
Sugar	kg	18.9	14.9
Eggs	kg	71.0	89.0
Rice	kg	3.9	1.7
Potatoes	kg	25.4	34.8
Fresh vegetables	kg	36.7	37.2
Per 1,000 households			
Refrigerators		16.4	7.0
Washing-machines		12.8	9.1
Radio sets		22.5	20.0
TV sets		20.1	12.3
Cars		3.8	2.8

Notes: Milk includes milk powder for 1980. Fresh milk products include cream, sour milk, etc.

Sources: Anuarul Statistic (1981: 512–13); *Buletin de informare* (1990/3: 9).

sharply as early as in 1981.[11] After that it oscillated at a level near that of 1989 for the rest of the decade. Regular 'over the counter' sales were much less than reported since most of the food supplied through the socialist trade system was used for barter by those working in the trade sector, sold under the counter to friends and relatives or 'diverted *en route*' in other ways. Large regional variations in supply were also experienced because of the poor distribution system and the official policy of 'territorial self-sufficiency', which bordered on autarchy.[12] The miniscule food rations obtainable through the socialist trade network cast in a starker light the failure of the regime to meet even the most basic needs of the population — forty years after World War II and twenty years after the collectivisation of agriculture. For example, in Cluj-Napoca, the largest city in Transylvania, rations in June 1988 were 750 g of sugar, 0.5 l of cooking oil, 2 kg of potatoes, 0.5 kg of wheat flour and 1 kg of macaroni per person per month. In addition, bread was rationed to 300 g per person per day. Moreover, all rations were subject to availability. Meat and dairy products were not formally rationed since there was nothing to ration. The rural population was not entitled to food rations, but could obtain industrial food products such as sugar and cooking oil only through barter, mainly with eggs, or contractual deliveries of privately produced food to the state.

As a consequence, the production and supply of food in the private sector increased in importance. In 1985 the private sector accounted for more than half of the total production of milk, wool, eggs and potatoes and for almost half of the production of meat and fruit, although it held only 13 per cent of the arable land. Its share in the total production of meat, milk, wool and maize increased significantly between 1980 and 1985. The significance of privately produced food in domestic consumption was even greater as part of the food produced in the socialised sector was exported.

The response of the regime to this development was determined by ideological rather than pragmatic considerations. In the early 1980s a 'new agrarian revolution' was launched by Ceausescu.[13] A key feature of this rather nebulous scheme turned out to be the incorporation of the entire agricultural sector into the centrally planned socialist economy. In 1984 the right of collective farm members to keep a private plot was linked to compulsory deliveries of food products by the households concerned to the state (Programul unic de crestere, 1984). The quotas were quite high, *viz.* one mature pig every two years, 10 kg of poultry per year, 800 l of milk per cow, 3,000 kg of potatoes per hectare, 8 kg of fruit per tree, and so on. Such procurement prices were less than a third of the market price for most produce (Ronnås, 1989: 554), and for animal products they were as a rule well below the cost of production. The same delivery requirements were also applied to private farms, except that these had to deliver a mature pig *every* year. The same programme also stipulated minimum production levels for a large number of agricultural products for both the collective farm member households and private farm households. A decree on the elaboration and implementation of agricultural plans in 1986 (Decretul 1986/78) further increased government control over private production since both private farms and the personal plots of collective farms were subjected to exactly the same type of central planning as state and collective farms. These unique measures made no economic sense. It must have been clear that they would have a detrimental effect on agricultural production and would further aggravate the already precarious supply of agricultural products in the domestic market. They can only be understood in the light of Ceausescu's personal abhorrence of private economic activities and his determination to create an all-embracing socialist economy and society at any cost.

Similar motives undoubtedly lay behind the revitalisation of the systematisation programme, originally adopted as far back as the Romanian Communist Party Congress in 1972.[14] The fundamental idea behind this programme was to structure all urban and rural localities into a well-defined hierarchy with a predetermined place and function for each locality and every region in order to ensure harmonious national development. The programme contained a strong element of physical planning, particularly in rural areas. Villages were to be restructured to resemble towns with a dense construction pattern of predominantly multi-storey buildings within a tightly drawn settlement perimeter. Rural development was to be highly discriminatory with special preference given to the some 300–500 villages selected for development into towns. At the other end of the scale, approximately half of Romania's 13,000 villages were considered as not having the prerequisites for development and were to be phased out altogether.

The primary motive behind the systematisation programme was explicitly ideological. The programme aimed at integrating the rural population into the socialist economy and was seen as a means of creating 'one unified population of workers' (*Scînteia*, 3 March 1988). As such, it was seen as a logical step after the collectivisation programme within the long-term strategy of making a 'socialist man' out of the Romanian peasant. Clearly, the relocation of the rural population from scattered homesteads and small villages to flats in larger settlements would also facilitate political control, particularly since such a relocation would also sharply reduce the degree of self-sufficiency in food production among rural households.

The programme sparked off a flurry of 'systematisation studies' in the 1970s, but its actual implementation was slow and came to a near halt around 1980 with the onset of the economic crisis. Indeed, it could only have been implemented within the framework of a dynamic rural development, and in the context of the rural demographic and economic decline that characterised the period after 1975 it was in fact a totally unrealistic scheme. Hence, it came as something of a surprise when Ceausescu put the programme back at the top of the agenda in early 1988 (*Scînteia*, 3 March 1988), particularly because there was a simultaneous upward revision of the targets. It cast light, especially internationally, on the extent to which Ceausescu had lost touch with reality and on his obsession with this particular strategy as a means for achieving his personal vision of a socialist society.

The strategy of 'socialising' agriculture and the agricultural population by force was clearly counterproductive. In the absence of modernisation, its main effects were an erosion of the production base and a further alienation of what was left of the Romanian peasantry. At the same time it undermined the capacity of the socialised economy to provide the population with food. Throughout the 1980s private production of and trade in agricultural products were even more important, in particular as a source of food for the non-agricultural population, than they had been in the 1970s when state food stores still provided an alternative to the peasant markets.

Emerging unemployment

One does not normally associate centrally planned economies, even when they function badly, with unemployment. Yet, available data clearly indicate that the economic stagnation in the 1980s severely impaired the capacity of the Romanian economy to absorb incremental labour, and that as a consequence an unemployment crisis gradually emerged. This crisis became acute after 1987 as the large cohorts born after the introduction of pro-natalistic legislation in 1966[15] entered the labour market.

Table 4.6 clearly shows the sharp decline in the rate of growth of wage employment after 1978. The annual rate of increase in wage employment fell from an average of 223,000, or 3.69 per cent, between 1970 and 1980, to 73,000, or 0.96 per cent, between 1980 and 1989.

Because of the relatively young age structure of the wage labour force, the attrition rate was low (though increasing) and the demand for wage employment among the new entrants into the labour force had largely to be met by additional

Table 4.6 Development of the labour force and of waged employment over previous year, 1975–89

	Absolute change (1,000)			Percentage change		
Year	A	B	C	A	B	C
1976	76	258	–182	0.6	4.1	–4.7
1977	37	181	–144	0.4	2.8	–3.9
1978	26	216	–190	0.3	3.2	–5.4
1979	30	227	–197	0.3	3.3	–5.9
1980	30	157	–127	0.3	2.2	–4.0
1981	25	95	–70	0.2	1.3	–2.3
1982	53	118	–65	0.5	1.6	–2.2
1983	30	47	–17	0.3	0.6	–0.6
1984	42	–15	57	0.4	–0.2	2.0
1985	86	76	10	0.8	1.0	0.3
1986	83	91	–7	0.8	1.2	–0.2
1987	50	38	11	0.5	0.5	0.4
1988	351	53	298	3.3	0.7	10.2
1989	(59)	(176)	(–117)	(0.5)	(2.2)	(–3.6)

A: Labour force (*populatia ocupata*)
B: Wage workers (*numarul mediu al personalului muncitor*)
C: Non-wage workers in the labour force (A – B)

Notes: All absolute figures are rounded off to the nearest thousand. The figures for 1989 are not totally comparable with figures for earlier years because of definitional differences.

Sources: Anuarul Statistic (1980: 113, 115); (1981: 121, 123); (1982: 60–1); (1983: 58–9); (1986: 50); (1987: 3); *Buletin de informare* (1990/3: 1–2, 8); *Scînteia* (4 February 1988; 4 February 1989).

employment opportunities (Table 4.7). According to the 1977 population census, some 81.4 per cent of those in the 20–24 year age range were in the labour force and 66 per cent had wage employment (*Recensamîntul*, 1977: 46–8). Using the latter figure as a somewhat conservative benchmark for calculating the gross incremental demand for wage employment, one can estimate that 910,200 new wage employment opportunities would have been required in 1977–81, 387,500 in 1982–6 and 670,200 in 1987–91, net of natural attrition (Table 4.7). During the first two of these periods the numbers of new wage jobs actually created were 876,300 and 315,900, respectively, indicating a total shortfall of 105,500 jobs. By a fortunate demographic coincidence the sharp decline in the growth of wage employment after 1979 coincided with a temporary fall in the net demand for such employment as attrition through retirement increased and as the number of new entrants into the labour market reached a trough.[16] This 'breathing space' ended abruptly in 1987 as the large age groups born after 1967 entered the labour market with full force. According to official statistics the labour force increased by some 351,000 between 1987 and 1988 (*Anuarul Statistic*, 1988: 3; *Scînmteia*, 4 February 1989), that is, a sevenfold increase over the preceding year. Of these, only 53,000 found wage employment, while the

Table 4.7 Estimates of demand and supply of waged employment

	1977–81	1982–86	1987–91	1992–97
Entrants to labour force				
– high estimate	1,356.1	1,103.7	1,692.7	1,525.0
– low estimate	1,118.8	910.5	1,396.4	1,258.0
Attrition	208.6	523.0	726.2	856.5
Net increment to labour force				
– high estimate	1,147.5	580.7	963.5	668.5
– low estimate	910.2	387.5	670.2	401.5
Actual increment of wage workers	876.3	315.9	(409.3)	n.a.
Discrepancy				
– high estimate	271.2	264.8	554.2	n.a.
– low estimate	33.9	71.6	260.9	n.a.

Notes: Estimates of attrition are based on the assumption that all male wage workers retire at 60 and female workers at the age of 55, i.e. at official retirement age for most categories. Estimates of entrants into the labour force are based on estimates of the population reaching the age of 20. The low estimate assumes that 66 per cent of all those reaching the age of 20 seek wage employment, i.e. the same as the actual percentage of wage workers in this age group in 1977. The high estimate assumes that 80 per cent seek employment. The estimated increment to the number of workers 1987–91 is extrapolated from the actual increment between 1987 and 1989.

Sources: Table 4.6; *Recensamîntul* (1977: 46–7).

remaining 298,000 must have joined the ranks of the more or less openly unemployed or of the non-wage agricultural labour force. Preliminary data suggest that the situation improved significantly in the following year, as there was supposedly an absolute increase of 176,000 in the wage labour force.[17] Yet, if the growth in wage employment in 1987–9 is extrapolated up to 1991 one arrives at a forecasted shortfall in wage employment opportunities of 260,900 for the entire 1987–91 period, in addition to the existing backlog in 1987.

As a result of the acute employment problem the transition of the labour force from agriculture to the non-agricultural sectors was not only halted, but reversed. The share of the total labour force in agriculture increased from 28.9 per cent in 1985 to 31.5 per cent in 1989, while the share in the services sectors fell sharply (*Anuarul Statistic*, 1986: 70; *Buletin de informare*, 1990/3: 2). In view of the much lower incomes in agriculture it can safely be assumed that this development reflected a shortage of wage employment opportunities rather than the changing preferences of the labour force.

In reality, the employment situation was much bleaker than Table 4.7 indicates, since there was an increase in underemployment and temporary unemployment among the regularly employed wage labour force. The increase took two forms. First, workers were laid off without pay as enterprises temporarily closed down, usually for lack of inputs. Second, employees suffered large declines in incomes as failure to meet plan targets, usually due to unrealistic targets or external factors beyond the control of the enterprise, was directly translated into a decline in incomes through the 'global piece-rate system' (*acordul global*) (Legea 1986/1).

Although the picture is still far from clear, various estimates made after the 1989 revolution indicate that the employment situation Romanians have inherited is indeed grim. According to one estimate (Ion Blaga in *Adevarul*, 9 January 1990), less than half of the new entrants into the labour force since 1985 have found wage employment. Another source (Mihai Ionescu in *Adevarul*, 21 February 1990) claims that in early 1990 approximately 8 to 10 per cent of the labour force were either unemployed or overqualified for their present jobs. This tallies with a survey in the county of Iasi, which estimated unemployment in the whole county to be 25,000 persons, of which 12,000 were in the city of Iasi alone (*Adevarul*, 22 February 1990). In addition, the industrial sector is estimated to suffer from overstaffing at about 25 per cent on average (*Adevarul*, 21 February 1990).

The unemployment crisis left behind by the old regime reflects a failure of the development strategy it pursued. First, the responsibility to provide adequate employment opportunities for the labour force is a logical and moral consequence of the obligation to work and the near monopoly position of the state as employer of labour for wages. Indeed, this responsibility is even enshrined in the Romanian constitution. Second, the failure to provide adequate wage employment opportunities in the socialised sector implies a failure of the overall strategy aimed at integrating the entire population into the socialist economy and society.

The legacy of Ceausescu

The legacy of Ceausescu can only be described as an unmitigated disaster on all fronts. The stagnation which characterised the entire 1980s eventually set in motion a disintegration of the socialist economy and economic system. This process was fuelled by incompetent dictatorial rule and extreme sectoral imbalances. As reported production results became totally detached from reality, the information base required for planning was eroded, yet the economy remained as rigidly planned as ever. In 1989 alone national income fell by an estimated 10 per cent (*Buletin de informare*, 1990/3: 1) to a level little more than half of that originally projected for 1990.[18] In spite of continued high investment rates throughout the 1980s, the physical capital in large sections of the economy, such as communication and transportation infrastructure and light industry, was severely run down. The agricultural sector was in a shambles.

More importantly, the human resources of the country were seriously neglected. The disastrous state of the health sector is well known. Although little quantitative information is yet available, it is clear that the physical well-being of the population deteriorated from an already unsatisfactory level throughout the 1980s due to malnutrition, lack of medical facilities, pollution, poor and often dangerous working conditions, and sheer physical fatigue. Infant mortality remains among the highest in Europe — 26.9 per thousand in 1989 (*Buletin de informare*, 1990/3:8) — and the average lifespan is low and falling.[19] The resources allocated to the educational sector declined throughout the 1980s, although the school-age population reached an all-time high. Higher education was particularly affected, as there was a pronounced shift from higher education to professional and vocational training. Hence, the number enrolled in universities fell from 192,800 in 1980/1 to 164,500 in 1989/90 (*Anuarul Statistic*, 1981: 579; *Buletin de informare*, 1990/3: 9) while the population in the 18–22 age bracket increased from 1,627,000 to 2,115,000. This shift to vocational training will be a major obstacle to the restructuring of the economy in the 1990s. It has produced a generation with a narrow educational profile, with an emphasis on specific skills rather than on general knowledge.

Developments since the revolution

The primary focus of the new regime during the interregnum between the fall of Ceausescu in December 1989 and the elections in May 1990 was on improving the supplies of food, energy and other basic needs to the population through reallocation of existing and imported resources, and on addressing some of the most glaring problems, particularly in the field of agriculture. The reallocation of resources had an immediate and impressive impact on the material well-being of the population. The supply of food on the domestic market increased substantially and quickly alleviated the acute shortages, even though rationing of key food products had to be reintroduced in early 1990. People's ingrained instinct to hoard whatever they might find in the shops gradually subsided as they got used to the idea that there would be meat in the shop the next day as well. The removal of restrictions on the supply of electricity and other forms of energy to the population had an immense impact on the standard of living at a comparatively low cost to the economy.

These reallocative measures were combined with a revocation of many of the more repressive laws and decrees imposed by the old regime, such as those on systematisation, on territorial self-sufficiency, on worker contributions to the social funds and not least those aimed at increasing the birth rate. These measures were both necessary and welcome, and nothing less than what would have been expected of any post-revolutionary regime. However, they did little to resolve the severe economic problems confronting the country, and in this sense their results were illusory. Indeed, they may well have had the negative side-effect of instilling a false belief among the population that the economic problems had by and large been resolved through the removal of Ceausescu.

Most of the population profess to be in favour of introducing a market economy, although a gradual transition is preferred to a rapid one.[20] However, this agreement in principle has yet to stand the test of reality. In contrast to Hungary and Poland, Romania has no past experience of repeated but unsuccessful attempts to reform the economic system. Consequently, the general public may not be convinced that the economic system cannot be improved, but needs desperately to be replaced. The highly personalised rule of Ceausescu has also served to obscure the shortcomings of the economic system and the industrial structure. This general lack of a sense of acute and profound crisis — a sense that is essential when a population is to accept the hardship and adjustment costs of reforms — clearly remains an important political obstacle to sorely needed economic reforms.

The sense of real improvements experienced by the population stands in sharp contrast to the picture given by the overall macro-economic indicators for the first half of 1990. Industrial production of final goods (*productia marfa industriala*) fell by 19 per cent in comparison with the first quarter of 1989 (*Revista romàna de Statistîca*, 1990/7: 45). Similarly, labour productivity in the manufacturing sector was down by 22 per cent, investments by 44 per cent and hard currency exports by 45 per cent.[21] On the other hand, hard currency imports were up by 53 per cent. Given the circumstances, it is understandable that Romania should live beyond its means for some time to come. The relatively small foreign debt gives the country some leeway in this regard and provides a certain breathing-space before undertaking a major overhaul of the economy. None the less, the slow pace of economic recovery during the first few months after the revolution gives cause for concern.

Attempts at reforms

Apart from agriculture, the attempts to reform the economy prior to the elections were piecemeal and somewhat half-hearted. Agriculture was the obvious first target for reforms. Not only were the problems in this sector particularly alarming, but the immediate remedies were uncontroversial and comparatively painless. Two decrees issued in early February (*Adevarul*, 1 and 2 February 1990) served to improve the autonomy and economic conditions of the collective and state farms. In hilly and peri-urban areas the collective farms were given the right to lease out all or part of the land to members on long-term contracts; in other areas, that is, on the plains, the personal plot could be increased to 5,000 sq m per active or retired member. A few weeks later the state procurement prices for agricultural products were raised by an average of 40 per cent. For animal produce the increases were considerably larger. The increase in farmgate prices provided a sorely needed stimulus to agricultural production. Previously prices had been well below production costs, particularly for animal products. The decrees issued in February seem to have been taken as a *carte blanche* for decollectivisation and throughout the spring the countryside was in turmoil as land was redistributed to collective farm members, often on the basis of former ownership. There can be no doubt that the measures taken will invigorate agriculture and improve agricultural production, even if in the short term it may suffer from the present uncertainties regarding holding rights. However, while the decollectivisation and price reforms may have solved the major incentive problems, production is likely to remain inefficient. Small and ill-equipped holdings do not form a sound basis for an efficient and modern agriculture. Furthermore, the rural infrastructure — social, economic and physical — is very poor.

By comparison, the non-agricultural sectors saw little change. The centrally planned state sector continued to function in much the same way as before, although outside interference in the running of enterprises decreased. Private enterprises are now permitted and officially encouraged. A law issued in March (Decretul Lege 54/1990) laying down the rules for private enterprises was overly restrictive, in particular because it limited the maximum number of employees to ten. This restriction was subsequently removed, at least informally, and generous support to new private enterprises, including heavily subsidised short-term loans has been introduced. However, the development of private firms, in both the manufacturing and service sectors, has so far been slow. A large-scale development of private enterprises seems unlikely as long as more comprehensive overall reform of the economy is absent.

The road ahead

Past experience in the socialist states, notably in Hungary, Poland and Vietnam, indicates that the path of small steps in the direction of a market economy favoured by the Romanian National Salvation Front is ineffective. Nothing short of a comprehensive and bold package of reforms, similar to those introduced in Poland and Vietnam, is needed to achieve a transition from the present economic system to a system based on the principles of a market economy.

A successful package has to include *inter alia* a relaxation of price controls for both producer and consumer goods and the introduction of real self-management of state enterprises, including the replacement of soft budget constraints by hard ones and a dismantling of the system of central allocation of inputs and guaranteed markets for outputs. Steps in this direction were taken in the second half of 1990. A comprehensive economic and legislative framework in support of a market economy will have to replace the centrally planned economic system.

A restructuring of the Romanian economy is inevitable and is likely to be a prolonged and rather painful process. The sectoral imbalances have been highlighted above. The economic structure is severely lopsided in the direction of heavy industry, while light industries producing consumer goods and, in particular, the service sectors are underdeveloped. Investment has been primarily based on ideological considerations and personal whims, with little heed paid to economic efficiency, comparative advantages and competitiveness. Technology is largely outdated. There can be little doubt that many enterprises have no future, and will have to close down sooner or later. Such closures will have high social costs because the labour force is both occupationally and geographically immobile, and local labour markets tend to be very poorly diversified. The economic base of small and medium-sized towns typically rests on one or two large enterprises. Clearly, the process of economic restructuring and the weeding-out of non-viable enterprises needs to be combined with concerted efforts to develop alternative local economic activities and employment opportunities to avoid mass unemployment and social unrest. Furthermore, there is a need for comprehensive and aggressive labour market policies aimed at increasing occupational mobility, including incentive for self-employment, and at providing an adequate material safety net for the unemployed.

Inflation has so far been kept reasonably under control. Indeed, the consumer price index may even have fallen in the first few months after the revolution as food prices on the private market fell somewhat and the supply of food products in the state shops, where prices are much lower, increased considerably. The increase in the state procurement prices of agricultural produce will sooner or later be carried through to the retail level, but the impact need not be very large since subsidies of retail food prices are still small.

Yet, strong inflationary pressure is rapidly building up. Personal disposable incomes were expected to increase by 90 billion lei in 1990.[22] Increases in wages, pensions and social benefits amounted to about 60 billion lei. In addition, repayment of earlier contributions to the now dissolved 'social fund' (*contributie cu parti sociale*) amounted to 29 billion lei (*Adevarul*, 8 and 9 March 1990). At the same time, labour productivity remains much below the level of 1989. This will inevitably result in increased surplus liquidity in the economy — which so far has been contained by increased imports of consumer goods — a cost explosion in the state sector and a rapidly increasing budget deficit.

However, it seems probable that it will be the rapidly deteriorating employment situation rather than inflation that will exert the strongest pressure on the regime to attend to the fundamental economic problems confronting the country. Given the demographic structure, the net labour force increment will exceed one hundred thousand per year in the coming five years. This is much above anything that the economy can be expected to absorb in its present state. Failure to address the fundamental economic problems and to embark on a programme of economic restructuring can only aggravate the situation. The measures taken so far to address the already acute unemployment problem have largely focused on the supply side — pension rules have been relaxed and maternity leave has been increased from three months to one year — and thus can only have a limited effect. The unemployment problem has important political implications as those hardest hit are entrants to the labour market, that is, those who sparked off the revolution and who already are at odds with the regime.

There appears to be a political consensus in principle on the need to move towards a market economy, although the programme put forward by the National Salvation Front prior to the elections revealed a strong preference for a mixed economy with a continued strong state sector and a reluctance to embark on radical reforms (*Platforma*, 1990: 4–9). A task force set up within the Ministry of National Economic Affairs has elaborated a comprehensive plan for the transition to a market economy and for restructuring the economy. According to the chief co-ordinator of this task force, Dr Tudorel Postolache, the aim is to achieve the transition as rapidly as possible, while safeguarding the standard of living and social security. The tentative target is ostensibly to establish the rudiments of a market economy by 1992, while the modernisation of the economy is expected to take at least five to eight years (*Adevarul*, 16 May 1990).

However, the crackdown on the opposition in mid-June cast serious doubt on the ability of the regime to lead the country through the transition to a market economy. The regime appears to be the captive of — to the extent that it is not part of — surviving power structures from the previous regime, which are likely to do their utmost to maintain the old order. It has also made itself the captive of the miners and industrial workers, who would be the hardest hit by radical economic reforms and privatisation.

The continued presence of the old power structures, including the security apparatus, makes the immediate and mid-term future look bleak. Indeed, these may well prove to be the most ominous of the legacies left behind by Ceausescu. None the less, in the long run there is no workable alternative to a fundamental restructuring of the economy and a dismantling of the centrally planned economic system in favour of a market economy.

Notes

1. Average wheat yields for the years 1956–60 were 1,125 kg/ha, compared with 1,090 kg/ha in the Old Kingdom in 1891–5 and 1,180 kg/ha in Transylvania in 1896. The corresponding figures for maize were 1,390, 1,000 and 1,330 kg/ha, respectively (Ronnås, 1984: 118, 134).
2. According to official figures national income grew at an average annual rate of 9.5 per cent between 1966 and 1975 (*Anuarul Statistic*, 1976: 46).
3. A highly though inadvertently informative case study of this locational policy is found in Constantinescu and Stahl (1970). For an overall analysis at the macro level, see Ronnås (1984: 59–73, 214–26, 259–67); Ronnås (1988); and Turnock (1987).
4. The National Statistical Commission (NSC) in Romania is currently recalculating the main economic statistics for the 1980s. Meanwhile, I was cautioned by a senior official at NSC against using the published economic data for the years after 1980. The recalculations of official statistics for 1988 and 1989 reveal large discrepancies for all types of production-related data, while information on investments, employment and retail sales, as well as demographic data, appear to have been more reliable.
5. Shafir (1985: 119–26) aptly labels the reforms in Romania, notably the introduction of the 'New Economic and Financial Mechanism' in 1978, 'simulated change'. Broadly speaking, the reforms decentralised the accountability for decisions which continued to be made at the top. The sanctity of the plan precluded any form of real decentralisation. For a full discussion of the 1978 reform, see Smith (1981).
6. For instance in the midst of economic crisis in the 1980s the growth target for national income was set at 9.9–10.6 per cent per year for the 1986–90 period (Pissulla, 1989: 185). Five years later, at the 13th and last party congress in November 1989, the target growth rate for the national income for the 1991–5 period was set at 6–7 per cent per year (*Scînteia*, 21 November 1989).
7. For example, in 1989 the grain harvest was reported to be over 60 million tonnes (*Scînteia*, 21 November 1990); the actual harvest appears to have been a mere 16.7 million tonnes (*Buletin de informare*, 1990/3: 5). Ceausescu's speech at the 13th Party Congress provides a wealth of similar examples.
8. This information refers to 1985, the last year for which a breakdown of agricultural production by types of producers is available.
9. This can also be inferred from the statement that the average *total* income of collective farm workers was 1,920 lei in 1989.
10. In 1985 it was less than 55 per cent of the national average in 11 out of 41 counties (Florian, 1988: 51–63).
11. 'There were reports of food shortages throughout 1981, and by 1982 Romanians in Bucharest were complaining that food supplies were scarcer than they had been since World War II. Prices of available food seemed to have tripled in just over a year' (Fischer, 1989: 251). This is in line with observations made by myself.
12. For a detailed review of the policy of territorial self-sufficiency introduced in the early 1980s, see Moldovan and Moldovan (1986).

13. For a comprehensive collection of statements made by Ceausescu on this issue, see Ceausescu (1987). See also Ghermani (1984a, 1984b).
14. For details see Conferinta Nationala (1972: 476–98) and 'Legea 1974/58'. See also Gabanyi (1989), Ronnås (1989), and Sampson (1982).
15. This legislation included a ban on all forms of contraceptives and abortions and a virtual ban on divorces. As a consequence, the number of live births increased from 273,700 in 1966 to 527,800 in 1967 (Decretul 1966/770).
16. It is unlikely that the decline in the growth of wage employment was a direct effect of a slower growth in the demand for wage employment.
17. Because of the preliminary nature of the figures for 1989 and a temporary change in definition, the figure for 1989 refers to the stock in September that year, while all the previous figures are based on the annual average number on payrolls. Comparisons between 1988 and 1989 should therefore be made with caution.
18. The Directives for the 1986–90 five-year plan predicted that the national income would reach 1,200 billion lei by the year 1990 (Ceausescu, 1984: 26).
19. It fell for men from 67.42 years in 1976–8 (*Anuarul Statistic*, 1981: 90) to 66.30 years in 1989 (*Buletin de informare*, 1990/3: 8).
20. A survey of some 2,500 people in May showed that 29 per cent wanted an immediate shift to a market economy, 39 per cent favoured a more gradual shift while 14 per cent wanted 'to wait'. Only 4 per cent wanted to retain the present economic system. The rest were undecided (*Adevarul*, 20 May 1990).
21. In all fairness, it should be added that the above figures are averages over a somewhat improving trend.
22. By comparison retail sales in the socialist sector were 297.3 billion lei in 1989 (*Buletin de informare*, 1990/3: 1).

References

Anuarul Statistic al Republicii Socialiste România (Bucuresti: Directia Centrala de Statistica, various years).

Ceausescu, Nicolae. 1984. *Raport la cel de-al XIII-lea Congres al Partidul Comunist Român* (Bucharest: Editura Politica).

Ceausescu, Nicolae. 1987. *Directii de dezvoltare a agriculturii socialiste românesti. Conceptul si obiectivele noii revolutii agrare* (Din gîndirea economica a presedintelui României). (Bucharest: Editura Politica).

[*Buletin de informare*, 1990/3] *Buletin de informare publica al Comisiei Nationale pentru Statistica.*

[*Conferinta Nationala*, 1972] *Conferinta Nationala a Partidului Comunist Român, 19–21 iulie 1972* (Bucharest: Editura Politica).

Constantinescu, M. and Stahl, H.H., eds. 1970. *Procesul de urbanizare in României: Zona Slatina-Olt* (Bucharest: Editura Academiei RSR).

[Decretul 770/1966] 'Decretul 770/1966 al Consiliului de Stat privind reglementarea înteruperii cursului sarcinii', *Buletinul Oficial al RSR*, vol. 12:60 (1 October).

[Decretul 306/1981] 'Decretul 306/1981 al Consiliului de Stat privind masuri pentru prevenirea si ombatatrea unor fapte care afecteaza buna aprovizionare a populatiei', *Buletinul Oficial al RSR*, vol. 17:77 (9 October).

[Decretul 313/1981] 'Decretul 313/1981 al Consiliului de Stat privind unele masuri referitoare la întarirea autoconducerii si autoaprovizionarii teritoriale, precum si la asigurarea aprovizionarii în buna conditii a populatiei cu pîine, faina si malai', *Buletinul Oficial al RSR*, vol. 17 (17 October).

[Decretul 78/1986] 'Decretul 78/1986 al Consiliului de Stat privind elaborarea si executarea planurilor de cultura si de productie, precum si a planurilor de productie în zootehnie ale unitatilor agricole socialiste, gospodariilor membrilor cooperativelor agricole de productie si producatorilor particulari', *Buletinul Oficial al RSR*, vol. 22 (11 March).

[Decretul-Lege 54/1990] 'Decretul Lege 54/1990 privind organizarea si desfasurarea unor activitati economice pe baza liberei initiative', *Monitorul Oficial al României*, vol. 2:33–4 (8 March).

Fischer, Mary Ellen. 1989. *Nicolae Ceausescu: A study in political leadership* (Boulder: Lynne Rienner).

Florian, A. 1988. 'Dimensiuni ale dezvoltarii socio-economice a ruralului si modul de locuire', *Viitorul Social*, 1, pp. 51–63.

Gabanyi, Anneli Ute. 1989. 'Ceausescus "Systematisierung". Territorialplanung in Rumänien', *Südosteuropa*, Jg. 38:5, pp. 235–57.

Ghermani, Dionisie. 1984a. 'Rumäniens angeschlagene Agrarwirtschaft (I)', *Südosteuropa*, Jg. 33:3/4, pp. 203–11.

Ghermani, Dionisie. 1984b. 'Rumäniens angeschlagene Agrarwirtschaft (II)', *Südosteuropa*, Jg. 33:5, pp. 261–70.

Jackson, Marvin. 1990. 'Rehabilitation of the Romanian economy', *PlanEcon Report*, vol. 6:5 (31 January).

[Legea 58/1974] 'Legea 58/1974 privind sistematizarea teritoriuliu si localitatilor urbane si rurale', *Buletinul Oficial al RSR*, vol. 10:135 (1 November).

[Legea 1/1986] 'Legea 1/1986 privind retribuirea în acord global si în acord direct a personalului muncitor', *Buletinul Oficial al RSR*, vol. 22:21 (10 April).

Moldovan, Toader and Moldovan, Liviu. 1986. *Conceptia Partidului Comunist Român, a tovarasului Nicolae Ceausescu cu privire la autoconducerea în profil teritorial* (Bucharest: Editura Politica).

Pissula, Petra, 'Rumänien 1988/89. Wirtschaftspolitischen unbeirrt in wachsende Isolation', in Klaus Bolz, ed., *Die wirtschaftliche Entwicklung in den sozialistischen Ländern Osteuropas zur Jahreswende 1988/89* (Hamburg: Verlag Weltarchiv), pp. 163–95.

[*Platforma*, 1990], *Platforma program* (Bucharest: Frontul Salvarii Nationale).

[*Programul-Directiva*, 1979] *Programul-Directiva de cercetare si dezvoltare în domeniul energiei pe perioada 1981–1990 si orientarile principale pîna în anul 2000* (Bucharest: Editura Politica).

[*Programul unic de crestere, 1984*] *'Programul unic de crestere a productiei agricole în gospodariile personale ale cooperativelor agricole de productie si în gospodariilor producatorilor particulari', Buletinul Oficial al RSR*, vol. 20:3 (19 January).

[*Recensamîntul*, 1977] *Recensamîntul populatiei si locuintelor din 5 ianuarie 1977*, vol. 2: *Structura socio-economica* (Bucharest: Directia Centrala de Statistica).

Ronnås, Per. 1984. *Urbanization in Romania: A geography of social and economic change since independence* (Stockholm: EFI).

Ronnås, Per. 1987. 'Agrarian change and economic development in rural Romania: a case study of the Oas region', *Geografiska Annaler*, vol. 69B:1, pp. 41–53.

Ronnås, Per. 1988. 'Städtewachstum und Raumentwicklung in Rumänien', *Osteuropa*, Jg. 38:11, pp. 1008–21.

Ronnås, Per. 1989. 'Turning the Romanian peasant into a new socialist man: an assessment of rural development policy in Romania', *Soviet Studies*, vol. 41:4, pp. 543–59.

Sampson, Steven. 1982. *The Planners and the Peasants: An anthropological study of urban development in Romania*, (Monographs in East–West Studies, 4. Esbjerg: Sydjysk Universitetsforlag).

Shafir, Michael. 1985. *Romania: Politics, economics and society* (London: Frances Pinter).

Smith, Alan H. 1981. 'The Romanian industrial enterprise', in I. Jeffries, ed., *The Industrial Enterprise in Eastern Europe* (Preager: Eastbourne), pp. 63–83.

Turnock, David. 1987. 'Romania', in Andrew H. Dawson, ed., *Planning in Eastern Europe* (London: Croom Helm), pp. 229–73.

5 The future of a failure: the Romanian economy

Alin Teodorescu

Introduction

For many people in the West, Romania remains a mysterious drama. The longest Stalinist dictatorship in Europe (apart from Albania) came to an end in December 1989 in a way that produced an international sensation. After Ceausescu's flight on 22 December 1989, Romania's borders opened and Europe began to witness the deep poverty and isolation in which this country had lived. As always after the fall of a dictatorship, what is striking about what is now coming to light in Romania is the enormous scale of the political and economic madness.

The Romanian economy has three characteristic features that distinguish it from the other countries of Eastern Europe: (1) it is a hypercentralised, socialist economy; (2) it had no external debt when Ceausescu fell; (3) it has the lowest material standard of living (with the exception of Albania).

These characteristic features facilitate, and at the same time impede, the process of transition to a market economy. On the one hand, the absence of external debt and the existence of unsatisfied demand for a number of important consumer goods should facilitate a 'take-off' in production. On the other hand, the socialist administrative and managerial structure renders economic reform more difficult.

The truth is that until now, no one has witnessed a socialist European economy moving rapidly, efficiently, and directly towards a market economy. The Yugoslav experience has gone on for thirty years, the Hungarian for twenty years, the Polish for ten years, and the Soviet for five years. Nowhere have results met expectations. The process of transition to a market economy has proved to be slow, violent, and with more negative effects than expected.

Things do not appear any better in the field of economic theory. The 'opening' of the socialist economies can be seen to be following one of two types of patterns. The first is the slow transition pattern, using experiments in small areas of the economy, with advances and retreats, depending on how the society reacts. Within the framework of this pattern, besides the negative effects of the transition itself, negative effects on economic trends appear, because an economy under transformation is more vulnerable than one of any kind which is stable and self-reproducing. The second pattern — frequently called 'shock therapy' — has often been theorised, but it has never been firmly implemented in any of the East European countries, with the partial exception of Poland.

A history of economic thought in Eastern Europe after World War II has yet to be written, but such a history might show that there may be no direct relation between the duration of the transition and economic theory. Polish and Yugoslav economists are best known from their works about the transition of a socialist economy to market economy. However, it is the East German economy that seems to hold the record, with its rapid steps towards a structure different from the socialist one. We should mention that one of the first decisions to this effect was to establish a direct relationship between the East and West German currencies.

Whichever view of things we might take, the complexity of the problems involved in transition has presented both Eastern and Western economists and analysts with a formidable challenge. The available data concerning the Romanian economy for example, are so few and so difficult to verify that no one, for the time being, can make a proper and thorough analysis. Moreover, the lack of good professional schooling makes economists, at least the Romanian ones, highly ineffective in the study of their own economy. In this regard Romania is in a difficult, but not unique situation. We can find similar problems in other East European countries.

Later in this chapter, I shall make an *ad hoc* analysis of the prospects of the Romanian economy, looking individually at the branch, national and international levels. I shall stress the specific character of the Romanian economy rather than its general characteristics. This is because when we study the transition from a socialist to a market economy, we must take into consideration the following:

- the socialist economies in Eastern Europe are very different from each other;
- existing transition theories attempt to explain the difficulties rather than suggest directly applicable solutions;
- East European economic processes are always intersected by specific political and ideological factors.

The cost of Ceausescu's external debt repayment policy

In April 1989 Romania could announce that it had completely repaid its external debt (which had amounted to almost US$10,000 million in 1981). It was a unique event in the recent history of the East European countries. The immediate procedure through which the payment was carried out was the achievement of surpluses on the balance of trade and balance of payments beginning in 1983 (4,000 million and 2,500 million, respectively in 1988). Starting in 1981, Ceausescu began continually increasing exports and decreasing imports in order to obtain surpluses that could be used to repay the external debt. The official figures seem to indicate that between 1981 and 1989 Romania paid US$10,000 million on its loans, plus US$6,000 million in interest, that is, US$16,000 million over eight years, an average of about $2,000 million each year.

This surplus seems quite small when abstracted from the Romanian economy.

However, it cannot be considered an indicator of the economic performance of Romania, because it was achieved under artificial circumstances. Ceausescu's policy of paying the external debt quickly, and at any cost gave rise to several unfavourable consequences:

1. The policy led to a sudden and general lowering of the standard of living in Romania. The country reached levels that were almost inconceivably low for Europe in the 1980s.
2. Compared with the situation in other countries, it increased the value of Romania's debts since Romania's debts were never cancelled or reduced. Many countries with external debts have been able to obtain massive reductions in their external debts. Romania consistently paid 100 per cent, since it was well known that Romanian policy was to pay off its debts.
3. The policy served to divide the Romanian economy into three separate and poorly interconnected sectors. These three sectors were:

   (i) branches and enterprises that imported, processed, and re-exported raw materials. The profit they obtained was not used to benefit modernisation. Instead it went directly to external debt payment;
   (ii) branches and enterprises that used, processed, and exported domestic raw materials. The profit here was also used to pay the external debt;
   (iii) enterprises that used domestic raw materials and produced for the home market.

Dividing up the economy this way gives us a better understanding of the mechanism that enabled Romania to pay off its debt so rapidly, and of why a holistic approach to the transition in Romania is not possible at present. Each element of this economy is so strangely structured and difficult to classify that it must be examined individually.

One fact worth considering is that once the repayment of the external debt was achieved, a decapitalisation of the country and a clear capital loss took place. This is due to the fact that the profit obtained from exports was not reinvested in technical modernisation, but was instead applied exclusively towards cancelling the external debt. This is why in Romania today one finds great production capacity, mostly underemployed, equipped with the heavily polluting technology of the 1960s, lacking in spare parts, and consuming great quantities of electricity and manpower.

The re-exportation sector (i) prevails in the oil, steel and chemical branches, and partly in the food industry. Between 1980 and 1989 great amounts of crude oil, iron ore, coke and electric power were imported and different sorts of oil products, steel goods, machinery and tools were produced, generally of low quality. For example, as indicated in Table 5.1, crude oil was imported from the Arab countries and the USSR, processed, and then re-exported (usually to the United States and the European Community). Romania became an oil-refining country with a processing capacity of about 32 million tons per year. In the meantime, internal crude oil production diminished, while domestic consumption decreased drastically. Consequently, the living standards of the population brutally deteriorated, hundreds of enterprises that produced mainly for the domestic market had serious difficulties in obtaining inputs, and agriculture suffered deeply due to the lack of fuel for irrigation, agricultural work and transport.

Table 5.1 Imports, domestic production, and exports of crude oil (in thousands of tons)

	1975	1980	1985	1989
1. Imports	5,085	15,961	14,626	21,809
2. Domestic production	14,590	11,511	10,718	9,173
3. Exports	6,176	8,754	9,691	13,030
Exports as percentage of 1+2	31.4	31.9	38.2	42.1
Sum 1+2	19,675	27,472	25,374	30,982

Sources: Anuarul Statistic (1986), pp. 104–5, 296–7 and 301; *Buletin de informare* (1990: 3), pp. 2 and 7.

The same phenomenon was registered in many other industrial branches. A steadily increasing percentage of domestic production was destined for export, while the respective branches did not benefit from the profit thus obtained. On the other hand, investments were carried out only in those branches where production was largely exported (railway carriages, trucks, ball-bearings, fertilisers, detergents, and so on; see Table 5.2).

Table 5.2 Production and exports of selected industrial goods production

	1975	1980	1985	1989
Production				
Railway coaches	14,334	12,287	12,178	11,213
Motorcars	55,511	79,321	114,353	122,800
Ball-bearings (thousand units)	70,577	101,927	115,631	n/a
Exports				
Railway coaches	9,126	6,582	10,732	n/a
Motorcars	17,526	14,705	71,177	79,172
Ball-bearings (thousand units)	21,755	50,817	59,506	79,348

Sources: Anuarul Statistic (1986), pp. 104–12, 295–302; *Buletin de infomare* (1990: 3), pp. 2 and 7.

A similar phenomenon took place in light industry, where cotton and leather were imported, and later, cotton fabric, leather footwear, and other products almost completely absent from the Romanian domestic market, were exported (Table 5.3).

Essentially, for three major industrial branches (metallurgy, chemistry and oil) huge amounts of raw materials were imported, processed at a low quality level, and products were then sold wherever they could be sold, without any estimate being

Table 5.3 Leather imports and footwear exports

	1975	1980	1985	1989
Raw leather imports (thousand tons)	36.7	42.6	29.8	43.1
Footwear production (thousand pairs)	86,888	113,401	117,152	111,400
Footwear export (thousand pairs)				
– leather	16,596	23,893	18,082	17,395
– other materials	n/a	6,765	11,000	n/a

Sources: Anuarul Statistic (1986), pp. 104–12, 295–302; *Buletin de informare* (1990: 3), pp. 2 and 7.

made of production costs. The important thing was to obtain any sum of foreign exchange, no matter how small, in order to pay the external debt. Many examples of this irrational policy could be given. Many of the most flagrant cases of decapitalisation are not yet known because of the complicated chains of transactions that were generated by this aberrant economic policy.

Turning now to sectors based on the exportation of products made from domestic raw materials, an analysis should be made, first of all, of the furniture and wood industry, the glass industry, part of the food industry, and textiles (Table 5.4). Unfortunately we do not have annual data at our disposal, but we can estimate that about 40–70 per cent of the production of these industries was exported, generally at very low prices. Therefore, furniture production increased in 1989 by 17.6 per cent compared with 1980, while the domestic consumption of furniture by the population decreased by 18.6 per cent.

Table 5.4 Furniture and clothing production, 1980–9

	1980	1985	1989
Furniture production			
(million lei)	14,142	17,399	20,475
out of which			
– for domestic market	7,829	5,631	6,372
– per cent	55.4	32.4	31.1
Clothing production			
(billion lei)	31.4	47.0	47.2
– for domestic market	14.0	–	19.2
– per cent	44.6	–	40.7

Sources: Anuarul Statistic (1986), pp. 104–12, 295–302; *Buletin de informare* (1990: 3), pp. 2 and 7.

The consequences of this policy of obtaining convertible currency at any cost were very serious. Among the most important are the following:

1. it retarded the growth of and led to a general decline in industrial and agricultural production;
2. it caused industrial equipment to fall into disuse and wear out;
3. it led to the creation of huge industrial units that are major consumers of energy and manpower and which function poorly but manage to sell part of their production at dumping prices;
4. it kept the public infrastructure at an extremely low level.

How was it possible to carry out such a policy? One can discern three main factors which allowed this:

1. by maintaining a high rate of wage employment in the labour force, even if poorly paid, which removed the danger of the social disturbances that unemployment would have caused;
2. the general and drastic deterioration of the quality of life by means of a system of economic, political, ideological and police practices that 'homogenised' the population and isolated the *nomenklatura* and its associates from the broad masses. In this way the economic inequality was less obvious, since everybody had some 'small advantages' and some 'small disadvantages' in an ever increasingly precarious existence;
3. the almost complete isolation of the country, in every field (tourism, information, culture, science, sports, and so on).

It is clear that only one of these factors is purely economic — namely the maintenance of a high rate of wage employment. Indeed, one of the fundamental features of the socialist economy, especially in Romania, was the differentiation between those employed for wages and the non-wage labour (i.e. mainly farmers) in the workforce. Wage labour had the benefit of a certain 'package' of advantages consisting of a constant wage, regular working hours, an annual holiday, a pension, a series of rights such as the right to settle in large cities, to have a house, and an allowance for one's children. In the socialist countries, the wage system is not only an economic relation, but also a social one. The employee becomes dependent not only on the activity cycle of the enterprise, but also on the entire state and party hierarchy. He is subject to — and he submits to — several extra-economic regulations and restrictions which limit his choice of action, but which increase his chances of promotion and hence of raising his income.

Technological pluralism as a factor in maintaining high employment rates

Immediately the question arises: How have the socialist economies managed constantly to increase the number and proportion of employees in the labour force, thus increasing the population's dependency on the centralised system of monetary and material allocations.

This phenomenon cannot be explained solely by the volume of investment. Instead, the main element is the 'technological pluralism' that prevails in these economies — the fact that a newly-built enterprise does not eliminate other outmoded ones of the same kind. The best example of this in Romania is the introduction of computer technology in industry. Between 1975 and 1989, several hundred electronic computer centres were created in all the industrial branches and all the counties of the country. Over 40,000 people work in this field, and investments are estimated to be about several hundred million lei. However, all these additional employees did not replace any existing jobs nor did they do anything to lower production costs.

A similar example can be drawn from the printing industry, where the establishing of a new printing-house, having technology on the level of the 1960s, for example, did not lead to the elimination of the older printing-houses which still used technology from the 1930s or even 1890s (one such printing-house does exist in Bucharest). All printing-houses work with the same budgeted production costs, with the same wages, and the same sales prices, and therefore it is difficult to characterise them on the basis of economic performance.

Thus, technological pluralism expresses the existence of several generations of equipmenting having the same purpose within each industry. This practice is maintained in order to avoid eliminating jobs. Because of this, unemployment only appears when the rhythm of investment is slowed down.

In the case of Romania the slowing-down of the economic processes due to the reestrictions on imports did not lead to a high unemployment rate until 1987. This was due to a peculiar and very specific situation: namely, in 1966 abortion became illegal in Romania. Since abortion had been the only contraceptive method available, the number of babies born doubled in the course of one year alone (from 273,700 births in 1966 to 527,800 in 1967, and 526,100 in 1968). Early in 1987, this age cohort, double the size of the previous generation, entered the labour market. The economy's capacity to absorb labour had in the meanwhile diminished a good deal as a consequence of the policy of restricting the production of goods not bound for export. This is why unemployment showed up all of a sudden, estimated at 5 to 7 per cent of the labour force. The generation that was 20–22 years old in December 1989, which as a result of Ceausescu's own policies was double the usual size, was also the most active in the mass rebellions that took place on 16–17 December in the city of Timisoara, and 21–22 December in Bucharest, and which led to the removal of Ceausescu. Ceausescu's anti-abortion policy had clearly backfired on him.

Debt repayment and the deterioration of the standard of living

The second major sacrifice to the repayment of the external debt was the sudden and general deterioration of the quality of life, and especially of public consumption. In 1989 state retail sales to the population were considerably lower than levels in 1980: meat sales were only 49 per cent, fresh dairy products 39 per cent, powdered milk 69 per cent, cheeses 60 per cent, butter and sugar 82 per cent, rice 46 per cent, refrigerators 44 per cent, washing-machines 74 per cent, TV sets 64 per cent, automobiles 79 per cent, and bicycles 61 per cent. Meanwhile the quality of the products worsened immeasurably. Salami contained only 40 per cent meat, 'coffee' was a mixture of unknown compounds, the butter was blended with margarine, and so on. Official state prices rose continually at an estimated rate of 15 per cent annually between 1981 and 1985, and 9 per cent annually between 1986 and 1989. The black market became more and more extensive, although not in the field of alternative production. Since private enterprise was a state offence, this was not possible. Instead, the growth was due to distribution now taking place at prices three times those of goods with state-set prices.

It may be difficult for a person in the West to imagine how Romanians lived in the 1980s. Because of the lack of statistics about real prices and availability of goods, I shall provide some examples from my own personal experiences which will perhaps serve to shed light on this question (see Table 5.5). In the month of January 1985 — one of the hardest winters in the past thirty years — my wage equalled the average wage in Romania, or 2,920 lei per month. My wife earned 3,220 lei per month. From both wages, 3 per cent was drawn for pensions. Also from our wages we paid the following: 300 lei for the telephone, 400 lei for electricity, 500 lei in rent, 500 lei for heating, water and gas, 400 lei for transportation back and forth to our jobs, and 1,000 lei for real coffee that we were able to get hold of on the black market (in 1989 this would have cost 1,500 lei). We spent about 100 lei per day on food, where one kilo of meat cost about 100 lei, 1 kg of potatoes 10 lei, 1 kg of apples 15 lei, and oil and sugar were given on ration once a month — 1 kg sugar cost 13 lei, and 1 kg oil was 19 lei. Our family was entitled to 4 l of oil and 6 kg of sugar per month because we were four persons in total (I have two daughters).

Table 5.5 The Teodorescu family budget, January 1985

Rent & utilities	500 + 500
Telephone and electricity	300 + 400
Transportation	200 + 200
Coffee	1,000
Food	3,000
Total monthly living expenses	**6,100**
Pension tax	184
Other taxes	100
Total monthly expenses	**6,384**
Total monthly income	**6,140**
Balance	**– 244 lei**

This was in fact a good month. My unfavourable balance was only 244 lei, a small sum. However, we did not buy clothes, detergents, medicines and books, nor did we see the dentist or any other doctor (an appendectomy would have cost us 3,000 lei), nor did we visit the cinema or theatre.

This presentation of my family budget would be misleading for the outsider if I did not add the following comments. We received electricity for only 6–8 hours per day and the temperature in our flat remained at about 8 degrees Centigrade (we would sleep with our overcoats on). We had warm water for 2 hours per week, and food was extremely difficult and time-consuming to obtain (5 kg of potatoes required 4–5 hours of queueing, and one could only buy one item at a time).

One might ask, why did the Romanians not revolt during this terrible period? For those who lived in Romania, this is not difficult to understand, but it is difficult to explain. The deterioration of the quality of life occurred gradually. As the quality of life went down, the intensity of the economic processes also decreased. People worked less and less, and they spent more and more time obtaining food. Moreover, the ideological pressure increased, reaching a frenzy in 1989. All print media, television (broadcasting only 3 hours per day), radio, and books were focused on maintaining the artificial state of the generalised lie. The enemies were said to be everywhere: the Hungarians that had claimed Transylvania, the Russians claiming who knows what, the capitalists who wanted to exploit us, NATO that was out there putting weapons into position, AIDS that was brought by foreign students, and so on. Somebody was always guilty of something — the pensioners who were queueing all day to buy up all the food, the peasants who refused to respect the fixed prices set by the government, the gypsies who were involved in speculation, and the whole population which was at fault because it did not work enough. Society was atomised, segmented, and people were becoming increasingly self-centred. There was also another essential element: the forces of repression were continually growing and were active everywhere. Telephone calls were intercepted, people were subject to searches and investigations, people mysteriously disappeared, sometimes so-called 'car accidents' occurred, the mail did not come, or if it came, it had been read already by someone else.

People's feelings of isolation and abandonment grew. Many Romanians believed that as long as Ceausescu managed to repay the debt to the West, and to provide the USSR with food and light industry products, he would not be removed as the head of Romania. In addition, there was the feeling of collective misfortune, as in the face of a natural disaster, because everyone seemed to find himself in the same situation. Only as late as the spring of 1989 did the idea that something must be done arise in the public consciousness. People began to understand that they should get rid of the two main enemies that had been identified a long time ago — the Ceausescu family and the Securitate secret police. The first of these was done away with.

This digression does have a point. It shows us how such an experience was possible and what its economic effects were. In terms of production, the Romanian economy is at present divided into a dollar sector, a rouble sector, and a leu sector. The level of technology and the industrial infrastructure are below mediocre. Currency reserves are not sufficient for the modernisation of production or for the acceleration of the economy. It will not be easy for Romania to obtain credit from abroad under the present political situation. The huge unsatisfied demand now characterising the market will bring about a rise in black market prices. This will stimulate the supply, first of job opportunities, and later of goods. More and more people will be tempted to produce something. However, in order to produce, one must have raw materials, which are still centrally allocated. Since the personal profit is larger in private production, entrepreneurs will use all possible means (beyond the legal ones) to extract raw materials from the state distribution chain. This will lead to corruption, obvious social inequality, and violence. Just look at the way Soviet co-operatives have developed after being established five years ago. The problem is that the communist ideology still has an economic function in the countries of Eastern Europe. When the ideology disappears, the downward pressure on public consumption will go with it. Pent-up consumer demand will be released, but there are still no means of satisfying it.

Reform proposals for Romania

At the time of writing (June 1990), there are only two economic reform proposals under discussion which are relatively coherent. I shall describe and discuss these below.

The programme of the National Salvation Front (FSN)

The FSN is a rather strange political body formed around a restricted group of people who were purely and simply pushed towards the leadership of the country in December 1989. Under Ceausescu, there had not been any opposition group with a leader well-known to the population, and therefore Ceausescu's flight created a genuine political vacuum. Because of this, leadership of the country was assumed by a strange collection of party activists (Ion Iliescu, Silviu Brucan), former members of the secret police (Dumitru Mazilu), and persons with a dubious moral background (Dan Iosif, Cazimir Ionescu), which called itself the FSN Council (23 December 1989). Immediately following this, well-known dissidents (Andrei Plesu, Doina Cornea, Gabriel Andreescu, Radu Filipescu, Mircea Dinescu) and other lesser-known persons were co-opted. Little by little, the FSN proved to be a group of the former *nomenklatura*, supported by the reactivated secret police, and incapable of making a firm decision to disengage the economy from the socialist system. The FSN adopted a populist economic policy of increasing wages, reducing the working week to 40 hours (it had been 44 hours up until December 1989) and raising the pensions of the peasants, and the population's disposable income. It has been announced that the disposable income of the population increased by over 60,000 million lei in only four months from the December revolution. Added to the 277,000 million lei already in their possession, this represents a sum of great inflationary potential and almost equals the state retail trade for 1989 (297,000 million as compared to 277,000 million lei). The people's purchasing power is diminished by the scarcity of merchandise and the high prices on the black market.

The FSN economic programme stipulates that

> the fundamental aim of the FSN economic policy is to ensure the welfare of the entire people and the quality of life in all respects. The Front considers that this objective can be reached under the circumstances of the gradual transformation of the Romanian economy into a market economy. (*Platforma program*, 1990: 4).

Both this objetive (which is an unvarying repetition of the Stalinist theory on the socialist economy) and its implementation are subject to the overriding goal of maintaining the 'country's political and social stability' and keeping inflation and unemployment under control.

The main measures suggested in the FSN programme are the following (*Platforma program*, 1990: 4–9):

1. to bring about a gradual 'liberalisation' of prices;
2. to develop a private sector in the economy;
3. to retain state ownership in the 'key branches' of the economy;
4. to attract foreign investment;
5. to allow agricultural land to be distributed by ownership or on lease;
6. for the state to invest in agriculture, industry and services;
7. to prevent the accumulation of so-called 'excessive' fortunes through taxes and duties;
8. to eliminate the state monopoly on foreign trade;
9. as a consequence of all these measures, it is suggested that the 'recognition of the international convertibility of the leu' should be reached; and finally,
10. not to allow 'chronic deficits in the balance of trade and payments which could lead to an overwhelming external debt'.

As one can readily see, the economic programme of the FSN is not much different from the innumerable programmes drawn up over the past thirty years by the theorists of 'reformed socialism'. The general characteristic of these programmes is that the state is to give up certain types of monopolies (the monopoly on ownership of the means of production and the monopoly on setting prices, the monopoly of foreign trade), but does not give up the key elements of the socialist economy, namely, the centralised allocation of the means of production, the command over the distribution of raw materials, production targets and investment. As one can see, the FSN programme does not grant the smallest amount of autonomy to state enterprises. These still do not have the right to decide on such matters as production, the supply of inputs and the marketing of their own products. Somewhat more freedom is granted in agriculture; liberalisation always seems to be less risky here as long as industry and investments are still supervised by the state (as in China's experience between 1984 and 1988).

The FSN won the election held on 20 May 1990 with 66 per cent of the vote. Nevertheless, it is not likely that their programme will have better success than had similar programmes in the USSR in 1965 and 1987, China in 1984, and Hungary in 1968.

The programme of the National Liberal Party (PNL)

The programme of the PNL, the third political party in terms of votes in the election is even more vague than that of the FSN. Like the FSN programme, it is not based on a sound understanding of the economic realities of Romania or on an analysis of the international context. It stipulates a series of measures, among which the most important are the observance and guarantee of the freedom to engage in economic activities and establish enterprises, speeding up the process of making the leu convertible, land allotment for peasants, and the increase in private consumption. Stress is placed on individual freedoms, which are to increase as a result of removing the administrative and political structures of the communist system.

The two reform programmes of the PNL and the FSN do not appear to represent more than mere electoral propaganda. They confirm the idea, suggested by many outside observers as well, that economic analysis and studies are in an extremely difficult situation in Romania. This situation has been brought about by a nearly total lack of information about our own economy and the evolution of the international economy. A second cause was the extremely nationalistic ideological approach in education and in economic research.

Prospects for reform

As far as methods go, I am a supporter of 'shock therapy' for bringing about economic transition in Romania. I believe one should start by granting greater autonomy to state enterprises and liberalising private initiative. At present, there it one single law concerning private enterprise, and it is very restrictive and unsatisfactory (as is pointed out by Per Ronnås in Chapter 4 of this book). As a matter of fact, we must distinguish between the privatisation of state enterprises and the creation of new private enterprises. Privatisation can be achieved by several means:

1. by granting property or the use thereof to the employees of the enterprise (as in Yugoslav self-management), with or without paying a periodic share to the state;
2. by selling certain enterprises or parts of enterprises to persons, associations, or non-state organisations, either foreign or local;
3. by dissolving certain enterprises and selling, piece by piece, the available equipment by auction (since the real value cannot be estimated), or using some price conventions; or
4. by transforming state enterprises into joint-stock companies perhaps after foreign appraisal experts have made an estimate of their value.

Experience shows that the creation of private enterprises alone cannot meet domestic consumption requirements, which are very large in Romania's case, and are worsened by the fact that the population is in possession of considerable sums of money. However, privatisation would have two immediate economic effects, namely:

1. it would pass large amounts of money from private persons to the state (the equivalent value of the equipment, raw material inventories, buildings, and so on) that cannot be used either as reserves, or as investments in branches showing a deficit (transport, telecommunications, services, and so on);
2. it would allow the population to engage directly in production, rather than in merely buying and selling goods and services, as we have commonly seen take place when private companies are created in the other socialist countries.

However, privatisation raises a sensitive moral question, namely that in Romania, the accumulation of capital (financial) is generally unequally distributed. The *nomenklatura*, members of the secret police, and certain employees of the state trade system have been able to amass large sums of money. This money is partly invested in goods that are scarce on the Romanian market: VCRs, colour television sets, radio cassette recorders, crystal, gold, silver, jewels and furs). It would seem advantageous to all to allow these people to buy the equipment of enterprises that work at a 'planned' loss every year and therefore allow them to put their capital to work in production. This seems in any case much more acceptable than allowing them to accumulate money because of their position in a counterproductive administrative system.

The process of making the state enterprises independent from the central and local planning authorities, as well as privatisation and the creation of new private enterprises must nevertheless be preceded by a radical devaluation of the national currency. The leu was devalued in February 1990 to a level of 21 lei to the dollar. On the black market in Romania, US$1 buys 100–120 lei. If the state decides to devalue the leu, fixing it at around the level of 100 lei to the dollar, then the black market would be effectively dissolved. And yet, the danger of hyperinflation would not be removed. It is necessary for the leu to be convertible at home too, not only abroad, and that the goods demanded on the domestic market can be found. For this, foreign trade must be liberalised in such a way that both the state and individuals should be able to gain from the import and export of goods and services.

A devaluation of the leu might have different effects in each of the three main economic sectors (the dollar, or re-export sector, the rouble sector and the leu sector). The huge metallurgical, chemical and oil works that are dependent on raw materials imports and state subsidies would surely be put in a very difficult situation. If US$1 were to cost 20 lei, then importing raw materials for US$100 would cost 2,000 lei. The production obtained with US$100 worth of raw materials must be sold for more than US$100 — something which rarely has been the case in the Romanian re-exportation sector, because raw material imports were often paid for in either food, textiles, furniture, arms or roubles. Whereas (after a devaluation), if one dollar were to cost 100 lei, then the price of importing raw materials would be five times greater, without any change in the quality, and the goods produced must be sold (in lei) at a five-times higher price. Since the domestic market cannot accept such a price, the state must subsidise this production. If the state does not subsidise it, then the enterprise will go bankrupt. Thus a devaluation would help to rid the economy of loss-making enterprises.

Moreover, a devaluation would make Romanian exports cheaper for foreign buyers and would stimulate the domestic production of goods and services based on domestic raw materials (agriculture, light industry, technical know-how). The enterprises that would benefit are therefore those making use of domestic raw materials whose prices might rapidly grow if production does not grow. I should therefore suggest the following package of measures:

1. liberalisation of foreign trade;
2. devaluation of the leu;
3. cancelling of subsidies that currently go to state enterprises;

4. privatisation of state enterprises, including land; and
5. reductions in the general expenditures of the state and state administration. This final item is in my view the key to the approach that will be very costly to avoid — a shock therapy.

We should not forget how the establishment of Stalinist regimes in Eastern Europe began with the arrival of Soviet tanks, and continued with the take-over of political power, nationalisation of enterprises, banks and trade, the revaluation of the national currency (1948 and 1952 in Romania), the closing of the borders, and the collectivisation of the agricultural land. This process must now be reversed. Political power has been lost by the communists, but the economic power remains in their hands. For the countries of Eastern Europe, World War II is finally over.

References

Anuarul Statistic al Republicii Socialiste România 1986 (Bucharest: Directia Centrala de Statistica).
Buletin de informare publica al Comitiei Nationala Pentru Statistica, 1990:3.
Lhomel, Edith. 1989. 'L'Économie roumaine en 1988: toujours à contre-courant', *Le Courrier des Pays de l'Est*, no. 341, pp. 64–72.
Platforma program, [Bucharest:] Frontul Salvarii Nationale, [March 1990].

6 The Bulgarian economy in the immediate post-Zhivkov era

Michael L. Wyzan

Introduction

On 10 November 1989 Todor Zhivkov, who had run the Bulgarian Communist party since 1954, and had been the unchallenged leader of the country since 1962, was forced from power in a 'palace coup'. He was replaced as both president and party leader by Petur Mladenov, who had served as foreign minister since 1971. Mladenov immediately set about making changes in the political system and undoing the five-year-old campaign to assimilate the country's large ethnic Turkish minority.

In early 1990, political events, including round-table talks between the communists and the opposition, the removal of the leading role of the party from the constitution, the establishment of opposition newspapers, and the disbanding of party cells in workplaces followed each other in rapid succession. At an extraordinary party congress that began on 30 January, Aleksandur Lilov, who had been purged from the Politburo in 1983, replaced Mladenov as party leader. On 1 February the ineffective Prime Minister, Georgi Atanasov, who had served since March 1986, was succeeded by Andrei Lukanov, an English-speaking party member who had been Minister for Foreign Economic Relations since Augsut 1987; a new government was appointed on 8 February.

Round-table talks began on 22 January between the communists, the multi-party opposition coalition known as the Union of Democratic Forces (UDF), and the Bulgarian Agrarian Party (BAP).[1] On 12 March the round table signed three agreements, on the role and status of the round table itself; on the peaceful transitioin to a democratic system; and on the nature of the future political system (see Gavrilov, 1990). Mladenov remained president — a post to which he was formally appointed by the National Assembly on 3 April — until 6 July, when he resigned after the appearance of a videotape in which he was heard advocating the use of tanks against demonstrators on 14 December 1989.

The spring of 1990 was marked by a rancorous political campaign between the erstwhile communists — since early April calling themselves the Bulgarian Socialist Party (BSP) — and a large number of opposition parties, the most important of which are grouped under the umbrella of the UDF. Simultaneously, *Rabotnichesko delo*, once the dour newspaper of a totalitarian communist party, became *Duma*, the livelier but generally less substantial paper of a ruling government struggling to retain power in a competitive election.

As a result of elections — the first openly contested ones since October 1946 — that took place on 10 and 17 June, the BSP holds the majority of the seats in the National Assembly (211 out of 400), while the UDF holds 144, the MRF 23, the BAP 16, and others 6 (V. Popov, 1990). The former communists did particularly well in small towns and rural areas, while the UDF triumphed in such larger cities as Sofia, Plovdiv, and Varna. Immediately after the elections, it appeared that the former communists would remain stronger than their counterparts in East Central Europe, a factor that may well have impinged on the country's ability to obtain assistance and co-operation from the West. Moreover, the turmoil in the country after the elections may have had a similarly negative effect on the confidence of foreign leaders and investors. However, on 1 August the National Assembly surprisingly elected UDF leader Zheliu Zhelev to replace Mladenov as president, after five unsuccessful rounds of voting among candidates nominated by the BSP, UDF and BAP. Some interpreted this event as a sign that the UDF would abandon its intention not to participate in a coalition government with the BSP. This turned out not to be the case, however, and Lukanov was forced to resign on 29 November, in the face of a general strike by Podkrepa and demands by the UDF for the key positions in any cabinet in which it would participate. Dimitur Popov, an independent judge, took over as a caretaker Prime Minister on 7 December; general elections are scheduled for late spring 1991.

In the first two months after Zhivkov's fall, little attention was devoted to economic matters. However, December 1989 saw a high degree of strike activity, which on the heels of the emigration of almost 400,000 ethnic Turks in the second half of the year wreaked havoc with economic performance in the final quarter. Indeed, the 1989 plan fulfilment report, published on 30 January, portrayed an economy in very bad shape at the end of the year. Moreover, the country has been afflicted by the worst foreign debt crisis in its history, forcing the Foreign Trade Bank to suspend unilaterally all principal payments on foreign loans on 29 March, and to do the same regarding interest payments on 26 June (Fidler, 1990).

The critical state of the economy stimulated in decisionmakers the necessity of putting economic reform at the top of the agenda. Accordingly, on 15 March the round table turned its attention to economic matters. The presentation of alternative economic proposals was an important component of the pre-election struggle. On 28 April, almost exactly one month after the government's presentation of its economic programme, the UDF began publication of its own economic programme in its newspaper, *Demokratsiia*. After their victory in the June elections, the Socialists did not put forward a budget and economic and stabilisation programme until October, by which time it was too late to save the Lukanov government and that programme was never implemented. Meanwhile, the economy has continued to deteriorate, although there has been some success in reducing the trade deficit with hard currency countries, largely by virtue of a major decline in imports.

In this chapter, and the companion chapter by Ognian Pishev, an attempt is made to come to grips with the current situation and future prospects of the Bulgarian economy during this pivotal and uncertain period in its history. My first task is to describe briefly the basic institutions and operating procedures of that economy in the late 1980s, in order to understand Todor Zhivkov's legacy to today's economic reformers. Second, I examine the reform programme of the Lukanov government. Third, I address the question of whether it could have represented the first steps in a successful transition to a market economy.

Bulgarian economic institutions in the late 1980s: Zhivkov's legacy

One cannot examine the economic policies of the Lukanov government, nor those proposed by the opposition, without a review of the legislation of the late Zhivkov era. Bulgaria had always had a fairly traditional centrally planned economy — despite a flirtation with Liberman-style economic reform from 1965 to 1968 (see, e.g. Lampe, 1986: 200–6) — when its leadership began to promulgate reform decrees in 1979. The so-called New Economic Mechanism was introduced in the agricultural sector in 1979 and in the rest of the economy in 1982.[2] As pointed out by Jackson (1986: 47), these reforms aimed at improving the functioning of central planning rather than replacing it with a market-oriented economy.

A period of major institutional upheaval began in 1986, when March saw the shutting down of most industrial branch ministries, after the creation of three 'councils', including one on the economy, in January. The publication in March of a new labour code and in January 1987 of *Pravilnik* (1987) ushered in a period of experimentation with the concept of 'self-management', which refers, as in Yugoslav practice, to workers having the right to elect management, as well as the obligation of enterprises to be self-financing. August 1987 saw a partial return to a ministerial system, with the creation of the Ministry of Economics and Planning to replace the Economic Council, the State Planning Commission, the Ministry of Finance, the Committee on Prices, and the Committee for Labour and Social Affairs (see Jackson, 1989b: 153–8; and Angelov, 1989, for descriptions of the reforms of 1987 and 1988). A decree in June 1987 allowed private and co-operative activity in the sphere of spare-time contract work at state industrial enterprises, as well as in retailing, construction, public catering and taxi services.[3]

The last important economic legislation of the Zhivkov era was Decree no. 56 of January 1989, along with its enabling legislation, which was passed a month later.[4] As it has turned out, the implementation of Decree no. 56 has been unusually confused, even by Zhivkovian standards. The decree called for the transformation of enterprises — formerly known as self-managing economic organisations — into new entities known as 'firms'. Many enterprises were required to make the formal, legal transition to this new status well before rules for doing so were promulgated (in May). None the less, the post-Zhivkov leadership has seen fit to amend the decree, rather than overturn it, and it is thus worthwhile to discuss this legislation in some detail before proceeding.

As noted by Grosser (1989: n.p.), Decree no. 56 made

relatively few changes within the system of economic instruments, the core of the new round of reform [being] a change in enterprise organization — the [establishment] of various forms of more independent enterprises goes hand in hand with relaxations for private enterprise and foreign investment.

The legislation may be seen as an attempt to create a modern business code to be applied to an economy consisting of firms of various types — their *ownership*: state-owned, municipal, co-operative, public (i.e. created by a public organisation) or individual (i.e. owned by individual citizens); and their *form*: joint-stock, unlimited liability, limited liability or sole proprietorship.

Firms are established, reorganised, and dissolved by the local district courts. They determine for themselves their internal organisational structure, the rights and obligations of their subdivisions, and the composition of their management. Provisions are established for the issue of inheritable staff shares — which can be kept upon retirement — to employees who have been with the firm for more than a year, and to members of the management board.

The internal structure of a firm is as follows. At the base of the pyramid is the general convention of workers. A management board is created, half of whose composition is determined by those providing the capital for the firm, and the other half by the general convention. In a decisive move away from the emphasis on worker self-management of the 1987 *Pravilnik*, the managing director, elected by the management board, is empowered to 'organise, direct and supervise the company's activities on the principle of one-man management and see to the proper use and upkeep of its property' (*Decree 56*, 1989:9). There is also a board of controllers, which is formed virtually identically to the management board, and which is charged with supervising the decisionmaking of the general convention and the management board, and with the upkeep of the firm's property.

In a joint-stock company, the stockholders' meeting is empowered to change the firm's constitution; set guidelines for a firm's activities; reorganise or terminate the firm; determine the numbers of members of the board of management and the board of controllers (as well as electing and dismissing them and setting their pay); approve the balance sheet, the distribution of income, and the board of management's annual report; decide on the issue of bonds and staff shares; decide on reducing or increasing the statutory capital; and appoint liquidators, should such a move prove necessary.

The board of management of a joint-stock company adopts the annual report and balance sheet; approves plans and programmes; proposes to the general meeting changes in the statutory capital; elects and dismisses the managing director (and sets his or her salary); elects a chairperson from among its ranks; approves the rules covering such matters as internal bookkeeping and wage-setting; decides on the creation and dissolution of subsidiaries, divisions, and representative offices, and on the firm's participation in joint ventures both within the country and overseas; determines the formation of the various enterprise funds and the procedures for dispersing them; and decides on the acquisition and transfer of immovable property, the use of investment credits, the granting of guarantees and warranties, the acquisition and transfer of licenses, and the participation in auctions and tenders.

A limited liability company is set up similarly to a joint-stock company, except that it is owned by partners who enjoy limited liability in the standard sense of

Western business law. A partners' general meeting replaces the stockholders' meeting of the joint-stock company. As in the latter, the limited liability company also has a managing director and a board of controllers. According to Grosser (1989: n.p.), this form is viewed as appropriate for foreign trade, construction, and transport activities. Unlimited liability companies are virtually identical to those of the limited liability type, with the major difference being that implied by their name.

More interesting, perhaps, is the enhanced encouragement of small firms owned by individuals. Such firms, for the first time, are allowed to hire labour — up to ten persons on a permanent basis plus an unlimited number of seasonal employees. Such 'individual' firms may be one-person operations, partnerships, or joint companies. The last of these types (only) is considered a legal person, with special rights and obligations. Such 'joint individual' companies are enjoined — as are presumably the other two types of individual firms — from exporting items produced by other firms; from importing items not directly related to their specific economic activity; from acting as representatives, brokers, or agents for foreign entities; and from making investments abroad or making partnerships with foreign bodies.

Decree no. 56 and its enabling legislation outline the first moves toward the creation of capital markets. Firms may float bond issues for specific investment purposes, with a maximum maturity of ten years, and a maximum interest rate of 5 points over that on private deposits. Such bonds may be purchased only by Bulgarian physical and legal persons. Staff shares may be issued up to a total value of 10,000 leva to a single person. The total value of bonds and staff shares must not exceed 50 per cent of the statutory capital of the firm. A telling peculiarity of these arrangements is the absence of a stock market: staff shares can be transferred only to other members of the firm's personnel. The new legislation also contains provisions for the bankruptcy and liquidation of firms.

State regulation of firms' activities is to include the use of 'taxes, duties and subsidies, currency rates, interest rates, rules of labour remuneration, depreciation rates, price-formation rules and government contracts' (*Decree 56*, 1989: 24). The state plan is supposed to contain only the main national goals; the overall material, financial, and currency balances; the main objectives of social development; macro-structural changes; the development of subnational territorial entities; trends in the nation's international economic activity; and a variety of normatives and regulators. The continuing use of state orders is provided for, but supposedly only in the context of the 'fulfilment of international obligations, for implementing the tasks of social policy, for achieving strategic, technological and market objectives, as well as for guaranteeing national security and major national balances' (*Decree 56*, 1989: 24).

State subsidisation of individual firms is provided for, although not for 'obsolete and unsaleable output [or] in cases when losses and low profits are due to subjective reasons' (*Regulations for the Application*, 1989: 26); individual exemption from taxation is also possible. The Council of Ministers and the trade union council are to formulate general rules for wage determination and starting salaries for personnel according to their skill qualifications. All pay is to be tied to the final productive results of the firm's activity. Subject to such qualifications, however, the firm sets its own wage bill. The firm is allowed to be serviced by and borrow from banks of its own choosing, with interest rates negotiated between the partners. The state is charged with maintaining competition between firms and preventing anti-competitive practices.

The firm draws up its own plan in a manner similar to the counterplanning that has been practised in Bulgaria for many years, taking into account state orders and other contracts and state-set normatives. The material on price setting in both the decree and the enabling legislation is vague, merely listing the factors that should be taken into account which include prices prevailing on international markets and domestic supply and demand. The prices of 'goods and services vital to the population's living standards, as well as the prices of certain prime and raw materials and transport services (*Regulations for the Application*, 1989: 22) are to be set or registered by the state; state organs will exercise 'methodological guidance and control and control over the correct formation and application' of other prices (*Regulations for the Application*, 1989: 23).

Firms must make payments to the state budget in the form of a value-added tax, a profit tax (generally 50 per cent), and a progressive tax on increases in the wage fund; they also must pay 10 per cent of balance sheet profit to the municipal council. Relatively greater freedom is allowed to firms in the distribution of their funds. Minima, which vary by sector, are established for the shares of profit that must be made into the 'development and technological renewal' fund (DTRF).[5] The firm's first priorities in the distribution of its profits are the repayment of credit, the profit tax and insurance. After meeting these obligations, it then pays into its investment fund, and pays the wage increase tax, the salaries of the managing director and the board of management, bonuses to personnel, profit shares to creative teams involved in certain research projects, and dividends. An interesting feature is that if profit is insufficient to cover the minimum deductions into the investment fund and to pay the wage increase tax, the difference must be taken from the wage fund.

The decree allows the expanded use of leasing arrangements — already encouraged since the June 1987 decree on the private sector — so that facilities can now be leased on a full-time private basis. The objects of the lease can be agricultural land, perennial crops, other rural property (e.g. dairies), hotels, retail establishments, restaurants, building equipment, transport vehicles and manufacturing plants. The lessors can be the state and municipal governents, social organisations or firms, but cannot be private operators. The period of the lease may be between three and fifty years. Lessees operate in a regulatory environment similar to that faced by other types of enterprises, first making a variety of payments, such as rent, credit instalments and insurance, among others, and then freely determining the use of their remaining funds.

Finally, the decree makes a number of changes in the sphere of foreign economic relations. Foreign persons are allowed to engage in economic activities on Bulgarian soil, both within joint ventures and through such enterprises as affiliated branches, trade representations, and wholly-owned subsidiaries. With the permission of the authorities, foreign ownership in a joint venture may now exceed 49 per cent in a limited liability company. A differentiated profit-tax regime is established for foreign persons operating in Bulgaria, with foreign branches and foreign participants in certain joint ventures (those in which such participants own more than 49 per cent of the capital) paying a 30 per cent tax, and independent foreign participants in the economy a 40 per cent rate (Grosser, 1989: n.p.). There is a total exemption from profit tax for the first five years for a foreign enterprise operating in a free-trade zone.

Bulgaria ended the Zhivkov era with a complex multiple exchange rate system, which the new regime has seen fit to complicate further in its attempts to move toward a market economy (see below). For example, as reported by Jackson (1989a: 34), on 1 August 1989, the *official* rate for commercial purposes was US$1 = 0.8415 leva, the *premium* rate for foreign transactions and non-trade payments with juridical persons was US$1 = 1.683 leva, and rate for purchases of dollars from foreigners and local *physical persons* was US$1 = 2.5245 leva.

The economic programme of the first post-Zhivkov government

As mentioned in the introduction, economic matters were generally not the most prominent in the debates between the government and its opponents in the run-up to the elections of 10 and 17 June 1990. Moreover, critics have charged, quite justifiably, that Lukanov failed to break sufficiently with the economic policies of the Zhivkov era; indeed, as mentioned above, Decree no. 56 remained in force and was subject to relatively minor amendment.

None the less, the Lukanov government promulgated a programme for crisis management and economic reform at the end of March and submitted a number of other pieces of economic legislation. This section will describe the main features of that government's economic policies.

On 15 March the round-table discussions between the communists and the opposition, which had continued intermittently since 22 January, turned to economic matters. A discussion paper, 'Osnovni printsipi' (1990), the result of the deliberations of a Working Group of Economic Experts from both the communists and the opposition, was brought out in preliminary form on 23 March. This report blames the economic crisis of the system on the 'command-administrative system of management of the economy, created under conditions of totalitarianism' ('Osnovni printsipi', 1989: 1–2). Proclaiming a market economy to be the goal of the reform, the report briefly describes the basic principles of reform in a number of areas: ownership, agrarian questions, the money credit system, the budget system, price-setting, the labour market, foreign economic relations and the valuta regime, the legal system and the social sphere. Even though the report was never actually discussed at the round table, many of its recommendations found their way into the Lukanov government's economic programme (*Programa za izlizane*, 1990)[6] that appeared about a week later.

This programme listed the following goals:

- active inclusion of all forms of property on the basis of their equal standing (*ravnopostavenost*) and legal defence;
- immediate change in economic conditions and regulators with a view to the encouragement of economic activity to increase the production of those goods and services that satisfy the requirements of the market;

- stabilisation of the internal market through better balancing of money incomes and goods supplies as price-setting is gradually liberalised; and
- measures to ensure the minimal standard of living of certain categories of the population. (*Programa za izlizane*, 1990: 2).

After presenting a number of measures of a crisis management nature, the government programme asserted that the

economic reform is based on the idea that for the development of a contemporary society there is no alternative to a market economy. The basic content of the reform is the realisation of a transition from a centrally-planned to a market economy, functioning analagously to the economies of those highly developed countries that carry out active social policy. (*Programe za izlizane*, 1990: 13).

Such an economy was said to be characterised by the equal legal position and encouragement of all forms of property — state, municipal, private, co-operative, joint-stock, that of social organisations, that of foreign subjects, and mixed forms. There should be interrelated markets for goods, capital and labour. The market was to be the basic regulator of production, exchange and consumption, and the engine of entrepreneurship and economic, technical and social progress. State regulation of the economy was to be effected by economic means and to include the amelioration of the unfavourable economic, social and ecological consequences of the functioning of the market. The state was also to defend the 'socially weak' elements of the population and to see to it that all individuals face equal initial conditions in the realization of their rights to work, income, accommodation, recreation, health care provision, education, access to cultural values, and favourable living and working environments. The economy was to be integrated into the world economy through the 'creation of competitive, export-oriented productive and scientific/technical potential, the carrying-out of a policy of encouraging exports and the attraction of foreign capital, as well as the diversification of foreign economic ties' (*Programa za izlizane*, 1990: 14).

Turning now to the Lukanov reforms themselves, in the sphere of ownership relations, the idea was to eliminate the monopoly of state ownership through the transformation of state property into other forms thereof. However, the constitution would specify those specific branches and firms in which the state will maintain 'controlling participation' (*Programa za izlizane*, 1990: 15). As for the remaining state firms, all or parts of them could be privatised or transformed into joint-stock companies that allow for the participation of domestic and foreign physical and juridical persons. Private property was to be guaranteed and private initiative supported. Property that had once belonged to co-operatives but that had subsequently been nationalised was to be returned to them. Leasing could be used to put buildings, land and other assets at the disposal of both co-operatives and individual citizens.

Little was said about agrarian reform — a separate law in this sphere was promised — except that 'agrarian reform begins with the returning of land to its owners from before collectivisation' (*Programa za izlizane*, 1990: 16). Those who do not want to work the land were to be compensated monetarily for their former property. At the beginning of 1990, state orders for agricultural products were eliminated. The profit tax for state and co-operative agricultural producers was set at 10 per cent; the interest that they pay for investment credit was set at 2.5 per cent. A separate decree on 15 February detailed conditions for providing land to the private sector permanently or under lease (mentioned in *Programa za izlizane*, 1990: 25).

On 16 May the Lukanov government proposed that private agricultural producers be allowed to own up to 200 decares of land in flat regions, and up to 300 decares in mountainous ones. An unlimited amount of land could be farmed privately under leasing arrangements. The land that one owns would have to be farmed personally and could not be leased out to others. Those who owned land but did not want to farm it could sell it to others, and those who wanted to farm but did not own any land could purchase land (Aleksandrova and Popov, 1990).

The programme expressed the intention to allow all agricultural prices, other than those for grain, milk, eggs, sunflower seeds and sugarbeets, to be set contractually by producers, consumers and purchasing organisations. Separately, on 1 February the retail prices of most vegetables, fruits and flowers were decontrolled. As a result, the price of vegetables rose by 55 per cent, that of fruits by 21 per cent, and that of flowers by 46 per cent, with all figures referring to the period from January through May of 1990 in comparison with the equivalent period during 1989 (Aleksandrova, 1990a). Due to popular fear of serious general food price inflation, on 23 March ceilings were set for the retail prices of bread, meat, milk, sugar, vegetable oil, and children's food. Simultaneously, however, the wholesale prices of these items were increased at the expense of the state budget (Nikolaev, 1990: 4).

In the sphere of money credit relations, a two tiered banking system was to be created, with the Bulgarian National Bank on one level and 'universal commercial banks' (*Programa za izlizane*, 1990: 28) on the other. Specialised financial institutions were to be created, such as trade banks, and investment, insurance, social insurance and health insurance funds; foreign participation in such ventures is allowed. An active inter-bank money market and a capital market, including a stock exchange, were to be created.

In line with creating a more active role for interest rates, the basic rate would be raised from 4.5 to 8 per cent; from the beginning of 1991, interest rates would be set entirely on a market basis. A proposal was prepared containing changes in interest rates paid and received by members of the public. Deposits left in the bank for five years were to receive a 6 per cent rate. Housing credit would be provided at a lower interest rate than other forms of household credit. An active credit policy would be used to stimulate the production of goods for domestic consumption and for export against convertible currency, through such measures as lower interest rates for bank credit to enterprises engaging in such activities.

The financial system was to have the following elements: a tax on profit that is undifferentiated by branch or firm; a unified, progressive tax on personal incomes; a value-added tax; an accounting system conforming to international standards; and a modern system of tax collection. A much tougher state budget policy was to be promulgated, with the reduction of subsidies to loss-making and low-profitability firms and activities; budget-financed capital investment; and expenditures on the administrative apparatus, on the maintenance of embassies and trade representations, and on national defence. State budget deficits would be financed by selling bonds rather than borrowing from the central bank. A variety of forms of tax relief would be employed in 1990, such as full freedom from profit taxes for firms producing additional goods and services for domestic consumption and for export against hard currency.

On price-setting, the programme alluded to the gradual reduction of state price regulation in given sectors in combination with the elimination of the monopolies of the state enterprises in those sectors. A market in means of production was to replace the system of material–technical supply. The share of goods and services with prices set contractually by the buyers and sellers was to rise from 12 per cent in 1989 to 40 per cent in 1990 and 60 per cent in 1991. The retail prices of luxury and delicatessen goods, most imported goods that are particularly important to consumption, and most public services were to be 'set freely' (*Programa za izlizane*, 1990: 26), as were the prices of luxury housing. (The situation regarding agricultural pricing was already discussed.)

The labour market was treated very briefly (although it must be admitted that the very use of the term would only recently have been deemed heretical). The level of wages was to be set via negotiations between the government, the trade unions and management; wage determination would be based on the worker's contribution to production, his or her qualifications, and the demand for and supply of labour power. As mentioned earlier, the tax system contained measures to prevent the growth of wages from outsripping that of labour productivity. As a measure to control wage inflation, the wages funds of ministries, administrations, people's councils, and of administrative personnel in non-material production were to be reduced by about 25 per cent.

In dealing with the social sphere, the programme recognised that the

> transition toward a market economy will be accompanied by a definite social insecurity and tension, linked to the freeing of surplus labour, the development of inflationary processes, and the reduction of the standard of living of certain layers of the population. (*Programa za izlizane*, 1990: 19).

A programme for registering, transferring, requalifying, and supporting the unemployed was to be created, as was a contemporary system of social services, including pension insurance, disability insurance, health insurance, unemployment compensation, social assistance and social insurance. Such matters should not be handled via the state budget but should be run analgously to the way such matters are handled in the West. *Glasnost* regarding the social aspects of the reform was to be maintained by making available information on inflation, changes in the standard of living, changes in real incomes, and the social consequences of the reform.

Turning to foreign economic activity, on 23 February Bulgaria applied for membership of the World Bank and the International Monetary Fund — which it obtained on 26 September — and on 8 May it signed an accord with the European Community covering trade in agriculture, mining, housing and energy. Another development in foreign economic relations was the agreement with the USSR announced on 23 April, that beginning on 1 January 1991, all bilaterial trade would be on a convertible-currency basis ('Bulgaria i Suvetskiiat Suiuz', 1990.)[7]

On 2 April the lev was massively 'devalued', or more precisely, the 'cash' rate for physical persons went to 9.5 leva to the dollar (for buying the latter) from 2.5245 leva.[8] This move was accompanied by a reduction to US$30 (from US$65) of the amount Bulgarians can purchase before travelling abroad. Exactly a month later, further changes were made in the exchange rate system. An 'official' (*ofitsialen kurs*) exchange rate was established at US$1 = 0.797 leva. A 'basic' rate (*osnoven kurs*), which is to apply to payments by legal persons and transactions between legal and physical persons, was established; on 1 August 1990 this rate stood at US$1 = 2.9299 leva. Finally, a 'market' rate (*obmenen kurs*), which was to be set via periodic auctions, and which applies to the purchase of currency from non-residents and resident physical persons, as well as to the purchase of 50 per cent of hard currency earnings from firms, was created; on 1 August this rate was US$1 = 6.995 leva for purchasing dollars, and US$1 = 7.1349 for selling dollars (the rates for 1 August are from *Duma*, 2 August 1990).

Under the Lukanov government's economic reform programme, firms representing all forms of property, including private property, were to be allowed to participate therein. State regulation in this sphere was to be carried out on the basis of tariff policy, exchange rate determination and interest rate determination. Steps were to be taken toward the creation of a unified exchange rate for the lev and toward its convertibility. Firms had to sell 50 per cent of the convertible currency from exports to the state at the market rate; the rest they could keep. All firms could purchase such currency at the same rate, although certain priority areas, such as for the production of goods to be exported against hard currency, were announced for 1990. The government expressed its interest in membership in international economic bodies and in the radical reform of the CMEA.

Other recent economic events include the following:

1. the publication in *Durzhaven vestnik* on 10 April of changes to the constitution, whereby a market economy and private ownership are mentioned in that document for the first time;
2. the founding of the nation's first private bank on 28 April (Sokolova, 1990);
3. the signing on 8 May of a trade agreement with the European Community ('Sporazumenieto', 1990);
4. the decision on 9 May by a tripartite commission — representing the trade unions, the government, and management — to declare a moratorium on layoffs by enterprises until after the election ('Weekly Record', 1990).
5. the publication in *Durzhaven vestnik* on 28 May of a new regulation stipulating a 300 per cent duty on the value of exported goods;
6. the announcement on 5 June that sixty-four decrees that had hindered the operation of the labour market or had given monopoly positions or granted special favours to individual enterprises would be abolished ('Government abolishes', 1990); and
7. the promulgation on 12 June of a decree requiring state licences for many types of imports and exports.

An evaluation of the Lukanov reform programme

Immediately after the election, it appeared unlikely that the newly elected government, in which the socialists hold 53 per cent of the seats in the National Assembly, would deviate from the programme put forward by its predecessor. Between the two rounds of the election, the BSP promised

> to lead the country out of crisis — without chaos, without breakneck inflation, without mass unemployment, without unbearable prices. No to shock therapy! Yes to accelerated economic development. No to the economics of the rich; yes to security for the millions of honest people! ('I na vtoriia tur', 1990).

The reform package that Lukanov attempted to introduce on 10 October contained some radical departures. It was very brief, however, and turned out to be dead on arrival at the Assembly. Thus, for the moment, the best insight into the unfolding drama of Bulgaria's post-Zhivkov economic policy can perhaps be gained from an assessment of the fairly extensive economic programme of the *pre-election* Lukanov government on its merits as the first steps on the road to a market economy.[9] The remainder of this chapter is devoted to this task.

It is convenient to view the processes of change in the East European nations as consisting of two distinct stages — macro-stabilisation and economic reform, with the focus of the latter being on privatisation of a major portion of state industry. The Lukanov regime also saw matters in this way, as can be seen from the title of its programme — 'The programme for crisis management and the development of economic reform'. Accordingly, I examine the two stages separately.

Looking first at the stabilisation side of the ledger, the obvious comparison is with the radical programme currently being implemented in Poland. These measures have included cutting subsidies on food, housing, energy and transport; pushing interest rates to above 40 per cent; devaluation of the zloty; and removing price controls while maintaining wage controls. The effects of this have been striking: inflation has fallen to about 5 per cent per month from about 80 per cent in January, and the value of the zloty has stabilised simultaneously with the creation of a growing trade surplus (Lloyd, 1990).

Without much reflection, it is clear that the Polish approach to stabilisation policy, which many have taken to calling 'shock therapy' was not followed by Lukanov. Subsidies of various types were contained in Decree no. 56, and although their use was forsworn for certain purposes in the government programme — e.g. loss-making firms were no longer to be subsidised — they were still to be used in certain contexts. Recall, e.g. that the wholesale prices of a number of food products were raised in March 1990, while ceilings were set for the retail prices of those items. State price regulation was only gradually to be lifted, with the share of goods with freely set prices only reaching 60 per cent in 1991.

As in Poland, interest rates rose, but, unlike Poland, they did not go up enough to create positive real interest rates. Like Poland, Bulgaria devalued its currency massively, but, unlike the former, under Lukanov it maintained a very complex exchange rate system, with highly unrealistic 'official' and 'premium' rates. It should also be noted that Bulgaria has not yet undergone a period of very high open inflation such as that which destroyed the real values of the hoards of money held by households and enterprises in Poland. Thus, a serious monetary overhang continues to exist. Finally, whereas Poland has come down very hard on wage pressure, Lukanov's only solution to this problem was yet another tax on 'excessive' increases in the wage bills of firms.

On the whole, therefore, one can say that Lukanov's stabilisation programme did not go far enough in dealing with the country's macro-economic imbalances. The partial decontrolling of prices and interest rates seems likely to have created the sort of fast tracks to wealth that were created by similar policies in the USSR and were taken advantage of by the co-operatives there (much to the resentment of the population). Only an immediate and general decontrolling of prices, interest rates, exchange rates, and so on, can prevent opportunities for arbitrage arising from temporary disproportions in prices.

Let us turn our attention to the economic reform programme *per se*. One cannot escape the impression that there was greater continuity between the Zhivkov era and the immediate post-Zhivkov era in Bulgaria than with transitions elsewhere in Eastern Europe. For example, Ivan Angelov, who was one of the chief designers of the Decree no. 56 (Angelov, 1987), played a similar role with respect to the Lukanov programme (he is referred to in the introduction to Angelov (1990) as one of the 'authors of the program for crisis management and the development of economic reform'). More substantially, the promulgation of masses of normative documents which attempt to cover every imaginable aspect of a given issue, which inevitably have numerous design flaws and inconsistencies, and which must be subsequently amended and replaced, seems to be continuing.

An ongoing feature of Bulgarian economic reform is the appropriation of the formal, outward aspects of a market economy without creating the substance of such an economy. Imitating the black market exchange rate by way of an enormous devaluation that only applies to certain transactions is not the same thing as having a convertible currency. However, such a move may be desirable from the point of view of eliminating the black market in foreign exchange. None the less, in order to have a genuinely convertible currency, there must be a real market for foreign exchange. This in turn is only possible when there are sufficient private sector agents, foreign or domestic, to make a market in the lev.

Similarly, having joint-stock companies that issue staff shares that cannot be resold outside the firm may have some effect on worker motivation. However, recent studies of West German and US firms have failed to discern significant positive effects of profit-sharing and employee stock-ownership on firm performance, although they do find such effects in firms offering employee participation in decisionmaking (Cable, 1988; Conte and Svejnar, 1988). Accordingly, the institution of staff shares seems unlikely to be of major benefit to the overall economy.

More interesting, perhaps, is the prospect of the establishment of a stock exchange in Sofia, which was supposed to take place by the end of 1990. The presumed motivation for such an action is the creation of a market for corporate control. However, such a market can hardly exist unless there is a relatively large number of buyers and sellers. This seems quite impossible, given the present poverty of the country, unless there is a considerable amount of foreign interest in the Sofia stock market and the relevant legislation encourages a free flow of capital into that market. It may be noted that the latter has been lacking until very recently, even in some of the most developed capitalist societies (e.g. Sweden and Finland).

None the less, it has been argued that giving members of the population an opportunity to hold shares is a valuable experience in and of itself (see, e.g. Åslund, 1990). In my view, however, until the value of such shares becomes clearer, these will be only worthless pieces of paper. This is equally true if the stocks are held by funds designed along the lines of pension-type funds. One may question whether people with such low incomes should be forced to bear the risk of fluctuating asset markets, particularly when the early days of small stock exchanges, e.g. the one in Kuala Lumpur, are generally characterised by great instability.[10] Mutual funds can ameliorate this risk in the usual way, but it is well to ask whence will come the competent fund managers to operate in such an uncertain environment.

It appears that in Decree no. 56 and in the more recent legislation an inordinate amount of attention is devoted to diverse forms of business ownership, when the state sector is likely to retain the bulk of firms for the foreseeable future. In the absence of genuine market conditions under which the worth of each firm and its assets can be appraised, it is impossible to value them. In my view, it is more important to have competent management that knows how to function in a market environment — even if it must be hired from abroad — than to deal with ownership questions at such an early stage of the reform. Indeed, from a nationalistic point of view, paid foreign management is probably preferable to foreign ownership of a significant share of the means of production.

One may also question the idea of the equality of all forms of property. This sounds laudable enough, especially when uttered by (former) communists previously committed to the primacy of the state sector. However, there are grounds for serious doubts about the Lukanov government's approach to this issue. At one level, one may question its sincerity about breaking the monopoly of state ownership, especially in view of its statement about maintaining 'controlling participation' in a number of sectors. The proposed limits on private landownership are also telling, especially in a country with a great deal of abandoned land.

However, even if the pledge had been kept to allow the fully equality of the forms of ownership, it is debatable whether this would have been sufficient to pull the economy out of its present dire straits. After all, the private sector is starting from a disadvantaged position and still faces a variety of restrictions, such as not being able to lease land to other persons and limits on how much land it can hold.

Moreover, one peculiar feature of state institutions must be recognised. Although they may not work well as economic institutions, they often function admirably as charitable ones. To take a concrete example, agricultural workers may wish to remain on collective farms because of the social benefits, regular working hours, and legal and illegal free access to building materials, fodder and other factors of production. Thus, saying that collective farm members are *allowed* to leave those farms and set up private ones will not be enough if they do not wish to leave. It is well known that such farms in socialist countries have had great difficulty preventing an alarming escalation in the cost of production. If price-setting is carried out on a market basis — i.e. Soviet-style subsidisation of retail food prices ends — and production of certain crops remains in the hands of collective farms, retail food prices will skyrocket.[11]

This is equally true outside agriculture, in fact more so, given the insignificant presence of private enterprise there. Unless private decision makers are in place to respond to market signals, there will be no one to take advantage of the phenomena that accompany the current austerity. The only solution is a policy that explicitly favours the private sector, so that it can put itself into a position quickly to contribute greatly to production in areas in which its presence has been marginal up to the present.[12] Otherwise, the austerity generated by reform and by dealing with the foreign-payments crisis will be what Ed Hewett has recently called 'shock without therapy'.

Notes

1. The BAP had been part of the government through the entire communist era but had had no independent decisionmaking role. When the new government was formed in early February, the agrarians refused to participate in it. Having also decided not to join the UDF, the BAP has been a third force at the round-table discussions and in televised debates. It might be added that a radical wing of the BAP, calling itself the BAP–Nikola Petkov, after the independent-minded agrarian leader executed by the communists in 1947, has joined the UDF. The UDF, formed in December 1989 as a coalition uniting ten political parties and organisations, contains sixteen such entities at present, including non-party organisations such as the environmental group, Ekoglasnost, the radical independent trade union, Podkrepa, and the Federation of Clubs for Glasnost and Democracy; parties from the pre-communist era which have come back to life, such as the Bulgarian Social Democratic Party; and new parties, such as the Green Party. There are a variety of smaller opposition parties outside the UDF, of which the most important is undoubtedly the Movement for Rights and Freedoms (MRF), which consists of and represents the ethnic Turkish minority.
2. In the interest of space, this section will largely ignore reform of the agricultural sector in the late Zhivkov era. Agricultural reform and performance during that period are treated in McIntyre (1988: 97–110) and Wyzan (1989a; 1990a; 1990b).
3. This is one of the few reform measures that appears to have had some effect on the observable performance of the economy. For example, taxi service in Sofia has been far better in the past few years, with as many as five or six co-operative firms competing with the former state monopoly, which has long been infamous for very poor service. The restaurant situation in the capital has also improved considerably with the addition of several private and co-operative restaurants. Interestingly, the prices of taxi rides and restaurant meals are actually *lower* than those for services of the same quantity (say, a ride of a given distance in a taxi) or quality (say, of restaurant food and service) in the state sector.
4. These are available in English as *Decree 56* (1989) and *Regulations for the Application* (1989). The most detailed English-language analyses of their contents are Grosser (1989) and Jackson (1989a).
5. These normatives were not contained in either the decree or its implementing legislation, but instead are found in a decree promulgated on 21 February 1990, as discussed by Jackson (1989a: 32, footnote 36). They vary from 8 per cent for firms in electronics to 1–2 per cent for firms in energy, metallurgy and agriculture (see also Grosser, 1989: n.p.). Other

normatives contained in the decree of that date are the percentage of wages that must be deducted for the social, housing and cultural fund (5 to 7 per cent); the percentage of profit that must be paid to the municipal councils (10 per cent); the percentage of the DTRF that must be turned over to municipal councils for infrastructural development (5 per cent); basic intereset rates of 4 and 6 per cent; and valuta coefficients (discussed below). These rates may be taken as examples of the manner in which the state intended to regulate the economy through the use of 'normatives'.

6. The government's economic programme is discussed in English in Nikolaev (1990). The discussions with the opposition which preceded the release of the programme are treated by Engelbrekt (1990). It should be observed that the three main contenders in the election, including the socialists, have their own programme. See 'Predizborna platforma na bulgarskata sotsialisticheska partiia' (1990); *Predizborna platforma na SDS* (1990); and *Programme of the Bulgarian Agrarian Party* (1990).
7. This move is widely expected to cause considerable difficulties for the Bulgarian economy, inasmuch as the Soviets will undoubtedly find it far more advantageous to export their oil and natural gas to Western countries than to their erstwhile CMEA trading partners. The effects of such a shift in trade patterns were foreshadowed in the summer of 1990, as the USSR, for domestic reasons, sharply cut back its oil deliveries to Bulgaria and other East European countries (see Karagiaurova, 1990), forcing Bulgaria to raise the price of petrol considerably on 22 July ('Povishava se', 1990). Another threat to Bulgaria's oil supply comes from its inability to honour its contracts for exports of fresh fruit and vegetables and conserves to the USSR. For example, it has managed to export only 146 tonnes of apricots to the USSR, as against a contractual obligation of 1500 tonnes; for a discussion of this problem, see Aleksandrova (1990b).
8. The absurdities created by this enormous devaluation are humorously discussed by D. Popov (1990). The motivation for this move was apparently as an attempt to stop black market activity in the lev.
9. For insightful, if highly partisan, critiques of the first 100 days of the Lukanov government and its economic programme, see Kostov (1990), Filipski (1990), and Pushkarov (1990).
10. Malaysia has had some interesting experience since 1981 with the National Unit Trust (known by its Malay acronym, ASN), a programme to distribute among a generally poor population corporate assets held by a public enterprise (the National Equity Corporation); see, e.g. Jesudason (1989: 115–6). It is tempting to conclude from that experience that such programmes are feasible, but two facts must be kept in mind. First, the shares are *sold* to the population at face value, not given away. Second, the shares represent titles to going concerns already operating in a capitalist environment, so that their value is known. In Eastern Europe, programmes that more or less give away free titles to fixed assets that may be of no value whatever — except perhaps for salvage purposes — would be of a quite different nature, and, in my view, of dubious value for the establishment of a market economy.
11. On the other hand, it may be argued that households who receive land, including those whose ancestors can be shown to have owned it, should pay for it, even if it is only a nominal amount. It is important to establish that this pivotal factor of production has a value to it and that its productive capacity must be maintained. Moreover, although in theory any member of the population may obtain agricultural land, in practice it is likely that only the rural population will wish to do so. When one considers that the standard of living of the average agricultural household is undoubtedly higher than that of one headed by an industrial worker (Wyzan, 1990b), it seems especially unfair to favour the former with a free gift of one of the few assets of genuine value left after forty-five years of communism. Credit institutions could be created to lend to families wishing to purchase land but lacking sufficient present funds. The necessity to pay back a loan at a positive real

intereset rate could be an effective device for disciplinary farmers and weeding out the incompetent among them.

12. In the words of Pero Filipski, writing in the new weekly newspaper published by the union of private entrepreneurs, 'When the producers are state [i.e. belong to the state sector], and the traders are state, but the prices — market, the word is not privatisation, but pauperisation' (Filipski, 1990).

References

Aleksandrova, Dimitrana. 1990a. 'Plodovete i zelenchutsite sa poskupnali s okolo 50 na sto', *Duma*, 5 July.

Aleksandrova, Dimitrana. 1990b. 'Chushki za SSSR chakat bulgarska visa', *Duma*, 2 August.

Aleksandrova, Dimitrana and Popov, Vasil. 1990. 'Selianite shte mogat da pritezhavat do 300 dekara, no da obrabotvat i poveche', *Duma*, 16 May.

Angelov, Ivan. 1987. *Strategiia za kachestveni promeni*, vol. 3 (Sofia: Partizdat).

Angelov, Ivan. 1989. 'Framework of the Bulgarian economic reform', in *Economic Reforms in the European Centrally Planned Economies*, United Nations Economic Commission for Europe, Economic Studies, 1 (New York: United Nations), pp. 13–19.

Angelov, Ivan. 1990. 'Pazarnoto stopanstvo sreshtu totalitarizma', *Duma*, 13 April.

Åslund, Anders. 1990. 'How to Privatise', May (mimeo).

'Bulgariia i Suvetskiiat Suiuz shte se razplashtat s konvertiruema valuta', *Duma*, 24 April 1990.

Cable, John. 1988. 'Is profit-sharing participation? Evidence on alternative firm types from West Germany', *International Journal of Industrial Organization*, vol. 6:1, pp. 121–37.

Conte, Michael and Svejnar, Jan. 1988. 'Productivity effects of worker participation in management, profit-sharing, worker ownership of assets and unionization in U.S. firms', *International Journal of Industrial Organization*, vol. 6:1, pp. 139–51.

Decree 56 on Economic Activity in the People's Republic of Bulgaria (Sofia: Sofia Press, 1989).

Engelbrekt, Kjell. 1990. 'Round-table talks on economic reform: gradual approach or shock therapy?', *Report on Eastern Europe*, vol. 1:13 (30 March), pp. 4–5.

Fidler, Stephen. 1990. 'Bulgaria asks to halt most debt payments', *Financial Times*, 27 June.

Filipski, Pero. 1990. 'Stote dni na Andrei Lukanov', *168 Chasa*, 22 May, p. 2.

Gavrilov, Vera. 1990. 'Communist party and opposition sign key political agreements', *Report on Eastern Europe*, vol. 1:14, (6 April), pp. 1–4.

Georgieva, Mara. 1990. 'Chastniiat biznes iska privilegii', *Duma*, 15 July.

'Government abolishes decrees restricting economic activity', *BBC Summary of World Broadcasts*, Part 2: *Eastern Europe*, EE/W0133 A/6 [21 June 1990].

Grosser, Ilse. 1989. 'Bulgaria: a new thrust towards economic reform', *Mitgliederinformation* (Vienna: Wiener Institut für internationale Wirtschaftsvergleiche), 7.

'I na vtoriia tur — s misul za Bulgariia', *Duma*, 13 June 1990.

Jackson, Marvin. 1986. 'Recent economic performance and policy in Bulgaria', in *East European Economies: Slow growth in the 1980s*, vol. 3: *Country studies on Eastern Europe and Yugoslavia. Selected papers submitted to the Joint Economic Committee, Congress of the United States, March 28, 1986* (Washington, DC: US Government Printing Office), pp. 23–58.

Jackson, Marvin. 1989a. *A Crucial Phase in Bulgarian Economic Reforms*, Berichte des Bundesinstituts für ostwissenschaftliche und internationale Studien, 72-1989 (Bonn: Bundesinstitut für ostwissenschaftliche und internationale Studien).

Jackson, Marvin. 1989b. 'The economics and politics of economic reforms in Bulgaria', in *Pressures for Reform in the East European Economies*, volume 2: *Selected Papers Submitted to the Joint Economic Committee, Congress of the United States, October 20, 1989* (Washington, DC: US Government Printing Office), pp. 152–68.

Jesudason, James. 1989. *Ethnicity and the Economy: The state, Chinese business, and multinationals in Malaysia* (Singapore: Oxford University Press).

Karagiaurova, Katiia. 1990. 'Potrebnosti ot benzin se zadovoliavat napolovina', *Duma*, 29 July.

Kostov, Ivan. 1990. 'Nekompetetnost ili viarna sluzhba?' *Demokratsiia*, 23 May.

Lampe, John. 1986. *The Bulgarian Economy in the Twentieth Century* (Beckenham, Kent: Croom Helm).

Lloyd, John. 1990. 'Poland's delicate balancing act', *Financial Times*, 14 May.

McIntyre, Robert. 1988. *Bulgaria: Politics, economics and society* (London: Frances Pinter).

Nikolaev, Rada. 1990. 'The Government's program for crisis management and economic reform', *Report on Eastern Europe*, vol. 1:17 (27 April) pp. 1–5.

'Osnovni printsipi i sudurzhanie na ikonomicheskata reforma'. Sofia: Rabotna grupa na ikonomicheskite eksperti, 23 March 1990 (mimeo).

'Parliamentary protest over taxation of private business', *BBC Summary of World Broadcasts*, Part 2: *Eastern Europe*, EE/W0138A/4 [26 July 1990].

Popov, Deian. 1990. 'Istinata e, che sme bedni', *Demokratsiia*, 11 April.

Popov, Vasil. 1990. 'Rezultatite ot izborite sa vrucheni na prezidenta', *Duma*, 20 June.

'Povishava se tsenata na benzina', *Duma*, 23 July 1990.

Pravilnik za stopanska deinost (Sofia: Ministerski suvet, 1987).

Predizborna platforma na SDS (Sofia: [SDS], 1990).

'Predizborna platforma na bulgarskata sotsialisticheska partiia', *Duma*, 16 April 1990.

Programa za izlizane ot stopanska kriza i razgrushtane na ikonomicheskata reforma (Sofia: Ministerski, suvet, April 1990).

Programme of the Bulgarian Agrarian Party (Sofia: 1 March 1990).

Pushkarov, Ivan. 1990. 'Goliamata iliuziia', *Svoboden narod*, 23 May.

Regulations for the Application of the Decree on Economic Activity in the People's Republic of Bulgaria (Sofia: Sofia Press, 1989).

Sokolova, Zina. 1990. 'Suzdadane e bulgarska chastna banka', *Duma*, 30 April.

'Sporazumenieto e podpisano', *Duma*, 9 May 1990.

'Weekly Record of Events', *Report on Eastern Europe*, vol. 1:20 (18 May 1990), pp. 46–7.

Wyzan, Michael. 1989. 'The small enterprise and agricultural initiatives in Bulgaria: a comment on Robert J. McIntyre', *Soviet Studies*, vol. 41:4, pp. 646–53.

Wyzan, Michael. 1990a. 'Bulgarian agriculture: sweeping reform, mediocre performance', in Karl-Eugen Wädekin, ed., *Communist Agriculture: Farming in the Soviet Union and Eastern Europe* (London: Routledge), pp. 290–306.

Wyzan, Michael. 1990b. 'The Bulgarian experience with centrally planned agriculture: lessons for Soviet reformers?' in Kenneth Gray, ed., *Soviet Agriculture: Comparative perspectives* (Ames, Iowa: Iowa State University Press), pp. 220–42.

7 The Bulgarian economy: transition or turmoil

*Ognian Pishev**

It is very difficult to assess correctly and impartially the revolutionary changes taking place in Bulgaria. The constant interaction between political reform towards a pluralistic democratic system and the ever-deepening economic crisis makes the task especially complex.

The economic component of the reform has come to the fore because of three critical and overlapping tendencies. The most fundamental of these is the inevitable collapse of the socialist economic model, which is not susceptible to positive modifications from within. The second tendency is the structural crisis of an overindustrialised and heavily polluting economy that has abandoned its historic traditions, its comparative advantages, and its agricultural and service sectors. This is the structural crisis of a small, but not open economy, vulnerable to changes in the international economic environment. Finally, there has been a cyclical downturn following several depressed years. All three factors raise the possibility of the collapse of the entire national economy.

The debates about the future of the Bulgarian economy are not purely academic. They reflect divergent theoretical views and types of thinking: the routine of socialist management and central planning vs the dynamism of market economics and entrepreneurship. Because of this threefold crisis, even Lukanov's government (made up of former members of the Communist party) was compelled to use market rhetoric. Hence, given the character of the political contest in our country, a careful study of different approaches to market reform as well as of the recent evolution of economic policy acquires even greater importance.

The economic programmes of the main contenders in the June 1990 elections

It is useful to compare the declared positions of the principal political forces that competed in the first free and democratic elections in post-war Bulgaria (10 and 17 June 1990). In general terms, the manifesto of the Bulgarian Socialist Party (BSP)

* *Editor's note:* This chapter was originally written in April 1990 when its author, at present the Bulgarian Ambassador to the United States, was an economic adviser to the opposition Union of Democratic Forces. The views expressed are the authors own as a private citizen and do not reflect those of the Bulgarian Government.

advocates the 'equitable competition of the co-operative, state, share-holding, communal and private forms of ownership'.[1] However, it points out quite vaguely that 'the interests of the citizens and the market will determine where and which will be preferred, where and which will be most efficient'. It is paradoxical to see how easily the former Communist party has renounced its hostility towards private property rights and the exploitation formerly associated with them. The same document equivocates in the following manner: 'it was a serious misconception to believe that socialism was incompatible with private property. However, it is another dangerous illusion to claim that our economy can develop only through private property.' Finally, the BSP tries to maintain credibility by speaking of 'democratic socialism' and a 'socially oriented market economy'. This sounds rather unconvincing, given the present situation.

In the Programme of the Bulgarian Agrarian Party (BAP) the principles of a market economy figure prominently.[2] This document has been strongly influenced by the theoretical and ideological legacies of the past forty-five years. The BAP is equally 'in favour of an open socially-oriented market economy' (*Programme*, 1990: 28), and of a 'free and efficient operation of all economic units' (*Programme*, 1990: 27). At the same time, however, it describes a limited but important role for state intervention, which is to 'set guidelines and rates of technical and scientific and socio-economic development; formation and distribution of raw materials, food, and foreign currency reserves of the country' (*Programme*, 1990: 27).

The BAP takes the view that the issue of ownership, which is central to any concept of a market economy, can be solved only if 'genuine socio-economic and legal guarantees provide for the equality and full-blooded operation of all kinds of property' (*Programme*, 1990: 29). The BAP rates the possible forms of ownership according to a different vision of their priority, viability and importance. First comes private property, followed by co-operative, municipal, state and mixed forms of property. The Agrarian party accepts without prejudice the idea of privatisation, which is conspicuously absent from the BSP platform.[3] In this policy document, the BAP declares itself in favour of 'the privatisation of state property to an extent and in a way that will lead to the rational utilization of the existing national wealth and the other means of production' (*Programme*, 1990: 31–1). In an accompanying commentary the BAP insists that the government should define the means of, and should guarantee for the foreseeable future the 'de-etatisation' of about half of existing fixed assets (*Predizborna platforma na BZNS*, 1990: 15).

Perhaps the most comprehensive analysis of the issue of private vs other forms of property is presented in the pre-election platform of the Union of Democratic Forces (UDF). Here I cannot claim impartiality because I am one of the authors of the platform, which unfortunately does not sound like a pre-election manifesto because it is short on unrealistic promises.

While proclaiming that the national economy should develop on the basis of the interaction and mutual enrichment (enhancement) of different forms of property, the UDF stresses the fact that a market economy cannot function without a significant private sector, and that private capital is the driving-force of economic development.[4] In contrast, while proclaiming the equality of all forms of ownership, the Socialist party has presented no clear views on how this equality can be achieved under existing conditions of state domination (95 per cent of the fixed assets are in the hands of the state).

For the UDF there are two major currents that would lead to the establishment of a strong and self-sustaining private sector positioned firmly at the heart of a mixed market economy. The first is the immediate transformation of state property, the second the spontaneous establishment of small and medium-sized businesses (*Predizborna platforma na SDS*, 1990: 17–20).

The issue of privatisation is being hotly debated in different parts of the world such as Western Europe, LDCs, and Eastern Europe.[5] It should be thoroughly discussed at the earliest possible stage of economic reform, together with the other crucial elements of a transition to a market economy. Before beginning my discussion of this issue, however, I shall present a systematic, although very brief, account of the three principal axes of market reform in Bulgaria. The first, the transformation of property relations in a state-dominated socialist economy, has already been discussed. Perhaps this, together with the second area — the creation of a genuine labour market — represent the two elements of the present economic system that are most resistant to change.

The third area, financial intermediation, has been almost non-existent. We shall have to create, or recreate, all the principal parts of a modern service sector: these include banking and finance, wholesale and retail trade, and various types of distribution channels. A wide range of producer services is needed, including contract R&D, engineering, marketing, consulting, information and telecommunication services, and computer software. Having built the infrastructure of the market, we can breathe life into it and assure its smooth functioning only if we can unfreeze, unbundle and combine in a much more efficient way the two main factors of production — capital and labour.

Systematic interaction along these lines of economic reform will cushion the structural shifts in the national economy, help redeploy large numbers of people, suppress non-viable enterprises, and create new jobs. Moreover, at the two extremes of economic policy we have the fundamental problems of privatisation and the formation of a safety net to alleviate the social costs of transition to a market economy.

The UDF Council of Economic Advisers was the driving-force of the economic discussions at the round-table talks (late January to late March 1990). Unlike the political issues, the economic ones have never been discussed in earnest by the Socialist party. This did not, however, prevent the Socialist one-party government from using the UDF's main economic ideas in its own policy documents.

It is true that whatever the outcome of the elections, there was no alternative to the economic policy proposed by the democratic opposition. In the next section, I shall briefly describe the views on economic change expressed by the economic experts at the round table in a document named 'Basic principles and content of the economic reform'.[6]

Fundamental features of a market economy

This chapter contains a brief description of a market economy and all the major elements of market reform as well as the goals of the reform. The economic experts of all political parties in Bulgaria have agreed that five fundamental features should be present in a market economy.

1. The market will be the principal regulator of production, trade and consumption. The market structure itself is formed by commodity, labour and capital markets and is based on the free mobility of factors of production and a developed monetary and financial economy. And quite naturally, competition and entrepreneurship are the stimulus to economic and technical development.
2. Variety (multiplicity) of forms of ownership: all forms of private, municipal and public (state) property of residents and non-residents are equal before the law and enjoy constitutional guarantees.
3. The government will regulate economic activity through flexible institutional structures servicing the market, but not vice versa, and will use indirect economic policy instruments (monetary, credit and tax policy, customs regulations, market exchange rates and so on).
4. Social aspects of economic development. The state is to create equal starting-conditions for every individual and assure the respect of basic economic and social rights.

   This idea was further developed by UDF experts to an all-embracing concept of a social safety net.
5. Integration into the world economy.

How such a general model would function depends on the actual pace and breadth of the reform, which includes the following elements:

- reform of ownership (property) relations;
- democratic agrarian reform;
- money, credit and banking reform;
- new approaches to public finance and the budget in particular;
- reform of the price system, based on rapid price decontrol, demonopolisation and competition;
- creation of a modern labour market;
- reforms in the field of economic information and statistics, in economics and business education;
- import liberalisation, reform of the external sector and consistent exchange rate policy;
- a comprehensive reform of the legal system based on the separation of commercial legislation (commercial code) from civil law.

There are not many original elements in this almost textbook description of a transition to a market economy. The emphasis on financial and monetary aspects of regulation itself is quite novel for us, but not to the world economy. Therefore it is unnecessary to describe the need to create an independent central bank and a second tier of specialised financial institutions (commercial banks, investment trusts and building societies, pension and insurance funds), to put government spending under strict budget control (a ceiling on deficit financing and public sector borrowing requirements), and to introduce trade in securities and of a stock exchange.

One of the features of the document from the round-table talks is the insistence on the long-term character of economic reform and the need of a non-partisan approach to its problems, especially regarding the proposal for the creation of a politically independent Centre for Economic Analyses attached to the National Assembly. The campaigning in the weeks between the formulation of the document and the elections greatly politicised the debate.

Domestic aspects of the present transition period

Here we come to the second group of questions dealing with the speed and degree of resolution of the economic reform. The initial gradual approach of the Socialist party was presented as the antithesis to 'shock therapy'. This proved to be a false dilemma. One simply cannot 'plan' an orderly transition from a centralised to a free market economy and know all the answers in advance.[7] There are several core elements in any reform package that must be introduced immediately and without hesitation. These include a rapid transition to a realistic market exchange rate for the lev, a series of measures to reinforce confidence in the lev (a halt to the dollarisation of the national economy, i.e. of the parallel functioning of several currencies in domestic transactions, and introduction of internal convertibility and anti-inflationary measures), a switch to market-based real interest rates both on credits and deposits, and so on.

Now we shall take a look at how the Lukanov government's stabilisation programme was actually prepared and carried out. The programme was based on the assumption that by administrative pressure, a smooth and gradual transition to a market system could be achieved while maintaining the standard of living.

The first post-totalitarian state budget did not deviate at all from the old centralistic tradition of redistributing 80–85 per cent of the national income; there was no detailed information or transparent budget procedures. This was not an anti-crisis budget because it contained provisions for a deficit of 1,200 million leva, financed by the Central Bank with a negative real interest rate.

The system of government institutions was 'enriched' by the re-establishment of many of the old ministries. Four or five of them competed for the management of the national economy, including the following: the Ministry of the Economy and Planning, Ministry of Industry and Technology, Finance Ministry, and the Ministry for Domestic Trade and Services. Even the old Stalinist-type Committee for State Control remained in place.

Nothing was done to secure the autonomy of the central bank, or to ensure the independence of the national statistical service, nor was there any serious attempt to assess the results of post-war economic developments or the stagnation of the last decade. With its inconsistent policies, which in many cases ran counter to the strivings for market reform, the Socialist government was preparing potential time bombs which would threaten the prospects for economic and political change. The main axes of government action were determined by the present condition of the economy. This condition was characterised by the following: a severe cyclical downturn; inflation; potentially high unemployment; weak private and public sector enterprises; and heavy external debt.

Inflation

The BSP opted for freely set but non-inflationary prices while at the same time government anti-inflationary measures lacked coherence. The internal public debt has been estimated at 9,000 million leva (it was only at the end of 1989 that its existence was made public). Even worse is the financial situation of public sector enterprises. According to former opposition economic expert and current Finance Minister Ivan Kostov, who applied the System of National Accounts methodology, the BSP contracted a 40,000 million leva debt to the budget and the credit system. This, together with private savings totalling 25,000–26,000 million leva, much of which is 'forced savings' due to shortages in the domestic market for consumer goods, has created a huge inflationary potential. This situation could lead to a price explosion comparable to those in a number of Latin American countries and in Poland.

Monitoring the consumer price index and other measures of inflation is of strategic importance when designing an overall and anti-inflationary programme. Surprisingly enough, the Bulgarian statistical office has not yet devised a price barometer and we must still rely on unofficial estimates. According to one of them (presented orally by Professor Liuben Berov at a recent conference in Bulgria), annual inflation was about 9 per cent between 1979 and 1989. By June 1990 retail goods prices were rising at a monthly rate of 3.4 per cent (Aleksandrova, 1990), and for all of 1990 the rate was 46 per cent (Dempsey, 1991).

Unemployment

The fall in material production of 10.7 per cent noted during 1990 implies that about 400,000 members of the workforce are more or less redundant. In fact, the redeployment of the labour force was delayed until after the elections. Together with the bloated civil service, this prepares the ground for massive short-term unemployment of 700,000–800,000 people. However, as of March 1991, 80,000 people were officially registered as unemployed (Sudetic, 1991).

In circumstances such as these, when the public sector loses steam it is natural to expect an immediate shift in favour of the private sector.

Private businesses

The Lukanov government stated its intention to help the fledgling small-business sector but this remained largely on paper. Instead of tax incentives it introduced unrealistically high tax rates that only served to stifle private initiative. Private entrepreneurs are taxed twice, as both physical and legal persons, so that the fiscal burden could even reach an astonishing 85 per cent of the income. Despite recent changes in the main legal documents that regulate economic activity (Decree no. 56), it is not possible to trade freely on the domestic market because there is practically no access to capital goods and other inputs, and credit is limited. Nor is free trade possible on the external market since individual enterprises must obtain an export/import permit from the Ministry of Foreign Economic Relations.

There are already some 23,000 private companies of various types of legal status. In May the private business association created its own First Private Bank, and began publishing the business weekly *168 Chasa*. But there is still a great deal of uncertainty about future state policy. The Lukanov government was not inclined to accept unconditionally the principle of private property rights as the basis for economic activity. It was opted instead for the less clear form of leasing, which was introduced in agriculure, commerce and the tourist industry.

Public sector enterprises

In Chapter 6 of this volume, Wyzan describes the intricacies of Decree no. 56, but, to put it bluntly, it does not create a normal environment even for the public sector enterprises that are still dominated by the state bureaucracy. Their declared autonomy bears no similarity to normal managerial practices. The law prescribes the way after-tax profits are to be distributed among the various company funds (the tax rate is often as high as 65 per cent). It regulates the labour force and wages and salaries, which means that no enterprise is free to manage its production, finances and marketing independently. Until now there has been no clear distinction between macro-economic policy and micro-economics, which hampers any progress towards autonomous corporate policy and further privatisation.

Foreign economic relations

External problems of the Bulgarian economy

During the second half of the 1980s, when the Bulgarian economy stagnated (and official figures had nothing to do with reality), the government resorted to heavy borrowing from abroad to compensate for the loss of competitiveness, chronic current account deficits, and shortages on the domestic market. At the end of the 1970s, we had had a similar experience and our external debt had become disproportionately large. However, thanks to several specific and unique factors Bulgaria was able to deal with its debt crisis. A relatively easy repayment of the outstanding debt was achieved by re-exporting Soviet oil and petrochemicals. The Iran–Iraq war provided a handy opportunity for arms exports, and this also contributed to the correction of these balance of payments difficulties.

We find ourselves in a similar situation but we are now without a magic formula to overcome the debt crisis. According to the official figures provided to the World Bank at the end of 1990 Bulgaria had a gross debt of US$10,400 million and a net debt of US$10,262 million (Crane and Telma, 1991, p. 2). The external imbalances of the Bulgarian economy are due to its inherent structural weaknesses and its peculiar role in the international division of labour, that of an intermediary-country (*pays-relais*). This is the first of several explanations of the trade pattern of the country.

Bulgaria's dependence on imports from the West is explained to a large extent by the constant use of dollar inputs to produce and export to the Soviet and other East European markets. Second, the commodity structure of Bulgarian industry is defined not by the comparative advantages it possesses but by the interests of its largest customer, the Soviet market. However, by having chosen such an unsaturated market, and one with such low demands on quality, competitiveness in Western markets is inevitably lost. And, third, borrowing from abroad was needed to allow traditional customers from the developing world to continue importing Bulgarian goods on credit.[8]

The increased vulnerability of Bulgaria's economy may be seen in Table 7.1. The concept of vulnerability seeks to measure whether the resources available to individual countries (i.e. reserves and unused credit commitments) are sufficient to meet requirements (the deficit on current account and debt amortisation), assuming no new borrowing is possible.

Table 7.1 Net vulnerability, 1984–9 (in US$1, 000 million)

	1984	1985	1986	1987	1988	1989
A. Total requirements	0.6	1.1	2.7	2.3	3.4	3.9
Current account balance	–0.7	0.0	0.9	0.0	0.7	0.8
Maturities	1.3	1.1	1.7	2.4	2.7	3.1
Long-term	0.4	0.3	0.6	0.6	0.8	0.8
Short-term	0.9	0.8	1.2	1.7	1.9	2.3
B. Total resources	2.0	2.7	2.1	1.9	3.0	2.3
Reserves	1.4	2.1	1.4	1.1	1.8	1.2
Unused credits	0.6	0.6	0.7	0.8	1.2	1.1
C. Vulnerability (B–A)	1.4	1.7	–0.6	–0.5	–0.4	–1.6*
As percent of imports of previous year	n/a	n/a	0.2	0.1	0.1	0.4

* Negative number: net vulnerability

Source: OECD Financial Market Trends, 1990.

Measured in various ways the debt crisis has assumed dangerous proportions. It is the single potentially most ruinous factor for a radical economic reform in Bulgaria. The net debt/export ratio (i.e. debt minus reserves over exports) of goods in convertible currency grew from 22 per cent in 1984 to 263 per cent in 1989. During the same period net interest payments reached US$425 million (compared with US$98 million in 1984) or 14 per cent of exports (compared with 3 per cent in 1984). Today, the debt service ratio is over 40 per cent while the previous year it was only 17 per cent. The OECD study named above includes Bulgaria (together with Hungary) in the category of countries whose debt level is such that it cannot be increased significantly but its current debt is manageable (OECD Financial Market Trends, 1990, p. 22).

I am sorry to contradict such an authoritative statement but in Bulgarian foreign economic policy the notion of debt management simply does not exist. If it had, we should never have developed a debt structure in which only one-quarter is public or publicly guaranteed, with the other three-quarters contracted with commercial banks in the Eurocredit market on ever-worsening terms. There has been no change in borrowing practices along the lines of syndicated loans, and no attempt to make use of new financial instruments or the general trend towards securitisation. The maturity structure of Bulgarian loans is burdened by the high percentage of short-term credits. This policy of perpetually refinancing debt obligations with short-term borrowing prepared the ground for the fatal period of 1989–90 when annual debt amortisation reached US$3,700–3,800 millions.

It was quite evident that the Lukanov government should have addressed a demand for debt rescheduling to its main creditors, but for several months after the end of 1989 it kept repaying debt obligations, draining reserves, and seeking at the same time fresh financing for imminent debt amortisation. Additional credits never materialised. Then came the declaration of a principal repayment moratorium at the end of March 1990. This operation was carried out in such a heavy-handed manner that it destroyed normal commercial relations and isolated Bulgarian enterprises from their traditional partners in the West.

Was the debt situation really 'tamed' as former Prime Minister Lukanov had proudly claimed (Naidenov, 1990)? Exports to the developed West during the first three quarters of 1990 were 88 per cent of exports during the same period of 1989. Such imports decline to 78 per cent of 1989's figures (Crane and Telma, 1991, p. 2). The overall trade surplus for the first three quarters of 1989 was equal to 585.1 million leva, compared to a deficit of 216.1 million for the first three quarters of 1990 (Crane and Telma, 1991, p. 19). Since the end of 1989 the currency reserves of the country have decreased from US$1,400 million to US$138 million, or less than one month's worth of normal imports (Crane and Telma, 1991, p. 2).

As of 31 March 1990 Bulgaria was owed US$2,357.3 million by a variety of Third World countries. The biggest debtor was Iraq, which owed US$1,239.0 million, followed by Libya (US$265.0 million), Nicaragua (US$195.0 million), Nigeria (US$142.0 million), Algeria (US$109.0 million), Yemen (US$76.0 million), Syria (US$74.0 million), Angola (US$71.0 million) and Ethiopia (US$54.0) (Crane and Telma, 1991, p. 32). Needless to say, the likelihood of ever being repaid much of this money is virtually nil.

The external debt is thus unmanageable, or at least could not be managed properly by the Lukanov government. The crisis has sapped Bulgarian production and trade potential, and future prospects for normal debt servicing are jeopardised by that government's hesitant policies which lacked coherence and logic. An example of the inherent contradictions of the Lukanov economic policy is the introduction of a very complex exchange rate policy that declared the obligation of exporters to cede to the state 50 per cent of their currency earnings at the administrative rate of 2.93 leva for 1 US dollar on 1 August 1990. There was an approved list of enterprises allowed to purchase hard currency at this rate. The rest could take part in auctions where, for example, the quoted rate might be 7.1 leva for 1 US dollar (*Duma*, 2 August 1990). These stipulations encouraged capital flight, and many

Bulgarian exporters sought to bypass the national banking system in their commercial dealings. Another negative result has been the further dollarisation of the domestic economy, where for quite a long time the lev has not been the only means of payment.

Economic policy, and exchange rate policy in particular, were not the only reasons for the rapid loss of creditworthiness. It is quite obvious that there also exist a certain political dilemma. It is doubtful that Bulgaria's creditors would have been eager to provide fresh money or reschedule the debt on behalf of the same people who spent the money so wastefully.

Bulgaria's relations with international economic organisations

Bulgaria has successfully completed negotiations and signed an agreement with the European Community along the lines of similar existing treaties (e.g. between Hungary and the European Community, between Poland and the EC). Title II covers trade and commercial co-operation; the contracting parties agree to accord each other Most Favoured Nation treatment and eliminate quantitative restrictions on imports (by 1995). The agreement also discusses in fairly general terms the possibilities of economic co-operation (Title III) and the establishment of a joint committee (Title IV).

Contacts with the European Commission play an important role within the general framework of the PHARE (Poland, Hungary Assistance for Reconstruction of the Economy), co-operation projects already extended to East European countries other than Hungary and Poland. A G-24 mission visited Bulgaria in mid-March 1990 to assess the needs of various sectors of the economy. Several areas were selected: agriculture, food industry, health, and environmental matters.

Bulgaria is among the founders of the European Bank for Reconstruction and Development but does not have yet a formal framework for the selection of specific projects, for performing feasibility studies, for providing guarantees against possible commercial and political risks, for intermediation between the national private sector and the Bank.

A Bulgarian delegation took an active part in the Bonn Conference on Economic Co-operation in Europe (19 March–11 April, 1990). One of its achievements was the introduction in the final document of an explicit reference to the problems of the transition period. The participating states

> stress the importance of the political and economic reforms taking place, and of a supportive international environment, recognize the particular economic interests and concerns of countries as they achieve a market economy, and acknowledge other difficulties, such as indebtedness, which are to be dealt with in the competent fora. (CSCE/KWZEB 15, Bonn, 11 April 1990).

The easy acceptance of the proclaimed market principles and of the importance of the private sector and competition for the reinvigoration of economic growth and resource reallocation is due to the rapid unfolding of a public debate on the problems of market reform. Bulgaria seems to have already accepted the discipline of the IMF and GATT to which it has applied for membership. It is too late to join the Uruguay round of Multilateral Trade Negotiations, and in any case Bulgaria does not expect to play an active role. However, what is important now is to review national legislation concerning our future international obligations.

Bulgaria's readiness for economic reform

It is my view that Bulgaria under Lukanov was not ready to implement the necessary reforms. Efforts have been outwardly oriented but almost nothing has been done to prepare the way for the integration of the national economy into the system of multilateral trading and payments. I shall name just two examples. The first is more of a technical nature, and the second concerns commercial legislation, but both are related to deeply entrenched centralist habits.

The deplorable state of economic information in a centrally planned economy is well known. The problem is exacerbated by Bulgaria's inability to introduce normal accounting principles, and to reorganise the statistical service according to the concepts of the System of National Accounts and accepted methods of calculating international trade and payments statistics. For instance, we have barely begun to introduce the UN Standard International Trade Classification, or the financial statistics used by IMF member-countries.

This situation has an influence on the more general matters of investors' confidence and the stability of the regulatory environment. The changes in Bulgarian legislation under Lukanov did not remove the existing hurdles. On the contrary, the exchange rate regulations and the reintroduction of export and import licences, together with the need for individual permission for private export businesses indicate a retreat from earlier promises.

The integration of the Bulgarian economy into world markets requires more than institutional and legal changes. As the UDF Platform stresses,

> the actual elimination of the state monopoly on foreign trade and payments is a necessary though insufficient condition for the liberalisation of our foreign economic relations. Administrative command and restrictions must be replaced by an active system of incentives and export promotion; foreign trade and exchange relations must be controlled through economic instruments; customs tariffs, a realistic foreign exchange rate, interest rates and export credit and insurance policy.

The centre stage of any future export-led growth should be occupied by the producers themselves, the specialised trading companies and other specialised intermediaries. The former quest for industrial specialisation in areas chosen at random or imposed from the outside is to be replaced by a flexible search for product niches, subcontracting, and intra-industry trade in the markets that best suit Bulgaria's comparative advantage, along with the expansion of modern commercial policy instruments.

The commercial policy of the Socialist government did not make a clear distinction between its relations with CMEA members and its relations with the West. In the midst of the most acute debt crisis in Bulgaria's history, it sent confusing signals to its trading partners.

Conclusion

There should be a way out of the dilemma I have described above. I should like to finish on a more optimistic note. The UDF's economic advisers are completely aware of the critical situation and the dangers associated with market reform. They fully recognise the need to regain international credibility and to improve Bulgaria's image in the West. An important step in the right direction was Bulgaria's admission to the IMF and the World Bank which took place on 26 September. The implementation during the next critical one or two years of the UDF advisers' stabilisation plan would be the first phase of the reform, although it would be better to leave periodisation to future historians. (I remember a bitter Polish joke from the mid-1980s: 'This is the next phase of the reform and after that we will have the reform of the phase'.)

The UDF Council of Economic Advisers has put forward the basic ideas of a stabilisation programme, and I should like briefly to introduce them.

The UDF proposes a two-part anti-crisis agenda for action that begins with a preparatory phase establishing the institutions and instruments indispensable to the reform, as follows:

- a review of the budget and a radical cut in subsidies;
- deregulation of a large portion of prices;
- establishment of an independent central bank and a halt to the uncontrolled financing of budget deficits;
- a comprehensive tax reform; and
- gaining membership in international financial organisations and ensuring external financing for the reform;

The second phase should accomplish the tasks of the radical transition to a market economy and the overcoming of the initial imbalances in the economy:

- deregulation of all prices and control of excessive price rises by means of monetary policy and the encouragement of competition;
- liberalisation of imports and introduction of uniform customs tariffs;
- market determination and regulation of interest rates;
- elimination of the majority of subsidies and sharp cuts in budget deficits; and
- introduction of a market exchange rate.

The most immediate results would be the emergence of genuine domestic and foreign competition; the appearance of a more active private sector with enormous employment potential; real incentives for exports and a reduced import propensity thanks to exchange rate policy; and the establishment of new non-inflationary equilibrium prices coupled with strict budget discipline. The resurgence of domestic activity will reduce the deficit character of the national economy, broaden the tax base, and increase confidence in the lev, provided we stop the dollarisation of the economy.

I believe that Bulgaria, which survived forty-five years of totalitarianism, possesses an enormous growth potential. The interaction between political democratisation and economic liberation assured by the transition to a market economy will make reform irreversible.

Notes

1. As given by the election platform of the Bulgarian Socialist Party ('Predizborna platforma na BSP', 1990).
2. Until quite recently this party was a junior partner in the coalition government led by the Communist party. During 1990 however, it distanced itself from its former ally, proclaiming an independent policy stance. For the first time in forty-three years they prepared a political programme, which was adopted at the 36th Extraordinary Congress, Sofia, 1 March 1990 (*Programme*, 1990).
3. The Socialist government of Lukanov did not follow the guidelines of the party manifesto. It eagerly incorporated the main ideas of the opposition on economic issues, including the notion of privatisation.
4. See the UDF Election Platform of April 1990 (*Predizborna platforma na SDS*, 1990).
5. On Eastern Europe see the April 1990 issue of *Institutional Investor*.
6. This document prepared by the economic experts of all the political formations that took part in the round-table discussions has never been officially agreed upon. This affair took a strange twist when the Lukanov government decided to introduce it to the National Assembly (the parliament elected during the Zhivkov regime) as its own policy document. The text is quoted from the newspaper *Svoboden narod* (A Free People), published by the Bulgarian Social Democratic party, a member of the Socialist International.
7. The latest *World Economic Outlook* of the IMF (May 1990) makes a very good case for the need for a rapid transition to market economy in Eastern Europe.
8. A recent OECD study stresses the importance of two factors that are responsible for Bulgaria's fast-rising debt: the widening deficit on the convertible currency current account and recourse to borrowing from the West to allow LDCs to purchase Bulgarian goods on credit (see OECD Financial Market Trends, 1990, p. 48); most of the data are quoted from that source, unless otherwise specified.

References

Aleksandrova, Dimitrana. 1990. 'Prez iuni zhivotut e struval s 4 na sto poveche, otkolkoto prez mai', *Duma*, 16 July.
Aleksandrova, Dimitrana. 1990b. 'Prez iuni zhivotut e struval s 4 na sto poveche, otkolkoto prez mai', *Duma*, 16 July.
Crane, Keith and Telma, Tomasz. 1991. 'Bulgarian foreign trade and payments during 1989 and the first nine months of 1990', *PlanEcon Report*, vol. 7: 4–5, 19 February.
Dempsey, Judy. 1991. 'Bulgarian interest rates soar to 45%', *Financial Times*, 7 February.
Ivanov, Nikola. 1990. 'Shte poluchim li obratno 3 miliarda dolara', *Duma*, 24 July.
Naidenov, Valeri. 1990. 'Pravitelstvoto ukroti dulgovete na Bulgariia', *Duma*, 4 June.
[OECD Financial Market Trends, 1990] 'The international trade and financial situation of Eastern Europe in 1988–1989', *Financial Market Trends*, no. 45 (February), pp. 11–55.
'Predizborna platforma na bulgarskata sotsialisticheska partiia', *Duma*, 16 April 1990.
Predizborna platforma na bulgarski zemedelski naroden suiuz (komentar) (Sofia: 1990).
Predizborna platforma na SDS (Sofia: [SDS] 1990).

Programme of the Bulgarian Agrarian Party (Sofia: March 1990).
Sudetic, Chuck. 1991. 'Budget gives poor humor to Bulgarians', *New York Times*, 6 March.
Todorova, Mariana. 1990. 'Istinata za vunshniia dulg', *Svoboden narod*, 6 June 1990.
World Economic Outlook (Washington, DC: International Monetary Fund, May 1990).

8 The Albanian economy in the 1980s: coping with a centralised system

Örjan Sjöberg

Introduction: the nature of the Albanian economy

Albania, of course, did not immediately share in the revolutionary experiences of the other centrally planned economies of East Central and South-Eastern Europe, which took place in late 1989. Nor did Albania follow them in earlier decades when reform was at the top of the agenda; Albania's leadership has charted a largely different course from its former allies. This is not to say, however, that the Albanian experience necessarily is unique in the sense that its leadership has pursued a brand-new type of policy. On the contrary, foreign observers are rather more impressed by Albania's conservative adherence to the orthodox model provided by early Soviet socialism. It is not without reason that Albania under the late Enver Hoxha viewed the other socialist politics of Eastern Europe as revisionist, that is, falling into the footsteps of capitalist-inspired development. From the vantage point of pre-1990 Albania, the CMEA member countries certainly moved in that direction.

In a recent article, Raymond Hutchings (1989a) challenges the rather widely accepted view — most forcefully if not originally put forward by Adi Schnytzer (1982) — that Albania is pursuing an economic strategy largely based on the classical Soviet model.[1] According to Hutchings, Albania displays a development pattern quite distinct from that found in Stalin's Soviet Union. In no small part, he contends, this can be explained with reference to the vast differences in size of the two countries, the lesser emphasis on the heavy end of manufacturing in Albanian policy,[2] and the more important role accorded to agriculture in Albania. Furthermore, Hutchings observes that the divergence from the original blueprint has increased over time, and from this he draws the conclusion that it is no longer particularly helpful, indeed not even correct, to speak of Albania as having maintained a Stalinist economic strategy.

If this is so, it may well have important implications for our understanding of the recent past, and as a result, for our capacity to interpret future events. However, it is my view that what would then pass for a new economic strategy is in effect no more than the application of the same or an only marginally modified orthodox model to a partially altered decisionmaking environment. In short, the observation that the ruling party adheres to Stalinist economic principles subject to the constraint that it remains in power (Lange, 1981; Schnytzer, 1982; and compare Schnytzer, 1981: 634–5) still holds true.

In other words, the differences regarding economic decisions and institutional set-up between Stalin's model of development and Albania during much of the post-war period are as likely to be due to dissimilarities in level of economic development, factor endowment, and events beyond the control of party and government as to a change in economic strategy. After all, circumstances and the vast differences in size may well give rise to somewhat deviating policy prescriptions, even though these prescriptions may have been based on a train of thought and world outlook which were for all intents and purposes identical.

Pursuing this line of reasoning, I shall argue that it is a complex web of external and nature-given circumstances, and above all failures patently of the leadership's own making, that have necessitated the periodic emphasis on agricultural production and consumer goods industry observed during the 1980s (Hutchings uses this as the litmus test).[3] It does not necessarily follow from this proposition, however, that the original objectives have been abandoned. It may be only that short-term concessions have been seen as advisable and perhaps even vital (compare Altmann, 1988: 291).[4] Rather, I shall argue that traces of a genuine move away from the orthodox Soviet-type strategy of development and its attendant central planning have appeared only *after* Hutchings wrote the article cited above (March 1988). And this still does not prove that 'real change' has already occurred. For all we know at the time of writing (autumn 1990), viewing developments during the 1980s as a series of temporary retreats of a tactical nature is as tenable as is genuine change (cf. Lhomel, 1990:14). Only time will tell which proved the better prediction. After all, the openly expressed concern over sluggish food and consumer goods production has so far resulted in only a marginal change in policy and the foundations of the pre-established system remain firm. Similarly, the priority of natural resource extraction over manufacturing, which is seen by Hutchings (1989a: 123) as a divergent pattern in Albania, could equally well be seen as a parallel to developments in the Soviet Union. In both cases it could be held that this pattern is a logical consequence of the preference for heavy industrialisation, which is inherent in the unreformed Soviet model of development with its gross failure to generate both desired productivity growth and badly needed export earnings. In neither case, however, would the measures taken necessarily imply that basic development priorities were being abandoned in the longer term. *A priori* it is as plausible to trace such a turn in policy to the need to redress unsatisfactory developments threatening the viability and security of the communist polity.

Finally, whether the changes named above should be ascribed to an internal power struggle between 'reformers' or 'liberals' on the one hand and the guardians of the heritage of Enver Hoxha on the other is perhaps best left to others. For the time being, it will suffice to note that step by step since the mid-1980s, and not without occasional backtracking, measures have been taken to create a slightly less centralised system of planning. The fact that basically the same recipes for 'perfecting the economic mechanism' (wage policy and monetary incentives, self-financing, local planning capacity, and so on, which were first announced in the mid-1980s), reappeared in the late 1980s suggests that barely any headway had been made. It might therefore be hard to identify the point when policy would have been put on a new course. If such a point can at all be found, it may well have been in the second half of 1990. To help put recent reform initiatives in perspective, in this chapter I shall trace the developments during the 1980s. On the basis of the pattern found, I shall also briefly indicate some implications for the more substantive set of reforms proposed during the spring of 1990.[5]

Highlights of economic policy in the 1980s

As was the case following its break with the Soviet Union in the early 1960s, Albania's disagreement and subsequent rupture with China in 1978 had an appreciable effect on short-term economic performance and perhaps more importantly on economic decisionmaking (compare Schnytzer, 1981: 645–7).[6] Albania's go-it-alone policy triggered a series of radical policy decisions that were conceived to prove the commitment to 'true' socialism.

Perhaps the most important of these policy decisions pertained to the organisation and the thrust of central planning. In 1978, just prior to the break with China, planning was reorganised and made more centralised than it had been until then (a description of how planning was supposed to work is given in *Njohuri*, 1981; cf. Schnytzer, 1981: 620–30; and Pashko in Chapter 9 of this volume). Regardless of whether this move was an attempt to regain command over the running of the economy, and to mould it into a monolithic whole, or simply an expedient because strict financial management became an imperative when Chinese economic assistance was withdrawn (Schnytzer, 1981: 629 *et passim*; Wildermuth, 1989: 37),[7] centralisation certainly served to reinforce the inclinations of a leadership raised on orthodox Marxist thinking. This more centralised mode of planning has maintained its position for much of the time since it was introduced in the 1970s.

Other key decisions concern rural areas and in particular agriculture, where post-1978 policy strengthened the dual objectives of autarchy in food production (in order to reduce the dependence on foreign trade and, by implication, foreign powers) and of tightening control over the rural population as a means of securing the desired levels of domestic agricultural production (Lange, 1981; Sjöberg, forthcoming). As was also the case during the late 1960s and 1970s, some effort was channelled into urban–rural equalisation measures, including wage policy, as well as the allocation of public funds for education, health services and social security benefits. These measures were explicitly used as a means to reduce urban–rural income and living standard differentials, which in turn, it was thought, would encourage people to stay on the land (Hall, 1987: 54–7) at times when other policy measures threatened to have quite the opposite effect.[8] More importantly, the long-cherished goal of gradually reducing private agricultural activities was maintained with the same if not increased vigour. This policy, which only stopped short of actually abolishing the household plot, was supplemented by late 1981 with the complete collectivisation of the remaining private livestock in lowland districts as well as all sheep and goats in the mountain areas (Sjöberg, 1989a: 18–24). The effect was disastrous: Albania plunged into a crisis with repercussions well beyond the confines of agriculture and the food supply to the population (Wildermuth, 1989: 74–7).

In hindsight it appears that economic policy during much of the rest of the decade was devoted to rectifying what had been destroyed by the centralisation efforts and the collectivisation campaign. Thus, some modifications implying a return to a more decentralised manner of managing the economy were put on the agenda in 1985–6.[9] The number of plan indicators was, on an experimental basis, to be reduced for some enterprises and farms in a few designated districts, which were to be granted more discretion in planning, finance and pricing (Wildermuth, 1989: 51–2, 57; cf. e.g. Konini, 1989). Beginning in 1990, the relaxation of agricultural planning is to be extended to the whole country (Gjyzari, 1989: 5–6). To support these changes in the planning system a state commission on economic and financial control was established in March 1987 (Lhomel, 1990: 14). In July 1987 the Council of Ministers issued a decision on the 'territorial co-ordination of sectoral plans', which was to be put into effect no later than 1990 in order to grant districts a more active role in planning (Sjöberg, forthcoming). Meanwhile, the policy of district self-sufficiency in food production was reaffirmed (cf. Wildermuth, 1989: 51). Other measures include the decision of April 1985 to use wage policy to encourage production, which in fact meant a renewed emphasis on the use of material incentives and increasing wage differentiation (e.g. Zanga, 1987: 3; Xhaja and Metohu, 1988; Gjyzari, 1989: 10–11). As importantly, 'self-financing' was increasingly to become a main target in industrial production.[10]

Regarding the collectivisation of livestock, the Party of Labour of Albania (PLA) tried to alleviate the grievances of a demoralised peasantry by granting only small concessions to regain previous production levels. As Wildermuth (1989: 100–1) has pointed out, this policy often merely implied that campaigning was replaced by an evolutionary approach rather than that the objectives were abandoned *per se*. Since these measures in general were only moderately successful, or not at all, further concessions had to be made to achieve the intended results. Meanwhile, town-dwellers had to put up with rationing of basic foodstuffs, which undoubtedly increased the urgency to do something about the dismal supplies of daily necessities — a recurrent theme in Party deliberations during a good part of the past decade.[11] In turn, this led to measures which were increasingly heralded as *përsosje*, or 'perfection', by the Albanians and 'reforms' by foreign observers, although 'retreat' and 'relaxation' might be more appropriate labels for the phenomena.

Although the collectivisation campaign, and in particular its implementation, were criticised by Ramiz Alia as early as the mid-1980s (Alia, 1986; cf. the recent assessment in Alia, 1990b), it is only very recently that the whole undertaking as such has been publicly condemned (Gjoni, 1990: 39–40).[12] In the interim, the first government response to the decline in production, which was apparently due to the widespread slaughter of privately held animals,[13] was to introduce more severe regulations, for example that peasants must cut back on their private plot so as to encourage a larger input of labour in the 'socialised sector' of co-operatives (Sjöberg, 1989a: 18–24; Wildermutyh, 1989: 74). Moreover, peasants who tried to sell their produce in town were harassed (Kaser, 1986: 21),[14] and, starting in 1983, co-operatives specialising in animal husbandry were established (Wildermuth, 1989: 89–92). The last move is in part an implicit recognition that the comparative advantages of mountain co-operatives lay not in grain production (which they still have to carry out to fulfil their domestic needs) but in stock-raising. However, this fact does not detract from the argument that the difficulties created by agricultural policy at first were simply met with 'more of the same'. After all, the units that would now specialise in animal husbandry did so with the animals procured by decree from among those belonging to their own members.

Obviously, these measures were not as successful as hoped, and by 1985 a new policy was introduced: the 'brigade herds'. Animals from the 'centralised herds' that had been formed when private animals in the early 1980s were collectivised were now allocated to the brigade (rather than to their previous owners) in the hope of increasing production by giving co-operative members a greater stake in the production of milk and meat. Each brigade was allocated a small number of cows and a flock of sheep and goats, the proceeds from the raising of which were to be divided between the members of the brigade. Despite the fact that this new system was incapable of fully compensating the shortfalls in production that resulted from the collectivisation of private animals (Wildermuth, 1989: 102–3), the outcome most certainly has been encouraging since the brigade herd was soon followed by the establishment of the 'brigade plot'. This piece of land was to supply peasants with vegetables, beans and potatoes. The decisions on how to allocate labour to the cultivation of these plots and the tending of the animals were left to the brigade, and the brigade herds and plots were soon charged with the task of furnishing peasants with a good part of their food needs (e.g. Alia, 1987b: *passim*; cf. Sjöberg, 1989: 24–6).

The Co-operative Congress, held in November 1988, and the subsequent 7th Plenum of the PLA, which was devoted to agriculture, elaborated on and further adjusted the measures taken or suggested to that point. Save for the willingness to supply agriculture with additional investments and inputs, little new thinking was forthcoming on these occasions. The system remained basically unaltered ('Vendim', 1989). The decision to allow co-operatives to sell more of their produce directly to towns was perhaps the only exception to this general pattern, and this appears to have caught on widely by the winter of 1989–90 (e.g. *Zëri i popullit*, 10 February 1990). Also, it was as late as the winter of 1989–90 that the gross failure of the collectivisation of animals was finally acknowledged, in deeds if not in words (*Zëri i popullit*, 30 December 1989; cf. Alia, 1990a: 2). Thus reports started to appear, claiming that cattle and small ruminants by the thousands were being allocated to peasants directly rather than to the brigades of which they were members (e.g. *Zëri i popullit*, 2 January 1990, detailing the distribution of animals in the district of Durrës). Appropriately, at about the same time it appears that livestock numbers at long last again reached pre-collectivisation levels (Alia, 1990b).

Patterns of unsatisfactory performance

The view of Albanian economic strategy and practice which I have presented has been suggested as an alternative to the assessment made by Huthcings (1989a). In order to substantiate my interpretation, supplementary data on economic performance will also be introduced. Thus, as evidence for my interpretation one would expect to find a pattern of sluggish economic performance over the period discussed. For example, as less than satisfactory results continually emerged, new concessionary measures were needed to shore up the economy. Conversely, any sizeable improvement, temporary or otherwise, in key economic indicators could be expected to bring about a change in attitude about the need to grant concessions (or about introducing reform).

The existence of important macro-economic imbalances, as attested to by the full range of phenomena, such as repressed inflation, an increasing savings quota, shortages of consumer goods, consumer subsidies and enterprises being bailed out by the state budget (see e.g. Hutchings, 1989b), certainly indicates severe difficulties. However, for lack of appropriate data, I shall not conduct a detailed inquiry into the extent and sources of these imbalances.

Rather, the traditional success indicators of the centrally planned economy such as national income, net material product and gross social product, are the only evidence we have on the actual performance of the Albanian economy. Although several uncertainties and gaps in the time series exist, such indicators as have been made available (or can be estimated) suggest that Albania has fared no better than other socialist economies in the 1980s. In an assessment of Albania's recent economic performance (Sandström and Sjöberg, forthcoming), a colleague and I reach the conclusion that growth was feeble throughout the 1980s (see Table 8.1). Indeed, taking into account the high average annual population growth of about 2.1 per cent over the past ten years (*Zëri i popullit*, 9 July 1989; cf. Höpken, 1989: 541), there are clear signs of stagnation and even decline in per capita production in industry as well as in agriculture.

Table 8.1 Estimated growth of industrial and agricultural production, 1981–8 (increase over previous year as a percentage)

	1981	1982	1983	1984	1985	1986	1987	1988
Sandström & Sjöberg:								
Industrial production	6.2	4.7	1.0	3.3	−1.4	6.4	0.2	2.0
Agricultural production	3.7	4.0	9.4	−3.5	1.6	4.2	−0.4	−6.4
Industry & agriculture	5.4	4.5	3.7	1.0	−0.4	5.7	0.3	−0.8
Wildermuth:								
Agricultural production								
– total	−1.0	3.0	6.3	0.0	0.2	−0.6	2.0	n/a
– per capita	−3.2	0.8	3.9	−2.2	−2.0	−2.7	−0.1	n/a

Sources: Sandström and Sjöberg (forthcoming), Table 3; Wildermuth (1989), p. 23.

Naturally, the track record varies over time and among branches of the economy. Thus, judging by the data assembled and calculations made in our study (Sandström and Sjöberg, forthcoming), 1986 seems to have been a year of above-average results for the economy as a whole. Industry performed well in 1981 and 1986, and reasonably well in 1982, whereas the 1.4 per cent decline in 1985 was a substantial setback (cf. Zanga, 1986). The final year in the series, 1988, recorded a meagre 2.0 per cent growth for indusry, which implies an increment on a par with population growth. In particular, most of the major export earning branches — oil, chromium, copper and electricity — made little progress over the decade and in some instances fell back from previously recorded production levels. The petroleum industry has proved to be the black hole of the economy, consuming investment, capital and labour resources out of all proportion. Concurrently the mining sector failed to capitalise on favourable conditions in the chromium trade, due partly to low production levels, and partly to low output quality. [15] Added to the shortfalls in agricultural production (see below), the less than reassuring performance of the extractive and manufacturing industries contributed appreciably to the need to reassess long-held dogma. It would not be an exaggeration to suggest that the accord reached with West Germany, which led to the establishment of diplomatic relations in late 1987 and subsequently to the extension of hard currency grants to Albania in 1988–9, must be seen in the light of the economic difficulties Albania has experienced during the past decade.[16]

Turning to the agricultural sector, it may be noted that production made good progress in 1983, and less progress in 1982 and 1986; at the other end of the scale, 1987 proved to be little short of disastrous, with only a 0.4 per cent growth, not to speak of the decline of 3.5 per cent recorded for 1984. As for 1988, the final year for which year-end data are available, the result (–6.4 per cent) is even more dismal than the corresponding figure for industrial growth.

In the most thorough study to date on agricultural policy and performance during the 1980s, Wildermuth (1989: 23; here reproduced in Table 8.1) bases his calculations on FAO production statistics. These figures, which are not fully comparable with ours, lead the author to infer that 1982 and 1983 showed reasonable progress over the previous year with negative growth recorded for 1980–1 and 1986. On a per capita basis only 1982 and 1983 gave any reason for satisfaction,[17] and the same could be said of overall food production in the 1980s as a whole. Despite some divergences between Wildermuth's and our results, the dominant feature that emerges is an unambiguous trend of decline (cf. Hutchings, 1989b: 332), which is consonant with a dire agricultural situation, in particular in animal husbandry.

If the statistics I present above are taken at face value,[18] and if it is assumed that the Albanian party and government reacted in a conscientious manner to the successes and shortcomings of the economy (allowing for the requisite time lag), then the fit with the pattern of economic policy-making is remarkable. For instance, we should reasonably expect an upsurge in 'reform proposals' following the bad years of 1984–5 and 1987–8, and in fact this is what we find. It is striking that little was altered and few initiatives were taken not only between 1981 and 1983 but also in 1988.[19] One might speculate that as long as Hoxha was still around, there was little scope for any decisions that might challenge his policies. However, this leaves us without an acceptable explanation for the passivity prior to the rather more frantic activities during the closing months of 1989 and the first half of 1990. Therefore, this leads us to conclude tentatively that policy prescriptions, as formulated in official materials, were reactive and short-term in character throughout much of the 1980s.

Conclusion

Despite ever-worsening economic performance, no doubt brought about by ill-conceived policies and increasing population pressure, it seems that only recently has it dawned upon the leadership that its orthodox objectives and methods of management have led the country down a dead-end street. More specifically, it is only since the late 1980s that poor economic performance has been addressed as a problem in its own right and of significant magnitude. Attempts at reform prior to the winter of 1989–90 were half-hearted and at times were seen by the leadership as less than urgent in the light of perceived, if only temporary, successes.

In fact, it is reasonable to conclude that Albanian economic policy during the better part of the past decade has conformed closely to the orthodox prescriptions established by the original Stalinist economic model. The various waves of 'reform efforts' are best understood as a succession of attempts to redress difficulties by marginal concessions. The efforts were not intended to reform the economic system as such, but rather conceived as a means of fending off the need for substantial change by making minor modifications. The measures implemented reveal an orthodox outlook on the part of the leadership, implying that during the better part of the 1980s there was little change in its views on running the economy.

Therefore, it follows that most of the work of reforming the economy remains to be done and that reform efforts may cause great alarm among those groups who stand to lose the most. Perhaps both the recent concern over the need to promote those with superior skills and abilities as well as the campaign against the bureaucracy which has been waged over the past years can best be understood in this light.[20] After all, by introducing new standards for promotion and rewards, those who have vested interests in the existing system should, in theory at least, become more vulnerable to criticism and demotion.

Even if the top leadership has a change of heart, implementing a reform programme may well prove quite a different issue altogether. It is safe to assume that any Albanian government bent on reforms will find it very difficult to carry out radical changes. Not only does Albania need to change the structure of investments, production, and export, as argued by Gramoz Pashko in Chapter 9 of this volume, but it has to make up for the previous lack of reform. When the other centrally planned economies of Eastern Europe set out on the 'first wave' of reform, Albania was still busy building its own centralised system. Now Albania is expected to move directly to a system more in tune with present-day demands at home and in international markets, a step that is by no means easy, even should the need to introduce substantial reform be acutely felt (compare the discussion in e.g. Winiecki, 1989a, 1989b).

Notes

1. Elsewhere, Hutchings (1989b: 328) contends that 'the Albanian economy diverges from

Stalinism in circumstances and policy but not in structure; however, the worst diseases of a centralised system are not experienced.'

2. See, however, Schnytzer's (1981: 648) conclusion that engineering has long been a high priority branch, primarily because it is the main supplier of spare parts.
3. I shall here consider neither external factors nor those that are determined by Albania's particular geographical characteristics. In keeping with this contribution's objective, I largely draw on the secondary literature on the topic rather than referring to Albanian primary sources (or what in Soviet and East European studies generally pass for primary sources). Only when bits and pieces are missing shall I draw upon Albanian materials — if these are available at all. This applies in particular to the closing years of the 1980s and the first months of 1990.
4. In fact, it was only at the 7th Plenum of the Party of Labour of Albania (PLA) in February 1989 that agriculture received extra financial support (e.g. 'Vendim', 1989).
5. As for the recent measures in 1990 intended to 'perfect the economic mechanism', which are the most thorough ever proposed in Albania, see Gramoz Pashko's Chapter 9 in this volume.
6. Although the actual break with China took place in July 1978, it has by now been established beyond reasonable doubt that the amiable relations between the two countries were dealt a serious blow when China appeared to approach the Soviet Union and accepted the overtures of the Nixon administration in the early 1970s (Pano, 1977: 36–7; Prifti, 1978: 245; Biberaj, 1986: chs. 4–5). Thus, for example, the Constitution of 1976, well-known for its negative stance on credits and loans from capitalist and 'revisionist' sources (Art. 28), must be seen as having been influenced by such attitudes, in a sense making it a counter-image of post-1972 Chinese policy. However, this must not be taken to imply (as suggested by e.g. Logoreci, 1977) that Albania ever pursued a policy modelled on or even similar to that of China during the Cultural Revolution (on this point, see e.g. Pano, 1974; Prifti, 1978: 144–5 *et passim*; Schnytzer, 1982: 2).
7. Thus, the budgetary system was progressively centralised starting in 1971 (since then districts' budgets have simply been handed down from above and incomes have been allocated from the centre), and then again in 1980. See Banja, Hilima and Koli (1988: 15–16).
8. In order to ensure that rural dwellers indeed stay on, rural retention policies employ a much wider selection of measures. Thus, urban–rural and inter-district equalisation is supplemented by administrative restrictions, which are intended to curb rural-to-urban migration should the more benevolent attitude towards the countryside as expressed by the equalisation measures prove insufficient (Sjöberg, 1989b: 112–3). Furthermore, a number of other programmes militate against economic equalisation among regions, e.g. the introduction of higher type agricultural co-operatives (Toepfer, 1985: 148) and the intensification scheme of the 1980s (Sjöberg, 1989a: 15–18; Wildermuth, 1989: 70–2). Also note, as rightly pointed out by Wildermuth (1989: 74), that the impact of the subsidies to highland farms inherent in the preferential procurement prices received is limited, given the relatively small amount of total production sold to the state by highland collective farms.
9. Of course, decentralisation does not necessarily imply deconcentration of power, which in fact remains firmly vested with the PLA and central government; indeed, the formal devolution of controls as suggested so far has not fundamentally challenged the vertical nature of decision making. See Lhomel (1990: 14), who notes that as of December 1989 no visible change had yet taken place.
10. However, it was only following the 9th plenum in January 1990 that 'cost-accounting' — which is certainly not a new concept even in the Albanian context — and profitability were established as the guiding principles of enterprises (see 'Vendim', 1990: 2, and e.g.

Zëri i popullit, 15, 20 and 21 March 1990 for sample articles; cf. Banja, 1990). On the important question of prices, many unclear and even contradictory statements were made prior to the promulgation (in May 1990) of the new law on prices and tariffs. For an authoritative statement immediately prior to the introduction of this new law, see Gjyzari (1989: 7–10).

11. By the mid-1980s, the lack of food was publicly acknowledged (*Keesing's Contemporary Archives: Record of world events*, vol. 32:3 (1986), p. 34251), and public discourse, including many speeches and writings by Party First Secretary Ramiz Alia, has since been replete with references to the problems of furnishing the population with the basics of everyday life. See further Sjöberg (forthcoming). Wildermuth (1989: 82) cites evidence indicating that a black market existed, thereby acknowledging the role of private initiative in making up for some of the frequently lamented deficiencies in officially approved trade; this is congruent with my own observations during visits to Albania in January–March 1986 and March–April 1988.
12. Xhelil Gjoni should know; he is First Party Secretary of the hard-hit district of Dibër (see Mitezi, 1985: 61). I am grateful to Andreas Wildermuth, who directed my attention to the article by Gjoni.
13. Wildermuth (1989: 20) appropriately quotes evidence to the effect that Hoxha himself is on record as having called it a 'massacre' (*kasaphanë*). However, other factors such as lack of fodder and insufficient care of animals (Sjöberg, 1989a: 22–4) as well as limited incentives for management to put scarce resources into animal husbandry (Bekteshi, 1987: 24–5) must also have contributed to the poor results.
14. The peasant market was abolished in early 1981, about half a year before the scheduled completion of the campaign to collectivise the remaining private animals (Sjöberg, forthcoming). By the mid-1980s, unofficial private marketing activities appear to have again been tolerated, although not yet legalised. Only following the Co-operative Congress in November 1988 did markets officially open again (see below).
15. As regards the contention brought forward by Hutchings (1989a) that the switch from heavy manufacturing towards extractive industry is essentially non-Stalinist it may well be that unsatisfactory developments in mining and related exports prompted a change in short-range policy rather than a change in economic strategy as such. It is not unrealistic to interpret this switch in policy as a move designed to shore up weak sectors by extending further resources to investment (investment of an extensive nature, at that), which indeed is entirely in keeping with orthodox behaviour. Not only capital investment, but also labour resources seem — on the basis of indirect evidence, such as an increasing share of rural inhabitants being employed in the state sector (Wildermuth, 1989: 15; Sjöberg, forthcoming) — to have been reallocated to mining.
16. Perhaps the recent and well-publicised visits by UN General Secretary Pérez de Cuéllar (*Zëri i popullit*, 12 and 13 May 1990) and in particular Vice General Secretary of the United Nations Development Programme (UNDP), William H. Draper (*Zëri i popullit*, 8 and 9 May 1990), demonstrate the need for foreign assistance and not only Albania's need to portray its human rights record in a more flattering light.
17. The years for which our estimates differ from Wildermuth's calculations are 1986–7. The latter records a growth of 2.0 per cent rather than a decline; on a per capita basis this makes for slightly negative growth. However, for 1987, which is Wildermuth's final entry, the FAO production statistics are estimates (or forecasts?) published in November, and year-end, and perhaps even post-harvest, figures are therefore not figured into the calculation. Our diverging results for 1986 are more difficult to account for, but could perhaps also be explained with reference to the preliminary nature of FAO data. More recently released FAO statistics confirm the stagnation in 1986–7 as well as a rather substantial decline in 1988–9 (again allowing for the preliminary nature of the figures for the final entry; see

Teopfer, H. 1985. 'Zur Entwicklung der Landwirtschaft in Albanien', *Zeitschrift für Agrargeographie*, Jg. 3:2, pp. 136–57.

['Vendim', 1989] 'Vendim i Plenumit të 7-të të Komitetit Qendror të Partisë', *Bujqësia socialiste*, 1989:3, pp. 1–5.

['Vendim', 1990] 'Mbi thellimin e masave për revohicionarizim e jetës së Partisë dje të gjithe vendit — Vendim i Plenumit të 9-të të Komitetit Qendror të Partisë', *Zëri i popullit*, 4 February, pp. 1–2.

Wildermuth, Andreas. 1989. *Die Krise der albanischen Landwirtschaft: Lösungsversuche der Partei-und Staatsführung unter Ramiz Alia*, (Wirtschaft und Gesellschaft in Südosteuropa, 6. Neuried: Hieronymus).

Winiecki, Jan. 1989a. 'CPEs' structural change and world market performance: a permanently developing country (PDC) status?', *Soviet Studies*, vol. 41:3, pp. 365–81.

Winiecki, Jan. 1989b. 'Eastern Europe: challenge of 1992 dwarfed by pressures of system's decline', *Aussenwirtschaft*, Jg. 44:3/4, pp. 345–65.

Xhaja, Bajram and Metohu, Diana. 1988. 'Shpërndarja sipas punës nxit shtimin e prodhimit e përmirësimin e cilësisë forcon regjimin e kursimit', *Probleme ekonomike*, viti 35 (6):4, pp. 27–33.

Zanga, Louis. 1986. 'Slump in Albanian economic development', *Radio Free Europe Research*, RAD Background Report/16 (Albania) (28 January).

Zanga, Louis. 1987. 'A more rational economic policy in Albania?', *Radio Free Europe Research*, RAD Background Report/23 (Albania) (3 April).

9 The Albanian economy at the beginning of the 1990s

Gramoz Pashko

Very rapid changes are taking place in Albania at present, but it remains a country beset by a multitude of problems. Tackling the legacy of the past presents enormous difficulties. Even greater problems lie ahead in building a European future. The way now seems to be open, however, for a start to be made in this direction. In this chapter, I shall address these two areas. I shall make an assessment of the performance of the Albanian economy during the last decade (focusing on the enterprise and the economy's structural characteristics)[1] and identify the first steps taking during the spring of 1990 towards a new type of development. Some of the problems likely to be encountered in the near future will also be covered.

Structural problems in retrospect: enterprises and industries

The Albanian economy differs from the other Eastern European economies in that it started its socialist development at a less-developed stage. This is in particular true of its inherited branch structure of industry and its high rate of population growth. After World War II, industry in Albania was oriented towards such natural resources as minerals and fossil fuels, in particular oil, since they offered an immediate source of income. Albanian industrial growth was initially financed by accumulation in agriculture and to some extent by Soviet credit.

I list these factors in order to highlight the background against which state control over production and allocation seems to have enjoyed legitimacy as an easily applicable and effective means of solving the immediate problems of the time. Under circumstances of widespread misery and abject poverty a centralised system can offer a very suitable mechanism for mobilising resources for growth and organising their allocation. Moreover, this model of growth is easily acceptable psychologically.

At the beginning of the 1960s Albania broke away from the Soviet bloc. Its centralised economic model, which had showed signs of effectiveness in mobilising resources in its earlier stages, was preserved, however, and indeed emphasised even more. This was partly due to the still low level of industrialisation, which required an extensive development strategy through a concentrated mobilisation of financial and other resources. It may have been more important, however, as a natural and strong psychological reaction to the suspension of financial aid and technological assistance from the Eastern bloc countries. In other words, the emphasis on centralisation was a response to the poor results in domestic accumulation and represented a kind of instinct for self-preservation on the part of Albania in this period of relative isolation.

In the following years centralisation increased to an excessive degree. There may have been some good reasons for this development. The strategy of extensive development was not crowned with success, however, that is, it never reached a point where productivity-raising development become self-perpetuating. The rapid growth of the population in the late 1960s and early 1970s and the concomitant demands for the creation of new employment opportunities, above all in urban areas, had some influence on the development strategy as well. Thus, hypercentralisation represented a reaction to previous experience and aimed at controlling the distribution of wealth and curbing the expanding internal aggregate demand under conditions of inadequate financial and technological resources.

Subjective factors, especially ideological ones, played an important role as well. Above all, as in the other Eastern countries, a mentality that was overly hostile towards modifications of the system was established and strengthened. In the 1960s and 1970s, attempts to reform the economy were strongly resisted. No decentralisation took place; on the contrary, the economy became increasingly centralised.

As a result, many resources in the Albanian economy were underutilised, the most important among which was the resource which should have been of primary importance — the labour force. The extensive growth strategy was more concerned with employing resources than with using them efficiently, aiming more at creating employment opportunities than at increasing productivity. This type of growth swallowed up many cheap resources, and failed to take real costs into account in a realistic way, since the system was incapable of setting appropriate prices.

The egalitarian system of income distribution was such that one's wages continued to appear as more of a gift granted from above than a result of one's work, while planners continued to regard material resources and assets as more valuable than labour. The deleterious effects of these policies remained internal, unperceived, thus lending credence to the myth of the correctness of hypercentralisation. It created safe jobs and guaranteed incomes, and it gave the impression that providence would provide the rest.

Even though the workings and performance of exceedingly centralised systems are well known and widely discussed, I think it would be relevant here to present a formal, largely normative scheme of the model that was used in Albania until very recently (Figure 9.1). It goes without saying that orders are passed down through the system and information is passed on in the opposite direction; other types of flows are indicated whenever relevant.

The diagram shows an economy which is a closed circuit, the decisionmaking centre being not the enterprise but the central authorities. In this way, 'sectoral *dirigisme*' and departmentalism became the rule. The centre of gravity is located at the branch of the sectoral level, in the name of which the ministry operated. According

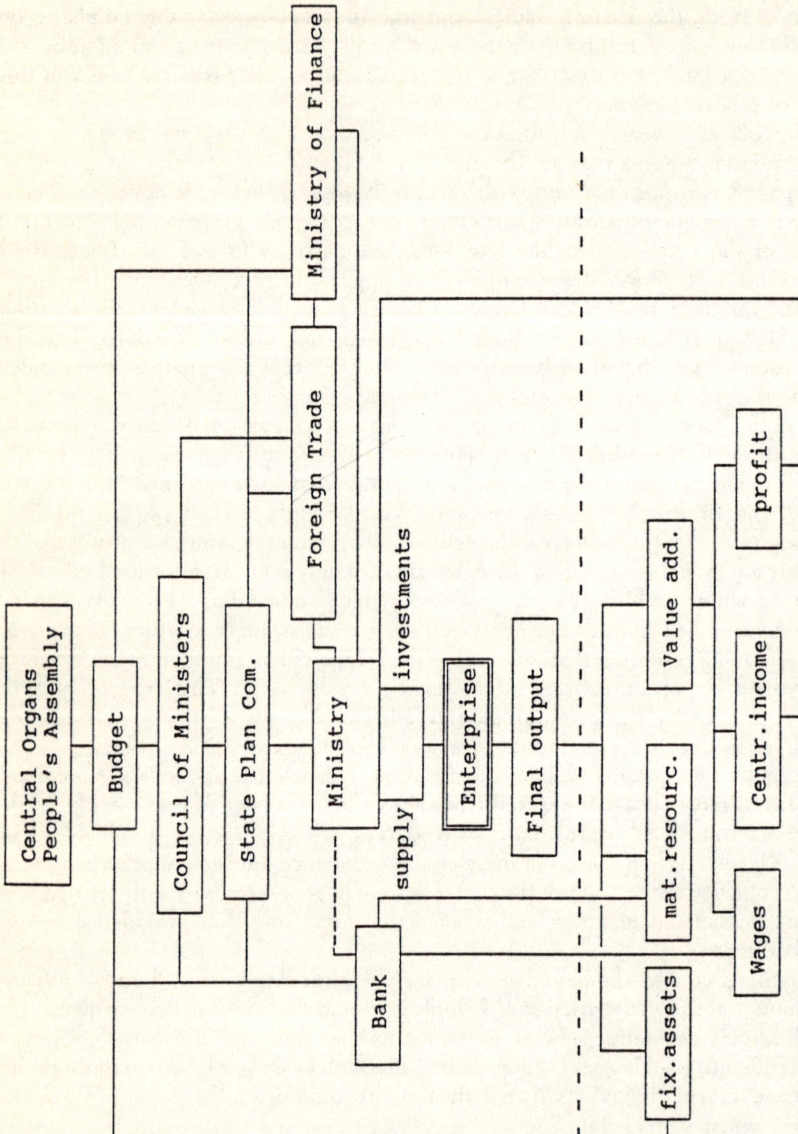

Figure 9.1 Albanian model of a centralised economy, in use until 1990

to the diagram, the enterprise had only one channel open for receiving directives and that was the one leading from the central government. In fact, the enterprise had no independent capacity for initiative. Political considerations had an excessive influence over the economic orientation of the enterprise and this was reflected to no small degree in the economic environment. Investments, supplies and the wage fund of the enterprise were all planned from above. The link to the bank shown in Figure 9.1 is purely a formal one; it merely reflects the creation of short-term bank deposits for administering the fund for wages and credits for material inputs.

Let me summarise this system of management in terms of three key points: how investment took place, how the supply of inputs worked, and how the wage system operated.

1. *Capital investments*

All economic activity originated from the investments made by the state through a single channel: the state budget. The firm in which the investment was made could manage only its initial capital stock. It was not allowed to dispose of or acquire new capital. It paid back to the budget a predetermined sum for its fixed assets, that is, as repayment for investments made. Nor was it allowed to reproduce independently its technology through autonomous new investments. These could be made only through the branch ministry, state planning commission or equivalent body. The enterprise was required to follow strictly an agenda laid down by higher authority. The autonomy of the firm as far as investment was concerned was limited to the possibility of reinvesting a part of the profits made (up to 100,000 leks), and then only in objects that were not related to the expansion of productive capacity (e.g. it could not invest in technology). The right of the enterprise to the assets it formally owned was merely juridical. It did not possess real economic power over them. Only the superior authority could decide — or more often dictate — the purchase from or, sale to an enterprise of basic capital stock.

2. *The supply of inputs*

All other material resources besides capital were supplied to the enterprise according to the centralised plan of the branch ministry or district Executive Committee. The enterprise could contract for supplies only within the planned quotas. The centre provided resources, the quantity and composition of which it determined by means of a mechanism which according to its logic was a rigid one. More often than not it hindered flexibility in production and any chance of modernising or expanding the enterprise. Thus, in this economic system, production was always conditioned by *ex ante* inputs. The problem of supply always remained the Achilles heel.

Such problems as shortages of inputs, inadequacies in their quantity, composition and delays in their delivery, which should have led to a failure to fulfil the overall plan or important structural components of it, were repeatedly disguised by budgetary cover-ups. The managerial staff of the enterprise were not subjected to any kind of economic sanctions for this. Only in recent years have the wages of employees been related to the fulfilment of plan targets, and the link has been very weak and it has been relatively easy to conceal non-fulfilment. The state intervened and covered losses even at the expense of efficiency and quality under the pretext of avoiding social tension. The enterprise that could arrange necessary supplies, no matter where they came from, was always lauded irrespective of its production costs while 'strategically important' enterprises (read: most of heavy industry) were always under the protection of the budget. Even though they operated under monopolistic conditions and were not subject to any test in the market-place, these enterprises were always presented as the vanguard of industry.

3. *The wage system*

What was true for the supply of inputs was true for wages to an even greater degree. These were also centrally determined. The enterprise was allocated a fixed fund for wages, a fixed number of workers and a fixed employment structure. The central government could increase the number of workers and the corresponding wage fund without additional specific demands on the enterprise regarding production, quality, efficiency and so on. Attempts to modify the wage system at the micro-economic level were made only recently, as incentives for overfulfilment of production targets were introduced, as were some wage restrictions in the event that enterprises failed to meet plan targets.

Hence, control of individual enterprises was facilitated by the hypercentralisation of all economic units. In the entire economic mechanism there were more than 1,300 centrally-determined indicators, most of which were expressed in terms of volume. This control by plan indicator was systematically implemented, but non-fulfilment was concealed (after some criticism of management). Only in recent years has fulfilment led to a 10 per cent cut in salaries for the managing staff. Under such conditions the enterprise could meet its production goals without possessing any managerial skill whatsoever, because competition was non-existent and non-scarcity prices made it very difficult to assess realistically the efficiency of the enterprise. Moreover, conflict between management and workers over questions of product quality or achievement of objectives was not permitted. This, together with the concealment of deficiencies in particular areas by focusing on aggregate results, created a parasitic system the effects of which spread throughout the whole economic apparatus.

Developments over the last decade have clearly brought to light the *structural defects* of this mechanism, which are related to both exogenous and endogenous factors. Many authors have analysed the shortcomings and collapse of this kind of system. The Albanian economy has, however, some peculiarities not only in time and space but also as a result of its distinctive economic mechanism.

There are a number of explanations for the distinguishing features of the system in Albania. Regretfully, it is still difficult to carry out a detailed analysis of the structural problems afflicting the Albanian economy. This means that the conclusions drawn here must to some extent be tentative. To make such an analysis would require an effort for which I am still somewhat unprepared, given the lack of data and of an adequate methodological and conceptual apparatus. Nevertheless, an outline of the structural problems presented by the growth dynamic of the past decade can be given.

In the Albanian economy, as elsewhere in East Central and South-Eastern Europe, heavy industry has been seen as the driving-force of the productive apparatus. Efforts were concentrated on processing minerals for export and on those areas of manufacturing where import-substitution could be achieved. Manufacturing industry concentrates mainly on metal processing, the main task being to produce spare parts. Basic chemicals is another important group of products.

Tables 9.1 and 9.2 show a relative decrease in the share of the light and food

Table 9.1 Shares of heavy and light industry in the total industrial output, 1960–88 (as a percentage)

Year	Group A	Group B
1960	48.9	51.1
1965	49.5	50.5
1970	57.0	43.0
1975	56.9	43.1
1980	64.0	36.0
1985	63.8	36.2
1986	64.8	35.2
1987	63.9	36.1
1988	63.9	36.1

Source: Vjetari (1989b), p. 69.

industries, as well as of the oil industry, since the 1960s. Relative growth was especially high in the engineering and chemical industries, but energy production, the copper industry and metallurgy all showed respectable increases. Nevertheless, these industries have not provided similarly rapid increases in exports.

The various branches of heavy industry swallowed up most of the available investment as well as the imports of technology and industrial infrastructure. Huge enterprises producing on a massive scale were set up, enjoying a monopoly as the only suppliers on the domestic market. They had good access to inputs and priority in obtaining imported raw materials. One consequence of this was a largely raw material oriented import structure. In the 1960s and 1970s, through Chinese credits, industries were created, which lacked clear strategic objectives and an awareness of economic realities.

It is also interesting to note the lack of complementarity between exports and imports. Both have displayed similar structures, in the sense that heavy industry has been insignificantly oriented towards the external market. Imports were, and still are, dominated by raw materials, with the aim of keeping such industry producing for domestic consumption, that is, mainly metallurgical products, spare parts, chemicals, and so on. Exports, which have a slightly different structure, have aimed at balancing

Table 9.2 Industrial structure by branches, 1950–88 (as a percentage of total industrial production)

Branch	1950	1960	1970	1980	1985	1986	1987	1988
Energy	0.5	1.1	2.0	3.6	2.9	3.7	3.3	3.1
Oil	18.8	15.5	14.9	9.2	5.7	5.6	5.3	5.2
Coal	1.4	1.6	1.5	1.3	1.7	1.6	1.6	1.7
Chromium	2.1	2.0	1.3	1.7	1.7	1.9	1.7	2.0
Copper	2.2	0.8	5.2	6.4	7.6	8.1	8.4	8.8
Iron & Metallurgy	–	1.3	2.2	3.0	3.4	3.0	3.2	3.8
Engineering	3.1	2.9	7.6	12.5	14.7	14.5	14.7	14.5
Chemicals	0.3	0.6	3.3	4.7	5.5	5.5	5.8	5.9
Building materials	3.3	4.7	5.6	7.9	6.3	6.3	6.2	5.8
Glass & porcelain	0.04	0.2	0.6	0.8	0.8	0.8	0.7	0.9
Wood & paper	6.7	11.2	8.0	5.8	5.8	5.7	5.4	5.1
Light industry	7.8	21.6	19.9	15.5	16.3	16.3	15.9	16.2
Printing	1.6	0.8	0.9	0.8	0.7	0.7	0.7	0.7
Food	64.1	43.5	30.4	25.6	25.3	24.5	25.2	24.7
Other	1.5	0.2	0.3	1.1	1.2	1.1	1.5	1.5

Source: Vjetari (1989a), pp. 46–8.

Notes:

1. In the last period the decrease in the share of any branch is often connected with an absolute decrease of the total value of its output.
2. The obvious decrease in the oil industry's share is due to a decrease in its total output. However, in the absence of absolute volume figures it is difficult to assess the real effect of the decrease in oil prices.
3. The branches are selected so as to include those having a total output of more than 1 million leks before 1950, more than 6 million in 1960, and above 20 million after 1970.

those imports. It can be observed that there has been no explicit correlative input–output relation between imports and exports. Moreover, there seems to be a vicious circle in which exports remain a means of financing the importation of inputs, most of which are used inefficiently within the industries that themselves produce the export goods.

The absence of a domestic market has favoured import-substituting industries, first by excluding their products from the competitive test of costs and quality, and, second, by allocating their output through the centralised system of distribution, making it available without charge. The inputs of these industries (mainly basic materials or spare parts) passed from the producer to the consumer through the state system of supply and distribution, well away from the firm's sphere of influence. The high costs thus passed on to the user reduced the efficiency of investment and of the national economy in general.

This 'sectoral *dirigisme*' gave top priority to heavy industry. Less attention was given to the needs of the light and food industries, of services and above all of small and medium-sized enterprises under district administration. The majority of the latter lacked the protection enjoyed by enterprises of national standing, that is, those directly subordinated to and hence under the protection of the ministries. Enterprises at the local level, administered by the Executive Committees, generally lacked the generous resource allocations and advantages which heavy industry enjoyed, such as investment, advanced technology and access to imports. This organisational structure gave rise to distortions at the enterprise and branch levels.

As Kornai (1986) has stated, centralisation creates its own conditions, reproducing itself and reproducing shortages. In fact, the Albanian economy can be seen as an economy in which the stimulus is not demand but supply. Demand should normally be generated by final consumption. In the Albanian case, however, demand has been restricted by the high priority given to heavy industry (Group A), by rapidly growing employment in that industry, as well as by the other factors mentioned above, which have meant that Group B industries have fared poorly. Demand has been generated by the state and by producers, but not by consumers. This has brought about a dystrophy in demand in general.

One would ordinarily expect that in a developing retail market, there would be a shift on the structure of consumption towards durable and other industrial consumer goods. There has, however, been no such shift, no change having occurred in the share of outlays on food, which remains the most important part of the retail trade. Table 9.3 illustrates these consumption trends.

Imbalances are continually created by the slower growth and lower productivity of the light and alimentary industries as well as in agriculture. This sluggish performance is made worse by the intense pressure for increased employment opportunities, as the annual net growth of the labour force is even higher than the already high population growth rate. At the same time, the increase in population has caused the demand for consumer goods to rise faster than for other goods.

Table 9.3 Growth of consumption, 1970–88 (calculated according to retail trade revenue)

	1970	1975	1980	1985	1986	1987	1988	1988 % share
Food	100	132	160	184	197	204	209	62.1
Non-food	100	130	150	172	189	192	195	37.9

Source: Calculated by the author on the basis of *Vjetari* (1989a), p. 160.

Note: The growth rate is between 2.3 and 2.7 per cent per year, very close to the rate of demographic increase and, at present, less than the annual growth rate of employment (about 3 per cent at the end of the period).

The weak development of services — due to the neglect of the infrastructure in general (physical, social and commercial) — is correlated with these imbalances and has negative effects on the productivity of the economy as a whole. The failure to create a viable infrastructure has been an immense handicap for Albania's economy; it is impossible to express the effects in quantitative terms. Lack of transport capacity and poor telecommunications are among the most troublesome factors. Less visible but no less important are the shortcomings in information services, trade networks and other specialised services. The investment quota in non-economic sectors (that is, those other than industry and agriculture) has been consistently low.[2] In reality it is rather difficult to make the data on the composition of total social product (corresponding to the Western concept of GNP) comparable with the measures used in international statistics. Thus, in the Statistical Yearbook of Albania there is no separate item concerning services. Percentage data are given on the share of transportation, trade and a few other areas. Information has been published in *Vjetari* (1989b: 121) showing a constant decline in that share since 1960. Starting at 10.6 per cent in 1950, it rose to 19.0 per cent in 1960, and then decreased gradually to 16.1 per cent in 1970, to 9.1 per cent in 1980, finishing at a marginal 8.3 per cent in 1988.

The economy has continued its orientation towards resource-intensive industry rather than towards labour-intensive activities which would make use of the supply of cheap labour. This orientation has come into conflict with the need to increase employment opportunities and the pressure created by the increase in the total wages bill. Of total industrial production, 35 per cent comes from seven resource-intensive industries, namely oil, coal, chromium, copper, iron and metallurgy, wood and paper. There are no available data on the distribution of the labour force between industries, but it is known that 22.9 per cent of the labour force is engaged in industry (*Vjetari*, 1989b: 59). Data on enterprise concentration by branch are also unavailable, as are data on how the workforce is distributed across primary and secondary sectors, administration, and so on.

This resource-intensive structure was also a result of the merger of economic units and a high degree of concentration in agriculture. The completion of collectivisation at the end of the 1960s marked the start of a new process: the merger of co-operatives. This in turn produced overly large units, and the resultant concentration of livestock was also strikingly less effective than small herds or flocks had been because it became nearly impossible for the agricultural co-operatives to be supplied with sufficient investment. These problems have been pointed out many times by the country's leadership as well as by Albanian and foreign scholars (e.g. Sjöberg, 1989).

The low level of investment in agricultural mechanisation and the high taxation of co-operatives introduced still more imbalances into the system. Thus, Ramiz Alia (1988b) noted that 25 per cent of state budgetary revenue in the second half of the 1960s came from the co-operative sector; today it is down to 12 per cent. Since 1971 the net contribution of agriculture to the state budget has been 20,000 million leks, meaning that it has provided one-third of the country's investment. Meanwhile, the increase of total agricultural output is said to have been at average 5,000 million leks in each five-year period.

Last but not least, the negative trends in consumption were shaped by the obligatory structure of agricultural production which, mainly for political reasons and despite unfavourable climatic conditions, stressed bread grain production to the detriment of more profitable crops and livestock-raising.

The demand for foodstuffs in Albania has risen faster than that for industrial products. For several years the growth rate of the volume of retail trade has remained quite close to the population growth rate, as can be seen from Table 9.3. The average rate of the increase in retail goods circulation was 2.5 per cent, nearly equal to the population growth rate.

The pathology of similar structures and mechanisms elsewhere in Eastern Europe has been widely analysed, especially by Kornai (1986) and Winiecki (1986, 1989). Quoting Kornai (1986), this mechanism 'reproduced difficulties' which were non-temporary, non-provisional and non-occasional, but presented themselves as a complex of phenomena which constantly reproduced themselves; this appears to be equally true for Albania as for the other, larger Soviet-type economies (STEs). However, a very important element that makes Albania different compared with other STEs is the shortcomings resulting from the absolute lack of real tests for exports. This has been because export goods, mainly raw materials, have been uncompetitive. Exports make up one-tenth of the gross social product (GSP) of

Table 9.4 Import structure, 1970–88 (as a percentage)

	1970	1975	1980	1985	1987	1988
Capital goods	32.8	45.2	21.7	25.1	26.2	31.5
Spare parts	7.2	3.8	2.5	5.3	6.7	4.8
Fuels, minerals and metals	21.6	21.4	35.8	27.0	28.2	23.1
Chemicals	9.4	8.3	14.9	14.1	14.2	12.7
Building materials	1.8	0.9	2.6	1.4	0.1	0.1
Non-food agricultural products	14.7	11.3	13.5	12.8	12.7	13.5
Food stuffs	3.4	5.0	4.0	8.3	5.4	8.1
Consumer goods	7.7	4.1	5.0	6.0	6.5	6.2

Sources: Vjetari (1983), p. 235; *Vjetari* (1987), p. 233; *Vjetari* (1989b), p. 167.

Table 9.5 Export structure, 1970–88 (as a percentage)

	1970	1975	1980	1985	1986	1987	1988
Fuels	27.4	25.7	29.0	15.1	11.7	11.0	7.9
Electricity	–	2.9	9.1	7.8	16.6	13.3	7.3
Minerals & metals	31.1	26.9	24.5	31.2	31.5	29.3	39.8
Chemicals	1.2	0.3	1.2	0.7	0.7	1.2	0.8
Building materials	0.1	0.7	1.5	1.0	1.1	1.3	1.5
Agricultural products	13.1	9.4	10.4	14.6	12.8	16.8	16.1
Food stuffs, processed	15.1	15.5	8.4	10.8	9.1	9.1	8.7
Food stuffs, unprocessed	4.4	6.3	5.4	8.1	7.0	8.2	8.2
Consumer goods	7.6	12.3	10.5	10.7	9.5	10.0	9.7

Sources: Vjetari (1983), p. 235; *Vjetari* (1987), p. 233; *Vjetari* (1989b), p. 167.

Albania (Alia, 1988a: 361). They may be divided into three groups, which alone account for 91 per cent of the total: (1) energy and oil products, copper, chromium, iron–nickel (which together account for some 57 per cent of the total); (2) agricultural products, mainly tobacco and vegetables (about 20 per cent); and (3) copper wire, cables and ferro-chromium, that is, intermediate products.

The relative insignificance of the manufacturing of final goods makes it difficult to assess domestic industry by comparing costs and productivity on a competitive basis. The rest of industry is mainly import-substituting and concentrates on producing spare parts or intermediate products such as metals, chemicals or fertilisers. These, because they are inputs themselves, cannot undergo a real efficiency test, and this is also true of the products made with these inputs.

The last structural problem I shall discuss is that which results from the demographic pressure. Population pressure creates a need to increase the number of job openings, which in turn has increased the extensive character of the economy. In the early 1960s each employed person supported two non-employed persons but currently supports only one. The absence of small enterprises meant that the labour force was drawn towards the big enterprises, which were obligated and indeed found it advantageous to make further unnecessary increases in employment. This led to an increase in the number of redundant work places. The production of intermediate goods (instead of final ones) discouraged and hampered mechanisation, and wasted material inputs and energy. The consequence was that unproductive enterprises were kept running in order to avoid social problems such as unemployment, thereby causing a general fall in productivity.

By the end of the 1980s, another problem made its appearance, one which is a particular feature of the structural difficulties affecting the Albanian economy. The greater part of the productive capacity introduced in the 1950s from the Soviet Union and in the 1960s and 1970s from China has become worn-out. To restructure that technology demanded financial resources and hard currency reserves and these were very limited in Albania as a result of its failure to introduce new trade techniques and the basic nature of its imports and exports.

Table 9.6 Productivity in industry, 1980–8

1980	1986	1987	1988
100	98.7	96.2	94.8

Source: Vjetari (1989a), p. 41.

As Winiecki (1989) has convincingly shown, large-scale industry in the STEs has been severely affected by the restructuring of the world economy. This restructuring has shifted the role of the driving-force of the economy away from large-scale industries with standardised products to those oriented towards production in smaller units according to the needs of customers, giving more importance to innovation, flexibility and management. Winiecki points out that this deprived the economies of the Eastern European countries of their only possibility of mobilising substantial financial resources for use in large scale projects. The effects on the Albanian economy of the restructuring of world industry are similar, but not identical, to those on many other East European countries. The structure of foreign trade has shown slight changes over a long time span (despite having been frequently redirected to different geographical areas from the late 1970s onwards).

The Albanian economy was never oriented towards exports. Exports always remained functional to imports, while imports served to fill the gaps in the economy in general. Without neglecting the role played by the drop throughout much of the 1980s in the world prices of raw materials, especially those of oil and metals, and by bad climatic conditions, which undoubtedly damaged agriculture and the production of energy,[3] one might say that it was clearly impossible to engineer further growth by the existing mechanism. As Ramiz Alia (1990) pointed out at the 10th Plenum, 'the improvements [of the economic mechanism] are a direct and logical consequence of the objective conditions created'. Ramiz Alia clearly stresses 'the weakening of centralism and hard discipline which were imposed by the indispensable accumulation' (*Zëri i popullit*, 13 May 1990).

Economic reform: solutions and problems

The proposed reform can be regarded as a sort of slow therapy, indispensable from one point of view and primarily valuable for helping to detect the inherent shortcomings and weaknesses of the economy. On 7 May 1990 the People's Assembly adopted a new law on the economic mechanism, originally studied and presented as a programme of measures at the 10th Central Committee Plenum held on 18 April 1990 (Çarçani, 1990; 'Ligj ër ndërmarrjet', 1990). This law, which comes into effect on 1 January 1991, aims primarily at reducing the bureaucracy, which has long been a burden to the economy. The basic principle introduced is the 'democratisation of economic relations', which will give more independence to enterprises as a result of their being granted self-financing status. The centre of gravity is to be partly relocated from the ministerial level to the enterprise.

The multiple links to the budget are to be dismantled at many points and significantly, subsidies seem to be partially cut. The same seems to be true of the 'unrestrained supervision' by superior authorities of the enterprises' activity. A concise presentation of the new role of the firm in three aspects may be of interest:

- the firm as initiator of economic activity, i.e. in relation to the market, including other enterprises;
- the firm as an agent of the state (a mere actor directed by the state), i.e. the firm in relation to the state;
- the internal operations of the firm.

The firm as an initiator of economic activity

Now the basic target laid before the firm by the superior organs will be the value of the goods sold, that is, sales (instead of goods produced, the target under the previous

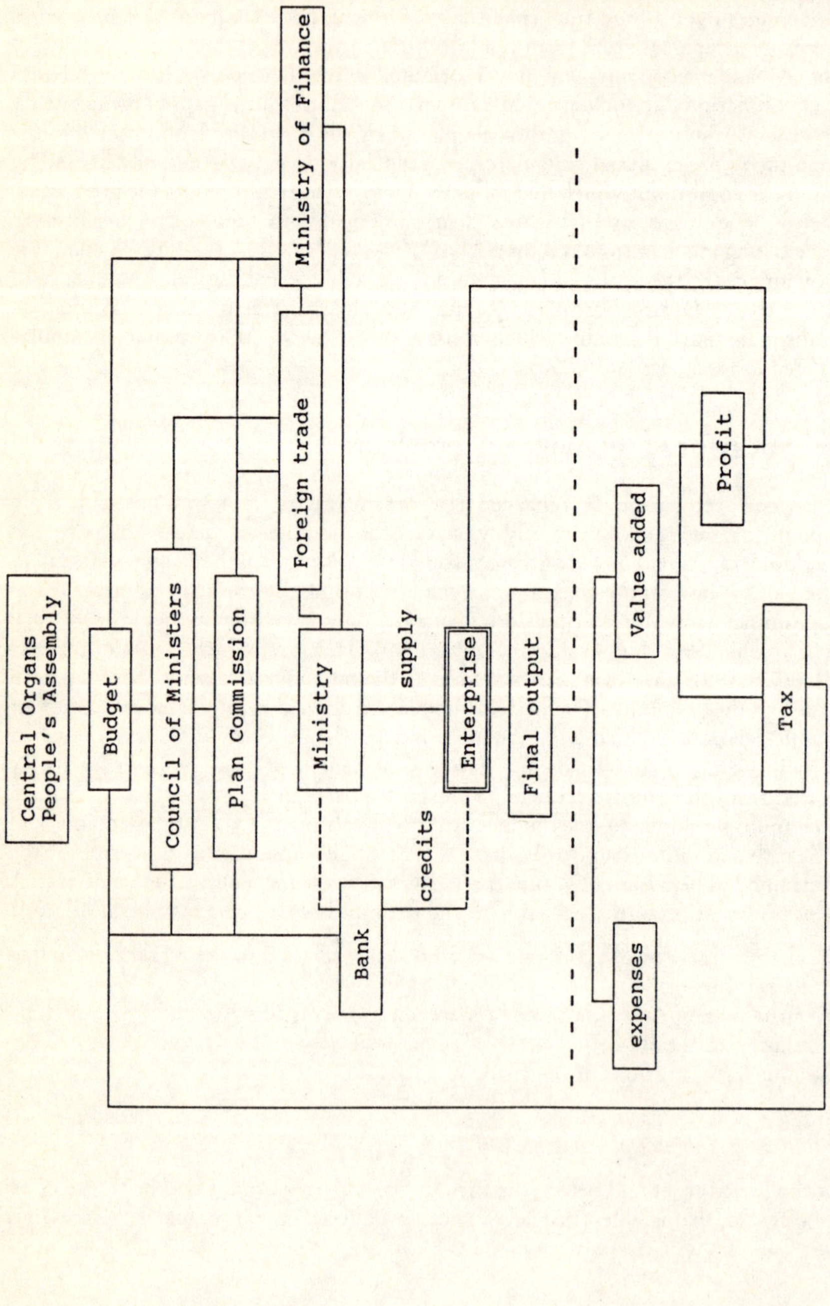

Figure 9.2 Model of the reformed Albanian economic system

mechanism). Centralised control will be maintained over this target. This is also true of cases where the main targets are expressed as volume indices. This encompasses enterprises producing goods considered to be of strategic importance, such as oil, chromium, copper, electric power, coal, textiles, flour, and goods for which the level of production is still set in physical units. The quantity of production destined for export or for supplying another district is to remain centralised. The firm is free to decide the quantity and assortment of the rest of production (*viz.* that part which is not centralised).

The planners have allowed the firm to employ 20 per cent of its productive capacity as it sees fit; the firm may decide what to produce and to whom to sell it. The firm is free to find inputs for this part of production. It may open its own shops and sell directly in response to supply and demand. In such industries as furniture, glass and ceramics, and so on, this freedom is extended further to the point where the firm has full control over its productive capacity.

It can be seen that this part of the reform applies in particular to small and medium-size enterprises, those subordinated at the district level as well as co-operatives, rather than to larger ones. The former are all the creators of their fates in the retail market.

The firm as an agent of the state

Under the new mechanism, the firm will be allowed to keep the return on fixed assets, which it used to pass on to the state budget after subtracting expenses. It transfers part of the value-added to the budget, while being allowed to retain the remaining 90 per cent as net income. On average, this is equivalent to some 40 per cent of the total after tax profit earned by the firm. It can be used for all kinds of activities, economic and otherwise, including investment in technology. Financing from the budget is largely discontinued, being practised only for creating new capacities of national importance, especially in infrastructure, railways, power-stations, and similar schemes. Figure 9.2 illustrates the links with the state the firm can have under the new system.

The importance of *the internal operations of the firm* is increasing. Under the new law the firm is allowed to invest using its own means, thereby enabling it to enlarge its productive capacities using its own profits. For the first time it can also use bank credits for this purpose, something which was strictly forbidden before (cf. 'Ligj për Bankën e Shtetit Shqiptar', 1990: Art. 8). Its powers now also extend to the labour force employed. The firm can, without restrictions, decide to increase the number of employees when capacity is expanded (until now the superior authorities have decided how many new positions should be added). The firm can also reduce the number of employees, but only with the consent of the authorities and only after finding new jobs for those laid off.

The enterprise is to create special funds for incentives and is also allowed to distribute half of the additional profit it has made in the form of wages (but no more than three monthly salaries per year). It can lower wages by 10 per cent in case targets are not met.

These three new roles considered at the micro and macro-economic levels can be expected to increase inefficiency and invigorate supply, but only to a limited extent. Furthermore, it has been declared that inefficient enterprises will not be tolerated, for example, when the enterprise is unable to honour its obligations towards the state budget, the bank and its clients or to guarantee the wages of its employees. Many examples of such inefficient enterprises are already evident.

In order to appraise the position of the firm, it is necessary to create a market and an adequate price mechanism. Such a mechanism will arise when enterprises have the right to come directly into the market as sellers. This would include those permitted to use 20 per cent of their productive capacity without interference from planning authorities; co-operatives and household plots in agriculture are also allowed to engage in market activities. It will, however, be only a partial market economy, in which the rest of prices continue to be controlled, which leaves little in the way of autonomous economic activity.

In combination with the restrictions imposed on wage rises, these cautious measures aim at preventing rapid inflation in an economy where wages and prices have so far been maintained at stable levels despite the latent pressures from the faster increase in demand than supply. In fact, due to the deficiencies on the supply side, an inflationary explosion is very likely to occur, especially since the total wages fund has risen over the years and further increases are to be expected.

Centralised price setting will continue to be the rule. But here as well steps have been taken to adjust the existing mechanism of price formation (see 'Ligj për çmimet dhe tarifat', 1990). The average cost of production at the sectoral level and optimal profitability are to be the general criteria for price formation in industry in future, instead of aiming to cover costs as has been the case so far. Prior to the introduction of the new law, in the mining industry the average cost of production in the poorest mineral-bearing areas formed the basis for pricing; costs in the least fertile areas did likewise for agricultural production. Though the new provisions could favour enterprises of average and/or above average efficiency, these provisions can again serve to promote (or at least do not exclude) the exploitation of marginal resources.

The new economic mechanism is accompanied by institutional modifications in the supply system. Among other changes, firms are given the right to enter into contracts with their customers and suppliers, provided that the quantities contracted for are kept within the framework planned from above for the bulk of production. As previously mentioned, supplies from other districts and imports remain under centralised control. Enterprises working for export do have the right, however, to dispose of a limited foreign currency fund; it is recommended that this fund be used for technological, as well as raw material imports.

Increased independence also makes its effects known at the sectoral or ministerial level. The new law does not authorise enterprises to become exporters in their own right. This remains within the competence of the ministries, which with a greater degree of independence are creating foreign trade enterprises at the sectoral level. The latter are in turn authorised to participate in all available forms of international co-operation.

Perspectives on the new economic mechanism in an international context

Albania is making preparations to become more broadly involved in the development processes of the continent and the world. The new economic mechanism represents a small step forward, a cautious and incomplete step but at the same time an indispensable one for future development. Originating as a reaction to the demands of both the domestic situation and the wider international context, it must at the same time be presented as a step, a premise in the logic of integrating Albania into the European economy and of the restructuring it is experiencing. Ramiz Alia has stressed that 'by now Albania's joining in the processes of European co-operation and security . . . is a demand of the time and meets our own interests' (Alia, 1990).

How successful will this mechanism be in bringing new life to the Albanian economy and achieving the stated goals? The new mechanism is by no means radical. Its cautious approach is justified by the possible risk of inflation and the creation of unemployment. The preservation of centralised control over most of the industries claimed to be of strategic importance constitutes an equally critical issue. The soft budget constraint has not been dismantled.

Criticism similar to that which has been raised by other authors on the occasion of the introduction of comparable mechanisms in the larger STEs (for example, see Kornai, 1986; and Winiecki, 1986, 1989) can be made of the new economic mechanism in Albania. It is, however, worth mentioning the special character and national features of the changes being introduced in Albania. The analysis of the system cannot be identical to that applied in Eastern Europe; there are specific problems and solutions which are linked to peculiarly Albanian circumstances.

The Albanian economy is broadly an economic system principally oriented towards supply rather than demand, as are the other STEs. The less the importance attached to the latter, the smaller the possibility of achieving real efficiency and the closer the situation is to Kornai's hydraulic analogy. Some differences are worth noting, however.

First, there is the general direction of development. The new mechanism introduced into the Albanian economy provides an incentive for increased production for those enterprises capable of providing such an increase. It does not, however, create conditions for a renewal of the existing productive capacity. Neither does it provide any real possibility of dealing with loss-making enterprises and sectors, which continue to be a considerable burden on the economy. This new mechanism seems unlikely to reduce this burden.

While the possibility for an enterprise to go bankrupt provides a partial solution, it does not completely resolve this problem. There is as yet no complete mechanism which can replace the role played by the market in resource and capital allocation; such a mechanism is a necessary corollary to bankruptcy. Prices, an essential lever for determining the real situation with respect to the cost and effectiveness of production, and which could also bring about the redistribution of capital to the more efficient industries or sectors, remain rigid and subject to distortion. The system of subsidies, which has operated for a long time, and the unrealistic cost structure have led to inert prices. In other words, the new economic mechanism cannot lead to scarcity pricing unless a real market is created.

Enterprises, especially those in heavy industry, which are giants by Albanian standards, maintain their monopoly in the basic sectors. Enjoying excessive privileges, well supplied with investment and other resources as well as credit, they maintain their operations irrespective of costs, spreading their deficiencies throughout the entire economy. Instead of being price-takers as a result of market participation, they remain price-makers because of the monopoly they hold. Worse still, because they are input suppliers these enterprises are not subjected to a realistic test either through the domestic customer or the foreign market. The buyer as an evaluator of their price and product quality is non-existent.

These enterprises are the biggest consumers of the country's total economic resources, in no small measure due to the 'do-it-yourself bias', to use Winiecki's (1989) apt terminology, and the fact that they enjoy the protection of a soft budget constraint. They have also the economic and administrative support of the élite (which derives benefits here), and furthermore enjoy the relative autonomy afforded by the self-financing of investment, disposal of a part of the foreign currency fund, and so on. A vicious circle in decisionmaking is thus created, rather than letting real market forces rule and/or introducing a stringent tax system. This means that increased sectoral autonomy, including influence over imports and exports, will continue to help bail them out to the detriment of enterprises at the district level. Under other circumstances, small and medium-size firms could be a great deal more efficient, and not least more beneficial to society, as a whole, for they are indispensable as far as the utilisation of marginal resources and marginal labour is concerned.

The real state of the big enterprises is hardly ascertainable. Assessment is carried out by the central authorities, which provides opportunities for bureaucratic concealment or distortion of the truth to protect giant enterprises of national importance which employ large labour forces. In the worst possible case, they will again receive assistance from the state budget, while bankruptcy as envisaged in the new law remains a very unlikely proposition. Hence, the big and inefficient mines, metallurgical plants and spare parts producers, which constitute the major part of the present economy — sectors in which technological renewal will require billions, and corresponding measures of time and effort — will in all probability remain unaffected in their role as a drain on the economy.

Second, there is the need to restructure foreign trade. In the absence of the general convertibility of the lek, and despite the limits now imposed, free access to foreign markets is still a privilege of the large enterprises. Moreover, no open test of their abilities in the world market will take place. As long as the lek is non-convertible, there will be no criteria for comparing domestic prices with those of international markets. Even if Albanian products were able to compete in the world market, and, under present conditions, this could hardly be realised for exports of inputs, this would not remove the negative influence of the inefficient enterprises. They would continue to spread their inefficiency throughout the economy through the mechanism of internal costs, material inputs, wages, and so on. In addition, considering their importance as a principal source of foreign exchange, the state will never let them go; the state budget will have again and again to bail them out, as Jeffrey Sachs (1990) puts it.

Third, Albania is powerfully caught up in the new European reality. It is too early to predict the potential and the scale of this involvement; serious problems deriving from eventual complementarity with Europe, or the lack of it, have not manifested themselves yet. Albania's output remains mineral and agricultural raw materials and these are central to its economic communication with the rest of the world. In the course of economic restructuring (and I have developed this more thoroughly in Pashko, 1990), products which are of strategic importance in an Albanian context hardly have that significance to the rest of the world. They cannot preserve this specific strategic character for long or indeed maintain their position of importance for economic interaction with the world economy. Raw materials have become vulnerable due to the secular changes in world industry. The restructuring of the priorities for industrial development has become an urgent problem for our economy.

Inherited backwardness and a refusal to face reality have led us to neglect the need for taking some very important steps. Hence, the idea of the necessity of integrating with the world economy was slow to be accepted; this makes it almost impossible for Albania to achieve present-day levels of technology and managerial skills.

Apart from the restructuring of existing industry, the solution in this case would be the gradual closure of inefficient enterprises, infrastructural improvements, and an economic orientation towards small and medium-size firms based on abundant labour resources. These could be services such as tourism but also processing industries in such traditional branches as the light and food industries.

Fourth, many problems must be tackled on both the micro- and macro-economic levels. In my opinion, the greatest danger would result from a possible wages inflation deriving from some sort of compromise between workers and managers in the division of additional profit through the use of special incentive funds. This compromise could also be at the expense of the quality of products. The possibility, or risk, cannot be excluded that enterprises will direct production towards those commodities which are in ample supply and which give the highest profit under the existing system of prices and costs, which of course do not reflect real scarcities.

Problems at the macro-economic level will arise because of the centralised relations of the enterprise regarding the supply of inputs. Despite the emphasis on financial rigour (Çarçani, 1990), there are considerable opportunities to avoid financial constraints as long as the assessment of enterprise performance is not based on objective criteria such as those supplied by an undistorted market.

Despite these reservations about the new mechanism, the Albanian economy has taken a step forward. The atmosphere and timing leave the matter of further modification open. Albania will be facing rapid population growth and the need for restructuring: two problems, the solutions to which could be mutually contradictory. How Albanian society will cope with the obstacles to its advance depends on how soon and to what extent it makes progress towards meeting the demands of this fascinating final decade of the century.

Notes

1. As for the overall nature of the planning system prior to the reforms of 1990, and the attempts to redress the effects of hypercentralisation, see Chapter 8 by Örjan Sjöberg in this volume.
2. In the 1981–5 period, transport, housing, education and culture accounted for 14.2 per cent of total investment, or slightly more than the corresponding figure — 13.3 per cent — for the 1976–80 period (*Vjetari*, 1989a: 134).
3. These events have been real enough, but their consequences have often been overestimated, thus diverting attention from the endemic causes.

References

Alia, Ramiz. 1988a. 'Planet plasqyrojnë interesat e popullit, për realizimin e tyre të mbahet përgjegjësi e plotë', in Ramiz Alia, *Fjalime e biseda, qershor — dhjetor 1987* (Tirana: 8 Nëntori), pp. 344–73.

Alia, Ramiz. 1988b. 'Kooperativizmi burim për begatine e jetës', *Zëri i popullit*, 22 November.

Alia, Ramiz. 1990. 'Demokratizimi i jetës ekonomiko-shoqërore fuqizon mendimin dhe veprimin e popullit', *Zëri i popullit*, 19 April.

Çarçani, Adil. 1990. 'Për përsosjen e mekanizmit ekonomik — Raport i paraqitur në emër të Këshillit të Ministrave, nga shoku Adil Çarçani, kryetar i Këshillit të Ministrave', *Zëri i popullit*, 8 May.

Kornai, János. 1986. *Contradictions and Dilemmas* (Cambridge, MA: MIT Press).

'Ligj për Bankën e Shtetit Shqiptar', *Probleme ekonomike*, viti 37 (8): 3, pp. 35–9.

'Ligj për çmimet dhe tarifat', *Probleme ekonomike*, viti 37 (8): 3, pp. 26–30.

'Ligj për ndërmarrjet', *Probleme ekonomike*, viti 37 (8): 3, pp. 20–5.

Pashko, Gramoz. 1990. *Krizat dhe ndryshimet strukturore në ekonomine botërore*, unpublished PhD dissertation (University of Tirana).

Sachs, Jeffrey. 1990. 'Eastern Europe's economies: what is to be done?', *The Economist*, 13–19 January, pp. 19–24.

Sjöberg, Örjan. 1989. *The Agrarian Sector in Albania during the 1980s: A changing regional focus*. (Studies in International Economics and Geography, 4; Rural Transformation in Eastern Europe, 6. Stockholm: Department of International Economics and Geography, Stockholm School of Economics).

Vjetari statistikor i RPS të Shqipërisë 1983 (Tirana: Drejtoria e Statistikës, 1983).

Vjetari statistikor i RPS të Shqipërisë 1987 (Tirana: Drejtoria e Statistikës, 1987).

Vjetari statistikor i RPS të Shqipërisë/Statistical Abstract of PSR of Albania 1988 (Tirana: Drejtoria e Statistikës, 1988).

Vjetari statistikor i RPS të Shqipërisë 1989 (Tirana: Drejtoria e Statistikës, 1989a).

Vjetari statistikor i RPS të Shqipërisë/Statistical Abstract of PSR of Albania 1989 (Tirana: Drejtoria e Statistikës, 1989b).

Winiecki, Jan. 1986. 'Are Soviet-type economies entering an era of long term decline?', *Soviet Studies*, vol. 38:3, pp. 325–48.

Winiecki, Jan. 1989. 'Eastern Europe: challenge of 1992 dwarfed by pressures of system's decline', *Außenwirtschaft* [Grüsch], Jg. 44:3/4, pp. 345–65.

10 The implications of change in East Central Europe for the Balkan socialist economies

Alan H. Smith

Political and economic thinking in post-Communist East Central Europe

The origins and impact of the social revolutions of East Central Europe

The social and political upheavals that swept away the communist political systems in East Central Europe in 1989 and the consequent free elections in the spring of 1990 have already resulted in those countries entering the transitional stage towards the establishment of a free market, private enterprise economy. The new governments of these countries have rejected the concept of a 'third way' (or regulated socialist market economy), which combines elements of a market economy with a national development strategy embodying socialist principles, not just as undesirable on political grounds but as unworkable on economic grounds. The idea that the establishment of a genuine pluralist society (which involves not just the right to vote in a multi-party democracy but extends to the creation of a civil society, the establishment of the rule of law and the development of independent movements with the capacity and right to question the prevailing orthodoxy), is essential for economic innovation, is central to the new thinking in East Central Europe.

There has been a growing acceptance in East Central Europe that political management of the economy in the form of centrally determined investment decisions for non-infrastructural developments, and arbitrary subsidisation of loss-making enterprises in order to preserve output and employment in the short run, regardless of cost, results in long-term losses of efficiency. The major area of debate on economic policy in the East Central European economies is no longer concerned with the desirability of establishing a market economy involving a major role for private (including foreign) capital and a limited role for the state, but with the more technical questions concerning the speed and optimal sequencing of marketisation, privatisation, and industrial restructuring, and in particular with the social costs of the transition, which will be expressed in the form of increased unemployment and rising prices for basic staple goods.

The failure of economic reforms under Communist governments

From the mid-1960s to the mid-1980s Polish and Hungarian economists in particular played a prominent role in both the theoretical and practical debates on the establishment and functioning of a market socialist economy. The Warsaw Pact invasion of Czechoslovakia and the enunciation of the Brezhnev doctrine resulted in the substantial modification of economic reforms in the late 1960s with only Hungary continuing to pursue market-oriented reforms, which stopped far short of wider-reaching social and political reforms and which did not challenge the leading role of the party.

During the 1970s the East European countries pursued the strategy of import-led growth which included importing Western machinery and equipment to modernise their economies and to update technology, largely as a substitute for more radical economic reforms. Investment goods were imported frequently on the basis of Western credits provided to East European governments, which enabled the East European governments to avoid the ideological pitfalls associated with genuine foreign ownership of capital or land on their territory. The major consequence was that Western suppliers had no material interest in the operation of equipment after delivery, while user-enterprises were divorced from the real costs of imported equipment, which they tended to view as a free addition to their capital stock. A major effect of this was that East European countries had no incentive to utilise imported technology efficiently, resulting in excessively long lead-in times before new plants were put in operation and problems arising from poor management of capital and low labour productivity including high operating costs and low quality output. Similarly the Western supplier had no interest in overcoming these problems or in updating the original technology in response to changes in Western supply and demand conditions.

As a result East European manufactured goods were frequently relatively obsolete, more expensive and of lower quality than products emanating from the newly industrialising economies of South-East Asia, where direct foreign capital ownership was permitted and where Western investors had a material interest in the efficiency of use of the capital and the competitiveness of the plant's output. This extended to the provision of advice and training in modern techniques of management, including cost and quality control and marketing. Consequently the East European economies failed to take full advantage of the benefits of international technology transfer while their manufactured goods were uncompetitive in terms of both price and quality in Western markets in comparison with exports from newly industrialising economies. This systemic inability to export was a major factor contributing to the East European debt crisis of the early 1980s (Poznanski, 1986).

Given the uncompetitiveness of manufactured exports, the East European economies were forced to respond to the debt crisis of the early 1980s by reducing imports. The major burden of import compression was borne by investment, which in turn widened the growing technology gap between Western and Eastern Europe and furthering the obsolescence of East European manufactured exports (Poznanski, 1988). Import cuts also contributed to a sharp deterioration in economic performance in the 1980s, including stagnation and even negative economic growth rates leading to falling levels of consumption. In the second half of the 1980s all the East European CMEA countries, with the exception of Romania, increased imports in an attempt to overcome their domestic economic problems, thus plunging deeper into debt.

The new economic thinking of Eastern Europe[1]

The failure of economic reforms in the 1960s and the import-led growth strategy in the 1970s have persuaded the body of market-oriented economists — many of whom come from academic and research backgrounds and are now either advisers or hold senior offices in the new governments in Poland, Hungary and Czechoslovakia — that their economic problems are systemic in origin and cannot be overcome by merely reforming the planning system within a socialist framework. They argue that the introduction of active retail and wholesale markets and profit-oriented state-owned enterprises within a socialist economy will not generate the efficient use of capital, and at the very least, reforms must extend to basic changes in the structure of ownership, which will provide for greater rewards for risk-taking, and in particular will require those responsible for poor investment decisions to bear the cost directly instead of dispersing it across the entire economy.

This will necessitate the creation of a competitive private sector, which will involve the widespread denationalisation of large-scale industry and the breakup of the existing highly monopolistic structure of industry as well as measures to facilitate the development of small and medium-size firms. This in turn will require the establishment of an active monetary system, involving the breakup of the monobank system and its replacement by a two-tier banking system composed of a central bank and independent private profit-oriented commercial banks and the development of capital markets. It is also argued that the economy must be open to foreign competition and foreign capital, thus leading to eventual full currency convertibility.

Market socialism and political change in the Balkan socialist states

Areas of differentiation between the Balkan socialist states and East Central Europe

Although the Balkan socialist states are confronted by very similar economic problems of a systemic nature as the East Central European economies, their situation differs from them in many important historic and geographic respects, which may well impinge on the process of economic reform and economic recovery. In the main the political traditions of the Balkan states have been shaped by subjugation to the Ottoman empire rather than to the traditions of the Habsburg monarchy. The Balkan republics are poorer and more dependent on agriculture than the East Central European economies, with substantially lower per capita incomes. They are also geographically more peripheral to the growing economic and political strength of a unified Germany.

Three of the economies, Albania, Bulgaria (*de facto* if not *de jure*) and Romania maintained highly centralised planning systems throughout the 1970s and 1980s and did not experiment with the principles of market socialism to any significant degree.[2]

Although Yugoslavia was the first socialist country to abandon the Stalinist model of central planning in the early 1950s and move to a model of market socialism incorporating workers' self-management, continued political interference in the day-to-day management of enterprises by local party organisations, the total unwillingness of republican authorities to bankrupt weak and losing enterprises, the growing tendency to regional autarchy and the virtual absence of free entry into the market have rendered the market elements of the system virtually inoperable. Consequently enterprises, although nominally operating in a market framework, are not subjected to genuine market discipline and can rely on easy sources of credit to finance losses.

In the Balkan socialist republics (with the exception of Bulgaria) the economies have been less dependent on trade links with the Soviet Union and the local Communist parties have been less dependent on Soviet support to maintain power. The Communist parties of both Yugoslavia and Albania formally split from the Soviet party and neither country is a full member of CMEA or the Warsaw Pact. Romania, although remaining a member of both the CMEA and the Warsaw Pact, reduced its trade links with the Soviet Union from the mid-1960s until the mid-1980s, did not participate in a number of Soviet-backed integration projects in CMEA, did not receive Soviet oil at the *de facto* subsidised intra-CMEA price in the 1970s and early 1980s, and does not allow Warsaw Pact manoeuvres on its territory. Bulgaria, however, remains highly dependent on Soviet energy supplies and Soviet markets for its manufactured goods. Historically and linguistically its people have a greater affinity with Russian culture and do not display the same antipathy towards Russia as has been shown in East Central Europe.

The adoption or imposition of the Stalinist policy of rapid industrialisation in predominantly agrarian economies, where as much as 80 per cent of the pre-war labour force was employed in agriculture, has led to the development of an industrial working class without the concomitant development of a cohesive independent working class movement, or a strong urban middle class capable of maintaining a sustained challenge to central authority.

In many cases the industrial community is largely composed of first and second-generation migrants from the villages, many of whom live in newly created townships without a strong pre-war industrial tradition, where a single large enterprise is the dominant source of employment and where many of the traditional functions associated with a local authority (welfare payments, social and sporting facilities, etc.) are provided by the workplace. Similarly industrial managers have been brought up in an environment where total obedience to central institutions brings direct rewards.

This is in marked contrast to the situation in East Central Europe. The initial challenge to the Communist bureaucracy in Poland emerged from an alliance of a genuine autonomous workers' movements, which arose in an area with a pre-war industrial tradition, and a liberal intelligentsia which maintained contact with mainstream liberal ideas and which had the support of a strong independent church. Similarly the revolutions in Czechoslovakia and East Germany involved intellectual movements which acted as a catalyst to protest by workers in industrial towns with a pre-war working-class tradition. In each of these countries conservative members of the party apparatus, who owed their authority almost entirely to Soviet support, relinquished power without a major struggle, while reform-minded communists were incapable of stemming the tide of anti-party feeling. Industrial workers, who will suffer the most from industrial restructuring and the introduction of a market economy in the short run, have shown little support for the restyled Socialist parties which have replaced the former Communist parties.

The absence of a more traditional working-class movement and of a strong independent middle class in most regions of the Balkan socialist states has resulted in greater support for indigenous Communist parties who promise to alleviate the harsher effects of industrial restructuring and marketisation on industrial workers. This could result in the survival of governments dominated, or at least strongly influenced by, reform communists or former communists who could exercise a major influence over economic policy well into the 1990s.

The example of Romania is the most disturbing to date. The social upheavals of December 1989 combined elements of a popular revolution against the Ceausescu regime with a political *coup d'état* which enabled a government dominated by former communists to take power, probably with the tacit support of the Securitate. The National Salvation Front and its presidential candidate Ion Iliescu subsequently won an overwhelming electoral victory, allegations of electoral malpractices notwithstanding. A major reason for the Front's electoral victory was that it had the support of industrial workers (who represent 40 per cent of the labour force), to whom it had already granted an immediate increase in living standards without the threat of either large-scale unemployment or price increases for basic items of consumption. Worker support for the Iliescu government was reflected in the violent suppression of student protests in Bucharest (in June 1990) by miners who had been transported into Bucharest for that purpose and were congratulated by the President. As a result the Romanian government has lost considerable credibility with Western governments and will be denied their economic assistance, and possibly more critically in the long term, favourable access to EC markets. As a result Western business interest in investing in Romania has been substantially eroded.

The events in Romania give a stark illustration of the dangers and divisions facing the Balkan states that do not create the basic elements of a civil society and the rule of law. Despite the widespread electoral support for the National Salvation Front, Romania is a highly fragmented society with clear divisions on ethnic, regional and class lines. Support for the Front is weakest in north-western border areas and the Timisoara region in particular, where four million people are reported to have signed the Timisoara declaration proposing to ban former communists from holding government office. The Hungarian Democratic Union, which stood only in the elections in the Transylvanian region, won the second largest share of the popular vote. However, the problems of youth unemployment, reflected in the Bucharest protests, present the greatest challenge to the establishment of national consensus. As a result of Ceausescu's anti-abortion policy, which started in the late 1960s, over 560,000 live births were recorded in 1968, tapering down to approximately 400,000 per annum in the 1970s. This compares with only 200,000–300,000 workers per year in their fifties and sixties (*Anuarul Statistic*, 1981) who may be expected to leave the labour force.[3] There is therefore an urgent need to attract capital to provide employment for a rapidly growing workforce if major social unrest is to be avoided.

There are growing indications of popular unrest in both Albania and Bulgaria in addition to the prospect of national disintegration in Yugoslavia. National elections in Bulgaria resulted in the return of a Communist government, but its leader Petur Mladenov has already been forced to resign as president, following his admission that he proposed the use of armed force to break up pro-democracy demonstrations. In Albania the growth of popular pressure for reform makes it debatable whether Hoxha's successor, Ramiz Alia will be able to utilise popular unrest against conservative opposition to implement 'reform socialism' or whether he too will be swept away by popular opposition.

The critical political question facing the Balkan socialist states therefore becomes whether the cultural and historical differences between East Central Europe and the Balkan states will simply postpone cultural and social revolutions or delay them indefinitely. Even if social revolutions result in the overthrow of Communist governments, will those countries tend more to the experience of Romania or will the Romanian experience become an isolated example?

This in turn raises a number of questions concerning the shape of economic developments. First, will the features of a socialist market economy, which have been rejected as unworkable by economists in East Central Europe, persist in some or all of the Balkan socialist states? If so, is the perception that a 'third way' or regulated socialist market economy is systemically unworkable justified in practice or is an alternative model more appropriate to the level of social and economic development reached in the Balkans? Finally, if the governments of the Balkan states remain under the control of former communists, will those leaderships be willing or capable of adopting a social-democratic form of economic system in which market forces predominate, but in which central authorities seek to alleviate the harsher elements of a market economy by establishing a welfare system and by applying economic policies in accordance with strictly determined *ex ante* rules, instead of on the basis of *ad hoc* judgements.

Economic prospects for the 1990s: the economics of transition

A broad spectrum of economic scenarios can be drawn up for each of the East European economies that are undergoing the transition from a centrally planned economy to a market economy, ranging from the most optimistic to the most pessimistic. The question then becomes: Where do the individual Balkan socialist states fall on the spectrum of scenarios?

The most optimistic scenario proposes that the problems that confronted the East European economies at the end of 1980s can be attributed to the nature of the economic system (including the nature of trade relations and the structure of output) and the relative backwardness of the capital stock. The economic system here may be taken to include an energy-intensive industrial structure which owes little to natural resource endowment and a trade structure which similarly owes little to comparative advantage. As a result, it is argued that major changes to the economic system (including industrial restructuring and a reorientation of trade away from the soft CMEA market to the international market, determined by the 'law' of comparative advantage), combined with a modernisation of the capital stock, will enable the East European economies to overcome their backwardness and catch up with a 'historic growth path' determined by the factor endowments of the country concerned, including skill levels, natural resources, and so on.[4] At its very crudest, this argument posits that in the long run the major difference between the productivity of industrial workers in, for example, East and West Germany, will be largely determined by differences in the capital stock and education and training, once systemic distortions are removed. The quicker the systemic distortions are removed and the capital stock is modernised, the smaller will be the productivity gap between East and West.

The optimistic scenario is largely derived from the experience of the more successful newly industrialising economies of South-East Asia, which attracted multinational investment seeking low labour cost production bases for exports back to high-income industrial market economies. This argument presupposes that labour costs in Eastern Europe will be low enough to make it profitable for multinational companies to establish production bases in Eastern Europe (either by constructing new factories in Eastern Europe or by taking over existing plants for modernisation) for re-export. For this to be the case, East European productivity levels will have to be sufficient to offset that part of the wage differentials between Eastern Europe and the newly industrialising economies which cannot be accounted for either by reduced costs of transport (e.g. to the EC market) or by higher skill factors.

The pessimistic scenario argues that the process of industrial restructuring and the transition to a market economy will be exceedingly painful, and will involve a significant increase in unemployment in the short run combined with a fall in output and consumption unless the fall in domestic production is offset by a compensating inflow of foreign capital and/or assistance.

An increase in unemployment in the short run will occur for a number of reasons. First, the development of an open-market economy will necessarily require a reduction in employment for workers in industries in which the country does not have a comparative advantage but which have been supported in the past by price distortions or hidden subsidies. This will occur either through the possibility of foreign competition and new entrants to the domestic market (although this is less probable in the short term until the currency is fully convertible), or through the application of market-determined prices which will make products uncompetitive in world markets. It could prove difficult or impossible to restore 'hidden' subsidies (even if these could be in the domestic interest of the country concerned, where, for example, marginal costs were below world market prices) if this violated international rules on dumping.

Second, one of the features of the 'full employment constraint' in the centrally planned economies has been that enterprises are encouraged to retain or employ labour, provided its marginal physical product is not negative. This has been one of the major factors contributing to low average labour productivity and to low value-added. The move to profit oriented market conditions will therefore result in enterprises reducing employment to the point where the marginal revenue product is equivalent to marginal wage payments, which will increase average productivity and will reduce total productivity and output in the short term until new employment opportunities become available. Finally, many enterprises in both the traditional heavy industrial sectors and the more modern petrochemical sectors may have to be closed down on grounds of environmental protection and worker safety.

The size and duration of unemployment will be determined chiefly by the mobility of labour and the speed of reconstruction of the capital stock. *A priori* reasoning indicates that labour mobility in the Balkan countries will be relatively low. First, industrial workers are familiar with an economic environment in which employment is relatively secure and consequently tend to have industry-specific skills and training and have little experience of the process of 'job search'. Second, industry tends to be concentrated in large plants (particularly in Romania), and industrial restructuring which results in plant closures will lead to high levels of localised unemployment. Third, housing is scarce and the market for housing and accommodation is underdeveloped. Industrial restructuring will also place considerable strain on the domestic construction industries and industrial relocation will be hampered by poor infrastructure including telecommunications, transportation and relatively undeveloped national energy grids. Finally, the pace of industrial reconstruction will depend on the speed with which inward investment can be attracted to the country.

The problem is further complicated by the existence of inflationary overhang. The removal of price controls under conditions of suppressed inflation will result in an immediate sharp increase in the aggregate price level. Enterprises will be confronted by pressure for compensating wage increases by workers attempting to maintain their 'real' wages, which they will be willing to grant under the prevailing monopolistic conditions, for they will be able to pass on cost increases in the form of further price increases. There is a very serious danger that this will become the first stage of a hyperinflationary process unless enterprises are subjected to hard budget constraints and an exceedingly tight monetary policy is employed.

Consequently, policies to remove the inflationary overhang and to break up the monopoly power of enterprises are a necessary prerequisite to the transition to a market economy. The removal of budget subsidies for basic staple goods and to loss-making enterprises is an essential part of this programme on the micro-economic grounds of price efficiency as well as on the macro-economic grounds of monetary stabilisation. However, this will give an additional impetus to the level of open inflation in the short term, while a tight monetary policy to counteract open inflationary pressures will drive up the level of unemployment more sharply than would be required by industrial restructuring alone.

The immediate consequence of the transition to a market under conditions of inflationary overhang is a redistributive increase in the price level. Increases in the price of basic staple goods and a rise in the level of unemployment will have the sharpest impact on industrial workers and the more disadvantaged members of society. This can bring about a number of pessimistic scenarios, particularly if the government does not enjoy popular support. The worst prospect is that of widespread popular unrest, triggered off by price increases for foodstuffs, which will stimulate ethnic conflicts and/or rural/urban conflicts, and conflicts between workers and intellectuals. This will create pressures for a return to authoritarian government, particularly in countries without a democratic tradition.

The fear of stimulating unrest poses real dangers, particularly for governments dependent on workers' support. This raises the critical question of whether governments in the Balkan socialist states will be able to withstand the short- and medium-term social problems that will result from the imposition of the deflationary policies required for the transition to a market economy. However, if these problems are not faced, it will prove exceedingly difficult to attract the inflow of foreign financial and physical capital required to stimulate the growth in productivity envisaged in the optimistic scenario.

The economic situation facing the Balkan economies at the end of the 1980s

Each of the Balkan economies was displaying symptoms of economic crisis at the beginning of 1990, which indicated the need for major systemic changes. Two critical problems may be identified. First, the question of domestic shortages in relation to monetary demand (repressed inflation), and second, the question of convertible currency scarcity, which is also systemic in origin.

The situation facing Albania with its low level of development is unique, and in many ways has more in common with the rural areas of the Soviet Union immediately following the death of Stalin than that of the economies of East Central Europe or the other Balkan states in the early 1990s (Hutchings, 1989). Hutchings, however, indicates that many of the problems associated with the traditional model of central planning in Eastern Europe, including repressed inflation, consumer shortages, and bribery and corruption, are starting to emerge in Albania, which will intensify pressure for reform. Hutchings also indicates that central investment projects with low or negative rates of return are also pursued, particularly in the raw material sector as mineral deposits are exhausted. More seriously, population growth may be running ahead of the growth of output of collectivised agriculture.

Bulgaria is displaying critical signs of excess demand, while new statistics published in January 1990 indicate a major degree of statistical falsification in the past. It is now admitted that gross convertible currency debt is around US$10,000 million, higher than previously believed by Western authorities, and that debt-servicing will take up over a third of Bulgaria's hard currency earnings. Equally alarming is the speed with which debt has risen from just US$2,000 million at the end of 1984 with annual hard currency balance of payments deficits in excess of US$1,000 million since 1987. The budget deficits in 1988 accounted for 11 per cent of GNP, while wages continued to grow substantially faster than nominal consumption in 1989 (which may even have declined), fuelling inflationary overhang. There is therefore a real danger that relaxing price controls will stimulate hyperinflationary pressures unless a steeply deflationary policy is pursued (*CPE Outlook/Centrally Planned Economies*, 1990).

Reliable data for the basic monetary aggregates have not been published since 1986 in Romania, and it is difficult to tell how severe a counterinflationary policy would have to be. Economic policy in the first half of 1990 was based on the premise that wage levels (as opposed to real consumption levels) were too low to sustain popular support, so the government implemented price cuts for electricity and has permitted *de facto* wage increases by rescinding fines for non-fulfilment of plan targets. Given the draconian cuts in domestic consumption brought about by the debt repayment programme, it would be churlish to criticise the policy of boosting domestic consumption by reducing net exports of energy and foodstuffs which contributed to annual hard currency trade surpluses of about US$2,500–3,000 million in the late 1980s, particularly as Romania was a net creditor nation when Ceausescu fell.

Romania, however, will still need a major input of capital. The debt repayment programme was conducted at an enormous economic as well as a human cost which will affect output well into the 1990s. An unofficial estimate indicates that approximately 10 per cent of GNP was directed towards running hard currency trade surpluses from the end of 1981 to the end of 1990. In addition, a significant, but as yet unquantifiable, sum was squandered on grandiose investment projects which yielded little or no productive capacity. Ceausescu's investment policy has been described as a 'strategy of underdevelopment', in which investment in modern industries was neglected to preserve the priority of more traditional energy-intensive heavy engineering industries and the petrochemical and refining industries. Import cuts during the 1980s bore beavily on imported machinery and equipment, and virtually no industrial modernisation has taken place during the 1980s, as a result of which the majority of industrial plants are using totally obsolete equipment. Investment in infrastructure including telecommunications, transport and power generation has also been badly neglected.

Finally, Yugoslavia faced major macro-economic problems at the end of 1989 with a gross debt of nearly US$20,000 million, an annual inflation rate approaching 1,000 per cent, and a regime in which enterprises faced exceedingly soft budget constraints, fuelled by inter-enterprise credit and the lax application of banking regulations. The crisis package of deflationary measures introduced by Marković bears strong similarities to the shock therapy treatment in Poland. It includes credit rationing to restrict the growth of wages and the introduction of a new convertible dinar pegged to the DM and worth 10,000 old dinars. The ability to sustain these policies in the long term and introduce a genuine market package will depend on political factors and on regional and republican relations in particular (*CPE Outlook/Centrally Planned Economies*, 1990).

The obstacles to economic recovery

What will be the commitment of the governments of the Balkan states to genuine economic reform and marketisation in the 1990s and how important is this for economic recovery? It is possible that the governments in Romania and Bulgaria will implement economic policies that will involve dismantling the old Stalinist system of central planning and replacing it with some form of market, but that this will entail a form of regulated market or market socialism rather than the essentially private enterprise market economic systems that are emerging in East Central Europe. This implies a far more gradual economic reform with a far slower pace of marketisation and privatisation and a far greater role for the state sector in the long term than those being conducted in East Central Europe and in Poland in particular.

A policy of gradual marketisation carries both internal and external dangers. On the positive side, a slower pace of marketisation will impose a lower level of immediate hardship on the population as it will imply a slower reduction of central budget subsidies, which will mean a lower initial rate of open inflation and unemployment. This could help to increase popular support for market-oriented reforms. However, it also carries the danger that reforms will be too cautious to permit industrial take-off. The main danger is that a slow transition to marketisation will extend the period over which the old system co-exists with the new, which will create a new set of problems associated with the transition process itself. This in itself may create renewed pressures for *ad hoc* central intervention to overcome the problems.

In practice the central authorities in socialist economies in both Central and South-East Europe have traditionally pursued paternalist or authoritarian economic policies, which provided workers with secure employment and guaranteed wages. This in turn necessitates the administration of soft budget constraints whereby enterprise losses are subsidised either by direct budget grants or soft loans or indirectly by enterprise-specific tax breaks. This necessarily stimulates micro-economic inefficiency even if rational market prices are introduced, as inefficient enterprises have no incentive to adjust their behaviour and in particular to innovate and introduce new products or cost-saving processes. Similarly, unless subsidies to inefficient enterprises and on basic staple goods are to be met by taxes on profitable enterprises or by taxes on income and other consumer goods, excess demand will be released. The policy of administering soft budget constraints owes as much to social policy as to central planning *per se* and historically has persisted under market-socialist type reforms in both Hungary and Poland. There is therefore a genuine concern that reforms within a market socialist framework will not be sufficiently deflationary to be effective, particularly when the government of the day depends on the support of those likely to be worst affected. Logically this suggests that the establishment of a state welfare system is an urgent priority in market-socialist countries to cushion the effects of tight monetary policies on those individuals worst affected by marketisation.

Equally seriously the implementation of gradualist reforms implies that some enterprises will continue to receive state subsidies while others will be exposed to market discipline. This again will mean that enterprise managers will continue to operate in an environment in which they have as much (or even more) to gain by bargaining with central authorities as by introducing genuine improvement to their working practices. In short, managers' and workers' expectations of how the economic system operates, will not be drastically altered as bad economic performance will not be punished, while efficient economic performance will not be rewarded.

The external economic environment facing the Balkan states will be significantly altered by the changes taking place in East Central Europe itself. This will affect the trade links of the Balkan states with both the East Central European economies themselves and with existing market economies. First, the East Central European economies were significant trade partners of the Balkan socialist states in the 1980s, accounting for over 20 per cent of the imports of Bulgaria and Romania, while East Germany was a major supplier of machinery and equipment to those countries. A significant proportion of this trade was conducted on a bilateral basis on soft currency terms. As the East Central European countries seek to redirect their trade to the industrial West and as long-standing CMEA trade agreements are rescinded, the East Central European economies will be willing to trade with the Balkan states only on hard currency terms. This will place increasing pressure on the Balkan republics to ensure that their export industries meet international price and quality specifications.

Equally critically the Balkan states will face growing competition from the East Central European states for inward investment. A relatively crude estimate indicates that Poland, Hungary and Czechoslovakia alone will be seeking net inward capital flows of at least US$10,000 million per annum in the early 1990s, in addition to any financial assistance in the form of debt or interest relief. These sums do not include the former East Germany, which is already proving a major source of attraction to West German firms. These sums will put a major strain on both the physical and financial capacity of Western firms and financial institutions. Although the requirements of the Balkan states will be much smaller, Western firms will be attracted to the economic environment that offers them the greatest opportunities for profit and the greatest control over their operations. The more rapid introduction of market principles will give the East Central European economies a considerable competitive edge over the Balkan economies in this respect. Finally, Western governmental assistance will be more readily available to economies that are creating the basis of a genuine civil society. This not only involves grant aid, but access to EC markets, which will be necessary if multinational companies are to be attracted to establish production bases in the region.

Conclusion

The Balkan socialist states will continue to face severe economic problems during the 1990s. The East Central European economies have demonstrated their commitment to a relatively rapid transition to a free market economy with a major role for private enterprise. They are also committed to a policy of reorienting their trade links to the West. This has major implications for the Balkan socialist economies, both as trade partners of the East Central European economies and as competitors for Western investment. Despite the political and economic changes that are taking place in the Balkan socialist states they are chasing a moving and even accelerating target in terms of their competitive position in the world economy. It is therefore exceedingly difficult to conclude that the Balkan socialist economies will fall within the optimistic range of the spectrum of scenarios, unless far-reaching political and economic changes are implemented.

Notes

1. A number of articles by East European economists who reject the concept of market socialism as economically and politically unworkable and who advocate the introduction

of a return to a free enterprise market economy have been published in the new journal *Communist Economies*, published by the Centre for Research into Communist Economies (London), which first appeared in January 1989 (e.g. Balcerowicz, 1990; Csaba, 1989; Dyba and Kouba, 1989; Kawalec, 1989; Klaus, 1989; and Rostowski, 1989). The majority of the authors of these articles could be considered outside the mainstream of critical analysis in their respective countries when they wrote the articles. Since the end of 1989 several of the authors have become members of their respective governments or economic advisers to the governments.

2. An important side effect of the experiments with market socialism in East Central Europe has been the introduction of market concepts into teaching and research in universities. Planners and officials in economic ministries in Romania, Albania and Bulgaria, with certain exceptions, are less familiar with market concepts than their counterparts in East Central Europe.
3. Cf. Ronnås's Chapter 4 of this volume.
4. The concept of an 'historic growth path' is derived from the works of Stanislaw Gomulka (see Gomulka, 1986).

References

Anuarul Statistic al Republicii Socialiste România 1981 (Bucharest: Directia Centrala de Statistica, 1981).

Balcerowicz, Leszek. 1990. 'The Soviet-type economic system, reformed systems and innovativeness', *Communist Economies*, vol. 2:1, pp. 3–23.

[*Centrally Planned Economies*, 1990] *Centrally Planned Economies Outlook* (London: The WEFA Group, April).

Country Report: Romania, Bulgaria, Albania (London: Economist Intelligence Unit), 1990:1 and 1990:2.

[*CPE Outlook*, 1990] *CPE Outlook for Foreign Trade and Finance* (London: The WEFA Group, January 1990).

Csaba, László. 1989. 'Some lessons from two decades of economic reform in Hungary', *Communist Economies* vol. 1:1, pp. 17–29.

Dyba, Karel and Kouba, Karel. 1989. 'Czechoslovak attempts at systemic changes: 1958, 1968, 1988', *Communist Economies*, vol. 1:3, pp. 313–25.

Gomulka, Stanislaw. 1986. *Growth, Innovation and Reform in Eastern Europe* (Brighton: Harvester Press).

Hutchings, Raymond. 1989. 'Albania', in *Pressures for Reform in the East European Economies*, vol. 2: *Study Papers submitted to the Joint Economic Committee, Congress of the United States, October 20, 1989* (Washington, DC: US Government Printing Office), pp. 38–46.

Kawalec, Stefan. 1989. 'Privatisation of the Polish economy', *Communist Economies*, vol. 1:3, pp. 241–56.

Klaus, Václav. 1989. 'Socialist economies, economic reforms and economists: reflections of a Czechoslovak economist', *Communist Economies*, vol. 1:1, pp. 89–96.

Poznanski, Kazimierz. 1986. 'Competition between Eastern Europe and developing countries in the Western market for manufactured goods', in *East European Economies: Slow growth in the 1980s*, vol. 2: *Foreign Trade and International Finance. Selected papers submitted to the Joint Economic Committee, Congress of the United States, March 28, 1986* (Washington, DC: US Government Printing Office), pp. 62–90.

Poznanski, Kazimierz. 1988. 'The competitiveness of Polish industry and indebtedness', in Paul

Marer and Wlodimierz Siwinski, eds, *Creditworthiness and Reform in Poland: Western and Polish perspectives* (Bloomington, Ind.: Indiana University Press), pp. 45–60.

Rostowski, Jacek. 1989. 'Market socialism is not enough: inflation vs unemployment in reformed Communist economies', *Communist Economies*, vol. 1:3, pp. 269–86.

11 Conclusion: the socialist Balkan countries will follow East Central Europe

Anders Åslund

A new time has arrived in the Balkans — a time to rethink, turn, decide and change. That was the very reason why we organised a conference on economic change in the socialist Balkan countries in Stockholm in June 1990. At long last it had become possible to invite good economists from all four socialist Balkan countries for a straightforward academic discussion of the state and future of their economies. A few months earlier such a conference was still impossible, but now the economists we had invited arrived not only from Yugoslavia but also Bulgaria, Romania and Albania.

This is a time of 'the return to Europe', as President Václav Havel calls it, with the formerly authoritarian East adopting the values and ideas of the liberal West. Such an atmosphere of a new spiritual European community was apparent at this conference. Its most striking feature was the degree of consensus among the score of participants. No divide between East and West was apparent any longer. We perceived the 'reunification of the language' in André Fontaine's words. These conclusions represent a partial and personal attempt to bring out the salient features of the discussion.

The Balkans certainly belong to Europe, but their status is similar to that of poor cousins also in comparison with the rest of Eastern Europe. The similarities between Bulgaria, Romania and Albania are considerable, while Yugoslavia is rather different and characterised by palpable regional disparities. Even so, the same problems were notable in all the countries. Nobody argued that the Balkans have to go their own way.

The economic problems of the Balkan countries are essentially of the same nature as in formerly communist countries in East Central Europe, though most developments have not reached as far in the Balkans. The differences involve lower levels of economic development, more centralised economic systems, and backward politics. However uncertain the future of Poland, Czechoslovakia and Hungary, the prospects of the countries to their south seem more precarious and distant. For all these countries, the ideal would be a swift 'Westerneuropeanisation', while the danger of 'Latinamericanisation', or worse, looms large. The four still socialist countries in the south-east of Europe form a natural tier in the new Europe, though the two northern republics of Yugoslavia, Slovenia and Croatia, might appear more akin to Central Europe. The historical boundary between the Habsburg and Ottoman empires remains distinct.

The exact states of these economies is difficult to assess. Yugoslavia excels with ample and good official statistics, and a lot of statistical studies, but large-scale unregistered economic activities remain a statistical question mark. A common perception is that the Yugoslavs live much better than the official statistics suggest. Traditionally, Bulgarian statistics have been of an average East European standard. Significant over-reporting takes place, but Bulgarian statistics are still usable, and a second economy compensates for some of the exaggerations. Romanian statistics have long been a joke with the most magnified claims to be found anywhere in the world. The new regime has released more statistics, but slowly, and figures tend to be given in relative rather than absolute terms. Little is known about the exact state of the Romanian economy. Albania has been more honest in its reporting, but instead has hardly reported any achievements at all, leaving students guessing.

In spite of the scant and unreliable statistics, the current state of these economies is too obvious to be missed. In Yugoslavia something big has happened. A deflationary stabilisation was initiated at the outset of 1990. Current questions are: Will the apparent success last? Will supplies be forthcoming? How much will the cure cost? How far will systemic changes proceed?

In the other countries, the decline in national income is not caused by reform, but by the collapse of the old command economy. So far, the situation looks worst in Romania, which is being hit by a massive drop in production, while Bulgaria and Albania are experiencing modest decreases.

Yugoslavia has already gone through hyperinflation, and the other countries are facing rising inflation which might very well approach hyperinflation, if they do not introduce restrictive financial and monetary policies in time.

For long, Yugoslavia has suffered from substantial unemployment. It has been revealed that Romania has had a considerable hidden unemployment that is now openly acknowledged, while Albania displays sizeable overpopulation in the countryside, partly because urbanisation has not been permitted. In Bulgaria, unemployment is expected to rise as a consequence of both external and internal shocks.

As pointed out in the various contributions to this volume, and summarised in Alan Smith's chapter, the burdens of foreign debts are varied. Yugoslavia has long had problems servicing its debt, but recently it has been well managed. At present, the crucial case is Bulgaria, which stopped its foreign payments at the end of March 1990. It is not likely to be able to service its debts without debt rescheduling. Romania had no foreign debt at the beginning of 1990, but currently it is running a massive deficit in its foreign trade, since consumption levels have risen at the expense of food exports. If its current foreign trade policy is not altered swiftly, Romania might end up with a huge foreign debt that has only gone to consumption. Albania is in a class of its own. Until recently foreign loans have been prohibited, which has rendered foreign payments cumbersome, but effectively proscribed the hardships of debt repayments.

In terms of economic development, Yugoslavia and Bulgaria come out on top, followed by Romania with Albania as a poor neighbour, though the picture is complicated by the extraordinary regional disparities in Yugoslavia. The level of development is reflected in the relative importance of agriculture, both in terms of output and employment. Albania looks like a classical developing country, and also Romania has a sizeable backward rural area. Socially, this means that not only the middle class but also the working class are poorly developed in the socialist Balkan countries.

This economic backwardness is not necessarily a disadvantage when effecting a change of economic system. Many unfortunate developments have not taken place. Notably, China and Vietnam have succeeded with swift reforms thanks to the perseverence of traditional agricultural techniques. The sector likely to be worst hit by a change of system is heavy industry, notably engineering and electronics, which are completely uncompetitive in world markets. Such industries are less prominent in the Balkans than in more-developed formerly communist countries. Possibly, Albania could more or less bypass some of the worst excesses of Stalinist industrialisation. The service sector offers growth potential, because it is so rudimentary and it can easily expand with little investment. The dominant agricultural sector can absorb more labour and easily feed more people in an austere transitionary period.

A Balkan problem that is not acute in East Central Europe is population pressure. Undoubtedly, the Balkans are to face very substantial unemployment, and it is uncertain what its political consequences will be. The optimist may point to the Iberian peninsula, where extensive unemployment does not hamper the evolution of liberal economic policies and fast economic growth, while the pessimist sees such an abundance of economic and social problems that he is reminded of societies that gave birth to fascism.

Yet, structural changes must be great. From 1 January 1991, the CMEA will switch from bilaterial barter trade to trade in hard currency at world market prices. Bulgaria and Romania will suffer sharply deteriorating terms of trade. In particular, Bulgaria will be hit, since the Soviet Union is its dominant trading partner. Bulgaria imports vast amounts of oil, gas, coal and iron ore at low prices from the USSR, and in return exports a lot of manufactured goods and agricultural produce at prices exceeding the world market level. Therefore, the quick shift to ordinary trade will be a big blow to Bulgaria and Romania, aggravating their already difficult structural problems.

As have other East European countries, the Balkans have pursued a policy of extreme protectionism and import substitution. It has proved even more harmful than in Latin America, promoting the production of obsolete goods of poor quality. For the future, the Balkans have no real option but to turn to the European free trade area. As Smith has pointed out in Chapter 10 of this volume, East European competition for foreign investment is growing, and the Balkans seem poorly equipped to attract foreign capital. A natural response to these problems would be a particularly far-reaching liberalisation.

Strangely, the differences seem greater in terms of economic system than in economic situation. Albania is reminiscent of the Soviet Union soon after the death of Stalin. Especially since 1978, it has pursued a policy of hypercentralisation. Something must happen, but nobody knows when or even the prospective direction of change. Romania has experienced a very particular form of one-family socialist dictatorship. Officially, Bulgaria has undertaken all kinds of reforms, but in real life little has changed. In fact, all these three countries might have had more similar and more Stalinist systems than has previously been perceived.

Yugoslavia is of course a very different case with its long-standing experiment with workers' self-management. From the outset of 1990, Yugoslavia's radical stabilisation programme has attempted to furnish the country with a comprehensive monetary and financial system. It is too early to assess the success of this attempt. The scenarios for Yugoslavia vary from disintegration to the new-found stability of a more normal market economy.

A remarkable consensus arose around the desirable developments of the economic systems in Bulgaria, Romania and Albania. In all three countries, it was broadly agreed, the old economic systems were swiftly coming to an end. For the future, no other rational choice than far-reaching marketisation and privatisation was conceived. Neither could the old systems survive for long, nor was any third road at hand, though Yugoslavia might remain an exception for another while. The reason for this consensus was that the economic problems are so great and manifold that no half-measures can possibly keep the society afloat.

Marketisation means the introduction of all the many institutions and practices of a market economy. At least some thirty new laws must be adopted, and much old legislation must be abrogated. The most sensitive issue is the liberalisation of prices. If proper checks and balances are not introduced before prices are freed, hyperinflation might be the result, as in Poland and Yugoslavia. First, restrictive monetary and financial policies must be introduced. Budget deficits must be properly recorded and eliminated in reality rather than through statistical tricks. Since it is very difficult to control inflation in a newly liberated economy, no Keynesian fine-tuning is possible. Anti-monopolistic measures have tended to be rather ineffective in the West, and they are likely to be even less effective in emerging market economies. Therefore, a third factor is needed to reinforce competition, namely an opening of the economy to foreign competition. A market-oriented exchange rate is required. Initially, the currencies should be given a low value. Otherwise, excessive protectionism and import quotas are necessary. By and large, this is the Balcerowicz programme, and it seems difficult to find a principal alternative to the current Polish approach. Critical remarks on the Polish programme tend to focus on timing or the value of various parameters, such as the exchange rate.

In short, the issue is whether marketisation should be introduced with a 'big bang', as in Poland, or gradually, as has been the case in Hungary. Essentially, the Polish model seems more attractive. Gradual changes of an economic system means that one distortion is replaced by another. Both in practice and in theory, the cost of cumulative distortions is likely to be very high. Besides, much time is lost in transition. The strongest argument in favour of gradualism would be that the nadir in the economy might be higher and less socially costly. Still, a successful gradual transition would require careful planning and scheduling. There is little reason to believe that the socialist Balkan countries will have the necessary data or staff for such a complex undertaking, not to mention the ample opportunities for the old bureaucracy to sabotage the whole project.

In real life, no alternative to the Polish model of a big bang ('shock therapy') is apparent. It is another matter whether the Polish approach will work. Competent management, a new work ethic and all kinds of new skills are also required, and they are patently in short supply in the ex-communist world.

While the requirements of marketisation are reasonably clear, privatisation is a big and open question. It is becoming ever more obvious that no real marketisation is feasible without an extensive privatisation of state-owned enterprises, but privatisation will be complicated from legal, political and economic points of view. Only Yugoslavia has a substantial private sector, while Bulgaria and Romania have recently allowed private enterprise on a broad scale. Property may be divided into large-scale enterprises, small enterprises and shops, agricultural land and real estate. Small enterprises and shops may be sold to emerging entrepreneurs; land may be distributed through a land reform, implying little payment by the people already tilling the land; real estate should be sold off gradually, providing the population with incentives for saving and the state with a source of revenue. A problem that requires a political solution is how former property rights are to be acknowledged.

The biggest headache is how to privatise large-scale state enterprises. First, they must be transformed into joint-stock companies. Many need to be broken up, but should splits take place before or after privatisation? Because of the large capital involved, ordinary sales to the population would take far too long. Instead, some form of more or less free distribution of shares to the population seems necessary. The technical and political solution of this task will be one of the major issues facing the formerly communist economies in the next few years.

The main difference between the East Central European countries and the Balkan socialist countries is to be found not in the economic sphere but in the political situation. In both Romania and Bulgaria, Gorbachevian reform communists retained power after the elections in May and June 1990, although they have changed political labels. In fact, this is the first time communists have won national majorities in free and reasonably fair elections. The ruling reform communists won with populist programmes, extolling what they would do for the standard of living of the population, while shying away from hard choices.

Ironically, the communists enjoyed most support in the countryside and small towns, while the modern working class and middle class took exception to them. This reflected the backward economic structure of the Balkan countries. However, as remarked by Alan Smith in Chapter 10, the main point is that these countries lack the civil society that has surfaced in full strength in Poland, Czechoslovakia and Hungary. The civil society of these countries seems to be a yield from their popular uprisings in the post-war period. Conversely, Albania, Bulgaria and Romania need to create a civil society before the full effects of democratisation can be achieved. One precondition for a civil society is independently and critically-thinking intellectuals of integrity, insight and international outlook. Another precondition is alternative political organisations, which are weak in Romania and Albania. Finally, the majority of the population must be convinced that communism, even of a populist variety, does not provide long-term welfare.

In the same way as it seemed difficult to perceive any other successful economic solution than the combination of marketisation and privatisation, democratisation appeared a necessary prerequisite for such a course in these countries, since they have been so imbued with far-reaching state control. The corollary was that the immediate post-totalitarian regimes in Albania, Bulgaria and Romania must collapse before any economic headway can be made.

One should never assume success. What would a failure look like? The natural alternative is Latinamericanisation, implying populist authoritarian policies with lasting macro-economic imbalances. The Polish alliance between the working class and the radical Right is a rare occurrence. Present political strains in Poland suggest that it is more likely to break up than to be repeated elsewhere. The reaction against the communists will probably be strong enough to keep socialism at bay, but an obvious danger is populism of the Right. While little remains of socialist ideology in the minds of the Balkan peoples, the ideology of equality persists. It will no doubt be aroused by large income differentials, which inevitably will emerge in poorly-functioning nascent markets. The cost of a transition to a market economy might simply seem excessive to the population, causing popular unrest, which might give rise to paternalistic populist regimes. A strong reason against such an unfortunate development is that the economic hardships will be so severe in any case that the Balkans cannot afford to fool around with their economic policies as some Latin American states have done. Moreover, the neighbourhood of an affluent and liberal Western Europe more or less imposes a certain choice of policies.

To sum up, the Balkans and the East Central European countries face similar economic problems, though the Balkans are more agricultural and more peripheral to the centre of Europe, that is, Germany. They are less mature in most regards. The main difference between the north and south of Eastern Europe seems to be the prior existence of a civil society in the north with free intellectuals and independent social forces in existence before the collapse of communism. In the south, communism lingers on in a populist form vaguely reminiscent of Edward Gierek's Poland, but the communists do not appear to have any workable economic alternative to offer.

Therefore, the first post-totalitarian regimes in Albania, Bulgaria and Romania must fall before the necessary economic changes can be implemented. However, the regimes will give way only when the majority of the population has realised that there is no other way out. Until the awareness of the Balkan populations has grown to such an extent that they throw out their still-socialist political leaders, little improvement in their economies is likely to take place. No time schedules for their systemic transitions have yet been drawn up.

An optimist would say that the Balkans can learn from the mistakes their northern neighbours will make in the next few years, but a pessimist would point to the recent past and argue that the socialist Balkan countries are more likely to make the same mistakes, though at an even higher cost.

Index